BASIC SPANISH

BASIC SPANISH

ESSENTIALS FOR MASTERY

Second Edition

Edward E. Settgast
Gerald F. Anderson

Stetson University

Harper & Row, Publishers
New York   Evanston   San Francisco   London

Sponsoring Editor: George J. Telecki
Special Projects Editor: Rita Pérez
Project Editor: Lois Wernick
Designer: Andrea Clark
Production Supervisor: Will C. Jomarrón
Picture Editor: Myra Schachne

BASIC SPANISH: Essentials for Mastery, second edition

Library of Congress Cataloging in Publication Data

Settgast, Edward E.
    Basic Spanish: essentials for mastery.
    1. Spanish Language—Grammar—1950–   I. Anderson,
Gerald F., joint author. II. Title.
PC4112.S45   1975   468′.2′421   74-10404
ISBN 0-06-045913-1

CONTENTS

PREFACE

The purpose of this text is threefold:

(1)   To present a flexible, concise, and orderly program that will provide students of Spanish with all of the essentials of the language and, at the same time, serve as a basis and a motivating factor for their further study.

(2)   To provide teachers of elementary Spanish courses with a framework for the presentation of the basic elements of the language that will allow a maximum of flexibility and freedom to engage in cultural work, conversation practice, and meaningful reading.

(3)   To provide coverage and practice of basic structures that will fit into a variety of systems of limited contact hours or flexible scheduling.

In recent years, many good, beginning texts have been published, but the majority of them are, by intention or fact, directed toward classes that meet more than three hours weekly. Even for those courses that meet more than three hours a week, some texts are often so all-inclusive that the time is spent almost completely on language instruction, leaving little opportunity for reading practice, culture, and conversation. The natural result of this type of comprehensive presentation for teachers and students alike is often frustration, rigidity of presentation, and neglect of the truly exciting aspects of language learning.

This text is organized in such a way as to carefully structure those essentials of the language that will be basic to the students' further study. Thus, all of the necessary language concepts have been presented, but no frills or unnecessary complications have been added that are, in any case, of doubtful advantage to first-year students. The text may be completed easily in one year in the traditional three-hour course with ample time remaining for other activities. In schools with a four- or five-hour-a-week schedule, the possibilities for a truly rewarding year of study would seem to be limitless.

The text avoids both extremes in methodology; the orientation is neither audio-lingual nor traditional. Memorization of a dialogue is not a required prelude to the mastery of materials that follow. The dialogue for reading and conversation practice is included at the end of each chapter and contains only grammar and vocabulary that have been mastered in the drills and exercises that precede it. It contains a balanced program of exercises for listening comprehension, patterns for manipulation, and reading and writing practice. The emphasis is always on a concise presentation of the grammatical structures. Those exercises usually associated with an audio-lingual text are presented but always in reasonable proportion to reading and writing drills of the traditional variety.

The basic elements of each lesson are as follows:

Basic Words and Expressions

This list is not intended as one students must memorize before proceeding to the Drills. Obviously, some familiarity with the vocabulary is desirable before beginning the Drills; however, students should be urged not to learn the vocabulary in isolation, but rather through usage. The list is intended primarily as an aid to students to provide them with a reference vocabulary as they proceed through each lesson.

Pronunciation

Certain vowels and consonants that present pronunciation difficulties are presented in Lessons 1–4 and are included in the tape program that accompanies this text. Additionally, a pronunciation chapter follows Lesson 5.

Basic Patterns

This section consists of a series of sentences that illustrate the basic grammatical and syntactical elements of the Drills that follow. Teachers should insist that they be studied thoroughly outside of class and in the language laboratory. By the time students have completed the Drills and Discussion and are ready to proceed to the Combined Exercises in any lesson, they should have completely mastered and understood the Basic Patterns. Like the Basic Words and Expressions, these sentences are intended as an aid: in this case, one that will provide students with examples of each point of grammar introduced in a lesson.

Drills and Discussion

Drills are presented prior to any discussion of grammar, since in some instances they can be mastered and the meaning made clear through the pattern presented. Where a grammatical discussion is necessary, students will find an explanation on the facing page under the same heading as the drill being practiced. This unique presentation helps students focus on one point at a time, both when learning grammar and practicing exercises.

Combined Exercises

These exercises, as the title implies, are an extension of the materials in the preceding section and an elaboration on them. They represent the heart of each lesson.

Reading and Conversation

This section brings together vocabulary and syntax in a connected dialogue that will offer little difficulty to the students who have mastered the preceding material. Beginning with Lesson 2, questions for oral responses are provided, and beginning with Lesson 4, additional exercises are included.

The Appendixes

(1) Readings: Eight readings are provided for additional practice. They are keyed to the four major divisions of the text and present cultural aspects of the Spanish-speaking world. All new vocabulary and structure are glossed in the margins.

(2) Translation Exercises: The correct responses to all translation exercises not on tape are found here. Thus, by utilizing this section and the tapes, students always have at their disposal a means of checking their performance before class recitation or tests.

(3) Verbs: A complete synopsis of the various verbs, tenses, and forms used in the text is given here for review and reference.

The Testing Program and Individualized Instruction

A separate Instructor's Manual provides practical suggestions for utilizing the text in a variety of ways. The emphasis is on making instruction more individualized, flexible, and personal. A complete testing program of Unit Tests, Two-Lesson Tests, and Lab Quizzes is provided with an alternate form for each test. Thirty masters of review material for preparing overhead transparencies are also included.

Suggested Assignment Schedule

Lessons 1–6 can be completed in two 50-minute class meetings per lesson. Lessons 7–20 can be completed in three 50-minute class meetings per lesson. Suggested assignments follow:

Lessons 1–6

First day: Pronunciation, Basic Patterns, Drills and the Discussion on the facing pages.

Second day: Combined Exercises, Reading and Conversation with Dialogue Practice.

Lessons 7–20

First day: Basic Patterns, begin Drills and Discussion on facing pages.
Second day: Complete Drills and Discussion, Combined Exercises.
Third Day: Reading and Conversation with Dialogue Practice.

About the Second Edition

This second edition provides the same brief presentation of the essentials of the language as did the first edition. In addition to changes in style, format, illustration, and clarification of many presentations, several major changes or additions should be mentioned separately. They are as follows:

(1) Familiar commands have been divided so as to present affirmative commands in one lesson and negative in another.

(2) Discussions and drills on prepositional pronouns and on the use of the subjunctive in indirect commands have been deleted from this edition. The authors believe that the pronouns can be taught through examples and that presentation of indirect commands at the introductory level only serves to confuse students in their study of the more fundamental forms of this mood.

(3) Eight reading selections are included in a separate appendix for instructors who may wish to provide this kind of practice without having to resort to a supplementary reader. These selections are graded as to grammatical difficulty, and the instructor is referred to them for their optional use at appropriate points in the text.

(4) A new tape has been added to the tape program, providing special reinforcement of those aspects of the language which have traditionally caused students the most difficulty. They are not merely drills, but self-teaching units to provide reinforcement in certain troublesome areas of language. The Instructor's Manual contains more specific information on this new tape, as well as on the general tape program.

(5) A program for individualizing instruction is included in the Instructor's Manual.

The authors wish to express their gratitude to Dr. Concha Bretón for her assistance in the preparation of the dialogues and to Ms. Jacqueline Kuechler for extensive help in the preparation of the manuscript.

E.E.S.
G.F.A.

Acknowledgments

(Page 4)   Cartoon—Cesc
(Page 8–9)   Cartoons—Mingote: From HOMBRE SOLO, 1970, Ediciones Myr, Madrid.
(Page 16)   New York Public Library Picture Collection
(Page 47)   *Top:* Reflejo, Woodfin Camp
                  Bottom: Heron, Monkmeyer
(Pages 48–49)   Spanish National Tourist Office
(Page 50)   *Top:* Trans World Airlines
                  Bottom: Spanish National Tourist Office
(Page 57)   Cartoons—Cesc
(Pages 84–85)   Cartoons—Cesc
(Page 103)   *Top and Bottom, right:* Mexican National Tourist Office
                  Bottom, left: American Airlines
(Page 104)   American Airlines
(Page 105)   *Top, left:* American Airlines
                  Top, right: Mexican National Tourist Office
                  Bottom: United Nations
(Page 106)   *Top:* Pease, Monkmeyer
                  Bottom: Edward E. Settgast
(Pages 140–141)   Cartoons—Mingote: From CHISTES VIII, 1965, Editorial Prensa Española, Madrid.
(Page 157)   *Top and Bottom, right:* United Nations
                  Bottom, left: Pan American World Airways, Inc.
(Page 158)   United Nations
(Page 159)   *Top:* Grabitsky, Monkmeyer
                  Bottom, left and right: Jane Latta
(Page 160)   *Top:* Jane Latta
                  Bottom, left and right: United Nations
(Page 161)   Jane Latta
(Page 162)   *Top:* Conklin, Monkmeyer
                  Middle: Jane Latta
                  Bottom: Gross, Monkmeyer
(Page 186)   Cartoon—Mingote: From HUMOR 1953–1955, Editorial Prensa Española, Madrid.
(Page 187)   Cartoon—Cesc
(Page 212)   *Top, left:* Grabitsky, Monkmeyer
                  Top, right and Bottom: Colombia Information Service
(Page 213)   *Top, left:* United Nations
                  Top, right and Bottom: Colombia Information Service
(Page 214)   *Top:* WHO—Paul Almasy
                  Bottom: Pan American World Airways, Inc.
(Page 215)   *Top:* United Nations
                  Bottom, left: Colombia Information Service
                  Bottom, right: Mann, Monkmeyer

BASIC SPANISH

PRIMERA LECCIÓN

Basic Words and Expressions

adiós good-bye
Buenos días, señor (señora, señorita)
  Good morning, sir (madam, miss)
Buenos días, señores (señoras, señoritas)
  Good morning, gentlemen (ladies,
  young ladies)
en casa at home
la clase de español the Spanish class
¿Cómo está usted? How are you? (*sing.*)
¿Cómo están ustedes? How are you? (*pl.*)
¿Cómo se llama usted? What is your
  name?
hasta luego so long, see you later
hasta mañana see you tomorrow
Me llamo . . . My name is . . .
Muy bien, gracias. Very well, thank you.
todo el día all day
todos los días every day

comprar to buy
estar to be
estudiar to study

hablar to speak, talk
necesitar to need
preparar to prepare

el alumno student
la casa house
el día day
el español Spanish, Spaniard
la lección lesson
la librería bookstore
el libro book
la mesa table
la silla chair

aquí here
bien well
en in, at, on
hoy today
todo all, everything
y and

Pronunciation

Certain consonants and vowels in this and following lessons represent sounds which differ from those normally associated with the same letters in English. Make a concentrated effort to master them at the outset of your study of Spanish. The explanations that follow will aid you in reproducing these sounds. Repeat the laboratory exercise for this section until you can imitate the model.

ll   This is considered a separate letter in Spanish and cannot be divided. It is pronounced approximately like the *y* in English *yes.*

        llama, llamo, silla, ella, ellos

r   This letter is pronounced with a quick tap of the tongue against the roof of mouth. It sounds much like the *d* in English *ladder.*

        señorita, comprar, librería

ñ   This letter is pronounced as the *ny* in English *canyon.*

        señor, señora, español, mañana

d   This letter, when between vowels or in final position, has a very soft sound similar to the *th* in English *they.*

        estudiar, usted, adiós, ustedes

    When in initial position, the *d* has a somewhat harder sound, though it is never as hard as the English *d*. The tongue touches briefly the upper gum and teeth.

        día, dónde

Basic Patterns

Study the following sentences thoroughly outside class and in the laboratory. They illustrate all the important structural items in any one lesson, and should be thoroughly mastered before beginning the Combined Exercises.

1.	**Los alumnos hablan en la clase.**	The students are talking in the class.
2.	**Estudio el libro en casa.**	I study the book at home.
3.	**Estoy en la clase de español.**	I am in the Spanish class.
4.	**Compran libros en la librería.**	They are buying books in the bookstore.
5.	**Necesito comprar los libros.**	I need to buy the books.
6.	**Usted habla español todos los días.**	You (*sing.*) speak Spanish every day.
7.	**Ustedes hablan todo el día.**	You (*pl.*) speak all day.
8.	**Las mesas están aquí.**	The tables are here.
9.	**¿Cómo está usted? Muy bien, gracias.**	How are you? Fine, thanks.
10.	**¿Cómo se llama usted?**	What is your name?
11.	**Me llamo Ricardo.**	My name is Richard.

Drills

Gender and Number of Nouns. Definite Article

Read the following exercise aloud, providing the proper definite article for each noun.

alumno / *el alumno*

casa, día, español, lección, alumno, librería, mesa, silla, señor, señora, clase, mañana, libro, señorita

Repeat the preceding exercise, changing the nouns to the plural.

alumno / *los alumnos*

Discussion

Gender and Number of Nouns. Definite Article

Gender of Nouns

Nouns ending in **-o** are usually masculine.

libro book

Nouns ending in **-a** are usually feminine.

casa house

Nouns ending in **-dad, -ión, -tud, -tad,** are usually feminine.

lección lesson
libertad liberty

The few exceptions to the above, as well as nouns which end in other letters, must be memorized as they appear.

Number of Nouns (Singular and Plural)

The letter **s** is generally added to words ending in a vowel.

libro book   **libros** books
silla chair   **sillas** chairs

The letters **es** are generally added to words ending in a consonant.

señor man   **señores** men

Definite Article

The forms of the definite articles are

	Masculine	Feminine
Singular	el	la
Plural	los	las

The definite article agrees in number and gender with the noun it modifies.

el libro the book   **los libros** the books
la casa the house   **las casas** the houses

The definite article is used before names of languages except directly after **hablar, en, de.**

Habla español.
Habla bien el español.

Subject Pronouns

Change the following subject pronouns to Spanish.

> I, we, he, she, they (*m.*), they (*f.*), you (*formal, sing.*), you (*formal, pl.*), you (*fam., sing.*)

First Conjugation: Regular -AR Verbs

Repeat the following model sentences and then make the changes according to the cues given.

1. Los alumnos hablan español en la clase.
   (*yo, tú, nosotros, ellos, él, Pedro, Ud., Uds.*)
2. Yo estudio la lección.
   (*nosotros, ellos, tú, Ud., los alumnos, el alumno, ella, ellas*)
3. Compran libros en la librería.
   (*yo, él, nosotros, tú, Ud., ellos, Uds., ella*)
4. Necesito comprar los libros hoy.
   (*él, nosotros, Uds., ellos, tú, yo, Pedro, ella*)
5. Preparo la lección en casa.
   (*los alumnos, tú, él, nosotros, yo, Uds., Ud.*)

ESTAR (to be)

Repeat the following model sentences and then make changes according to the cues given.

1. Estoy en la clase de español.
   (*nosotros, él, tú, Juan, ellos, yo, ella, Ud., Juan y María*)
2. Las mesas están aquí.
   (*las sillas, el alumno, la casa, los libros, la mesa*)

Subject Pronouns

Subject pronouns are often not necessary in Spanish. With the exception of **usted** and **ustedes,** they are often omitted, since the verb ending usually identifies the person.

yo	I	? nosotros	we
tú	you (*fam., sing.*)	*	
él	he, it (*m.*)	ellos	they (*m.*)
ella	she, it (*f.*)	ellas	they (*f.*)
usted (Ud.)	you (*formal, sing.*)	ustedes (Uds.)	you (*formal, pl.*)

Tú is used among close friends, students, or members of a family. **Usted,** the more formal form of address, is used with strangers and when a tone of respect is desired.

First Conjugation: Regular -AR Verbs

The present tense of regular verbs whose infinitive ends in **-ar** is formed by omitting the **-ar** and adding the following endings:

hablar (to speak)

habl *o*	I speak	habl *amos*	we speak
habl *as*	you (*fam., sing.*) speak		
habl *a*	he, she, it speaks; you (*formal, sing.*) speak	habl *an*	they, you (*formal, pl.*) speak

The present tense may be translated three different ways: *I speak, I am speaking, I do speak; he speaks, he is speaking, he does speak; etc.*

ESTAR (to be)

In this lesson, **estar** is used to state location and to express a temporary state of being (**¿Cómo está usted?**). It is irregular in the first person singular.

estar (to be)

estoy	I am	estamos	we are
estás	you (*fam., sing.*) are		
está	he, she, it is; you (*formal, sing.*) are	están	they, you (*formal, pl.*) are

---

* **Vosotros,** the familiar form for the second person plural, is common in Spain but little used in Spanish America. It will be omitted from verb paradigms in this text but its forms and usage will be illustrated in the Appendix. In Spanish America the **ustedes** form is used instead, and thus serves as both the formal and familiar equivalent of *you* (*pl.*).

Negation

Read each sentence aloud and then change to the negative.

El alumno está aquí. / *El alumno no está aquí.*

1. Estudio en la clase.
2. Compro el libro.
3. Los alumnos hablan bien el español.
4. Ella estudia la lección.
5. Juan está en la librería.
6. Necesito la mesa.
7. Ud. compra la silla.

Negation

To make a sentence negative in Spanish, the word **no** is placed before the verb.

Juan habla español.   John speaks Spanish.
Juan no habla español.   John doesn't speak Spanish.

Combined Exercises

A. Write the following in Spanish and be prepared to give them orally in class.

1. the student, the houses, the lesson, the bookstore, the day, the tables, the chairs
2. I buy, he studies, they speak, she needs, they prepare, he is here, we study, you (*fam., sing.*) buy, I prepare, you (*formal, sing.*) speak
3. every day, all day, good morning, the Spanish class, at home, good-bye, see you later, see you tomorrow

B. Write answers to the following questions and be prepared to give them orally in class without referring to your notes.

1. ¿Cómo está Ud.?
2. ¿Cómo se llama Ud.?
3. ¿Cómo están Uds.?
4. ¿Compra Ud. libros hoy?
5. ¿Compras libros en la librería?
6. ¿Necesitan Uds. mesas?
7. ¿Compran Uds. sillas?
8. ¿Estudia Ud. la lección hoy?
9. ¿Está Ud. aquí?
10. ¿Hablas español todo el día?
11. ¿Habla Ud. todos los días?
12. ¿Está aquí la librería?
13. ¿Preparas la lección todos los días?
14. ¿Necesitan Uds. los libros en la clase de español?

⊕* C. Write the following sentences in Spanish.

1. Good morning, students. How are you (*formal, pl.*)?   2. I am in the Spanish class today.   3. The tables are here.   4. He studies every day.   5. We speak Spanish here.   6. He studies at home.   7. We prepare the lessons.   8. The table and the chair are in the house.   9. You (*formal, pl.*) buy books in the bookstore.   10. You (*formal, sing.*) prepare the lesson at home.   11. I need the books.   12. They are here today.   13. You (*fam., sing.*) are in the bookstore and need to buy the book.   14. The tables and chairs are in the house.   15. We study all day.   16. What is your name?   17. My name is . . .   18. In the Spanish class, we don't speak Spanish well.   19. The students buy books in the bookstore today.   20. The books, the tables, and the chairs are in the Spanish class.

* The symbol ⊕ indicates that a drill has **not** been taped.

Reading and Conversation

La Primera Clase de Español*

El profesor Buenos días, alumnos. ¿Cómo están ustedes? Hoy estamos en la primera clase de español. Ustedes necesitan comprar libros en la librería y necesitan estudiar la lección todos los días. Preparamos las lecciones, estudiamos en casa y hablamos español en la clase.
Adiós, alumnos. Hasta mañana.

Paco y Cecilia

Cecilia Buenos días, Paco. ¿Cómo estás?
Paco Muy bien, Cecilia. ¿Y tú?
Cecilia Estoy bien. ¿Estás en la clase de español?
Paco Sí, estoy en la clase. Necesito comprar el libro.
Cecilia Hasta luego.
Paco Adiós.

Dialogue Practice

⊕ A. After you have studied the dialogue for this lesson, write out the following paragraph filling in the blanks with the proper word. Use the dialogue and reading selection as models.

Se llama Pedro y está en _____ _____ de español. Necesita _____ libros. Prepara _____ lección en _____ y habla español en _____ clase. No habla muy _____ y necesita estudiar _____ los días.

B. Rewrite the above paragraph, changing all verbs from the third person (él) to the first person (yo).

----

* **La primera clase de español** The first Spanish class

LECCIÓN DOS

Basic Words and Expressions

¿Cómo? How?
¿Dónde? Where?
¿Por qué? Why?
¿Qué? What?

abrir to open
aprender to learn
aprender a + *inf.** to learn + *inf.*
comer to eat
entrar (en) to enter
escribir to write
leer to read
vender to sell
vivir to live

la carta letter
la hermana sister
el hermano brother
el hombre man
la madre mother

la mujer woman
el padre father
la pluma pen
el restaurante restaurant
la tienda store

bueno good
grande large
hermoso beautiful, handsome
interesante interesting
nuevo new
pequeño small
viejo old

con with
hay there is, there are
mi my (*when thing possessed is singular*)
muy very
pero but

* This type of entry will be seen often in this text. Any number of infinitives may be substituted to extend its meaning.

     Aprendo a escribir. I am learning to write.
     Juan aprende a leer. John is learning to read.

Pronunciation

b, v   These consonants have identical sounds. When they appear at the beginning of a sentence or group of words, or after *m* or *n,* they are pronounced somewhat like the English *b,* but not as explosively.

> **V**enden libros. **B**uenos días. **V**ivo aquí.
> el hom**b**re, un **v**aso, **b**ien, **v**iejo

In all other positions the sound for *b* or *v* has no close English equivalent. Try to say an English *b* without making the lips touch. The escaping air should keep the lips barely apart.

> nue**v**o, escri**b**ir, vivir   (*Note the two sounds of* **v** *in* **vivir.**)

j   Similar to English *h* in *Hi!* but more strongly aspirated.

> vie**j**o, mu**j**er

h   This is the only silent consonant in Spanish. It is never pronounced.

> **h**ablar, **h**asta, **h**ombre, **h**ermoso

Basic Patterns

1. **¿Por qué escribe Ud. la carta?** Why are you writing the letter?
2. **¿Qué vende el hombre?** What is the man selling?
3. **Aprendemos a hablar español.** We are learning to speak Spanish.
4. **Un alumno escribe una carta interesante.** A student is writing an interesting letter.
5. **Hoy comemos en un restaurante bueno.** Today we are eating in a good restaurant.
6. **Necesito comprar un libro nuevo.** I need to buy a new book.
7. **La mujer vive en una casa grande.** The woman lives in a large house.
8. **Leo un libro muy viejo pero interesante.** I am reading a very old but interesting book.
9. **Necesito comprar unos libros nuevos.** I need to buy some new books.
10. **Abro un libro pequeño.** I am opening a small book.

Drills

Indefinite Article

Place the proper indefinite article before the following nouns and read aloud.

alumno, casa, lección, mesa, silla, señor, clase, día, carta, hombre, mujer, tienda, pluma, restaurante, padre, madre

Plural Use of *Some*

Repeat the model sentence and make the changes according to the cues given.

Necesito comprar unas sillas.
_____ plumas.
_____ libros.
_____ mesas.
_____ casas.

Second Conjugation: Regular -ER Verbs

Repeat the following sentences and then make the changes according to the cues.

1. ¿Qué vende el hombre?
    (*yo, tú, él, nosotros, ella, Uds., Juan*)
2. Aprendemos a hablar español.
    (*él, Uds., yo, tú, María, ellos, Ud.*)
3. Hoy comemos en un restaurante.
    (*él, Ud., yo, ella, Uds., ellos, tú, Paco*)
4. Leo un libro muy viejo.
    (*María, nosotros, ellos, tú, Ud., Uds., él*)

Third Conjugation: Regular -IR Verbs

Follow the same instructions given in the drill above.

1. ¿Por qué escribe Ud. la carta?
    (*tú, él, ella, nosotros, yo, Uds., ellos, ellas*)
2. La mujer vive aquí.
    (*yo, tú, ellos, Ud., él, ella, nosotros, el hombre*)
3. Abro un libro pequeño.
    (*él, tú, nosotros, ellos, Uds., María, ella, mi hermano*)

14

Discussion

Indefinite Article

The forms are: **un** (*m.*) *a, an*   **una** (*f.*) *a, an*
They agree in gender with the noun they precede: **un hombre**   **una casa**

Plural Use of *Some*

The forms are: **unos** (*m.*) *some, any*   **unas** (*f.*) *some, any*

Some and *any* are normally expressed only in the plural. They are used when emphasis is desired and agree in gender with the noun they precede.

> **Vende unos libros.**   He is selling some books.
> **Vende unas plumas.**   He is selling some pens.

Second Conjugation: Regular -ER Verbs

The present tense of regular verbs whose infinitive ends in **-er** is formed by omitting the **-er** and adding the following endings.

vender (to sell)

vend *o* I sell		**vend** *emos* we sell	
vend *es* you (*fam., sing.*) sell			
vend *e* he, she, it sells; you (*formal, sing.*) sell		**vend** *en* they, you (*formal, pl.*) sell	

Third Conjugation: Regular -IR Verbs

The present tense of regular verbs whose infinitive ends in **-ir** is formed by omitting the **-ir** and adding the following endings.

vivir (to live)

viv *o* I live		**viv** *imos* we live	
viv *es* you (*fam., sing.*) live			
viv *e* he, she, it lives, you (*formal, sing.*) live		**viv** *en* they, you (*formal, pl.*) live	

Number and Gender of Adjectives

⊕ Give the feminine singular, and the masculine and feminine plural of the following.

nuevo, viejo, interesante, hermoso, bueno, pequeño, grande

Position and Agreement of Adjectives

Say the following in Spanish.

a new book, an interesting letter, the big store, the new houses, a beautiful woman, the small tables, an old pen, a good restaurant, the old chairs

Number and Gender of Adjectives

Adjectives ending in **-o** form the feminine by changing **-o** to **-a**:   viejo   vieja
Adjectives ending in **-e** do not change: **grande** (*m.*)   **grande** (*f.*)
Both types form the plural by adding **s**:   **viejos   viejas   grandes   grandes**

Position and Agreement of Adjectives

Descriptive adjectives normally follow the noun they describe.

un libro pequeño, un libro interesante

Adjectives agree in number and gender with the noun they modify.

una mujer vieja, un hombre viejo, unos libros nuevos, unas casas hermosas

Combined Exercises

A. Complete the following phrases orally, using the unnumbered one as a model, and make all the necessary changes suggested by the cues.

	una	casa	grande	*Correct response*
1.	___	___	grandes	unas casas grandes
2.	___	libro	___	un libro grande
3.	___	___	interesante	un libro interesante
4.	___	___	interesantes	unos libros interesantes
5.	___	lección	___	una lección interesante
6.	___	___	buena	una lección buena
7.	___	señorita	___	una señorita buena
8.	___	___	hermosas	unas señoritas hermosas
9.	___	mesa	___	una mesa hermosa

⊕ B. Write sentences using each of the following words. Begin with the example and be sure that each new sentence is based on the preceding one.

   una casa grande / *Aquí está una casa grande.*

   interesantes, libro, casas, lecciones, buenas, mesa, vieja, hombre, señorita, hermosa, mujeres, pequeña

C. Read each sentence aloud and then change all parts to the plural.

1. Leo una carta interesante.   2. Él come en un restaurante bueno.   3. Ud. escribe con una pluma nueva.   4. Un hombre viejo vive aquí.   5. Necesito una pluma nueva.   6. Hay una tienda nueva aquí.   7. Ella lee un libro nuevo.   8. Tú compras una silla aquí.   9. Tú entras en una tienda pequeña. 10. El hermano abre la tienda.

D. Write answers to the following questions and be prepared to give them orally in class. You may follow the response given on the taped program or write your own.

1. ¿Qué venden los alumnos?   2. ¿Dónde viven Uds.?   3. ¿Hay sillas nuevas en la clase?   4. ¿Qué estudias hoy?   5. ¿Aprendes a comer en la clase de español?   6. ¿Vende Ud. libros en la clase?   7. ¿Qué necesitan Uds. comprar en la librería?   8. ¿Escriben Uds. la lección en español?   9. ¿Cómo escribes la lección?

⊕ E. Write the following sentences in Spanish.

1. The men are entering the small restaurant.
2. My brother lives in an old house.
3. We need to write a letter today.
4. The new chairs are in the store.
5. Paco and I are learning to read.
6. In the bookstore there are interesting books.
7. The beautiful girl (*Miss*) is opening a letter.
8. They are writing some interesting letters.
9. Do you (*formal, pl.*) need some books?
10. Why do you (*fam., sing.*) prepare the Spanish lesson?
11. There are large stores in New York.
12. A very old man lives here.
13. The lady (*Mrs.*) eats in a restaurant every day.
14. Some students write letters every day.
15. You (*fam., sing.*) sell some very beautiful pens.
16. Where does the woman live?
17. We read and study at home.
18. We open the store every day.
19. You (*fam., sing.*) are learning to read Spanish.
20. Why do you (*formal, sing.*) live here?

Reading and Conversation

En la Casa de Juan

Paco   ¡Juan! ¿Dónde estás?

Juan   Estoy aquí, en la casa. ¿Por qué no entras?

   (*Paco entra en la casa.*)

Paco   Buenos días, Juan. ¿Qué lees? ¿Estudias?

Juan   No, no estudio. Leo una carta. Mi hermana Elena está en Nueva York y escribe todos los días.

Paco   ¿Vive ella en Nueva York?

Juan   Sí. Hoy mi padre y mi madre están con ella. Necesitan comprar una mesa nueva y unas sillas.

Paco   En Nueva York hay muchas tiendas grandes y unos restaurantes muy buenos.

Juan   Sí. Todos los días ellos comen en un restaurante pequeño pero muy bueno.

Paco   ¿Dónde comes tú hoy, en casa o en un restaurante? ¿Por qué no comemos en un restaurante?

Paco come con Juan en el restaurante. Paco necesita comprar una pluma nueva y entran en una librería. El hombre vende libros nuevos y viejos. Juan compra un libro viejo pero interesante. Paco compra una pluma hermosa. En casa, Paco abre el libro de español y estudia la lección. Juan lee un libro y escribe una carta.

Dialogue Practice

A. Prepare oral responses to the following questions.

1.   ¿Qué lee Juan?
2.   ¿Dónde vive Elena?
3.   ¿Qué hay en Nueva York?
4.   ¿Qué necesita comprar Paco?
5.   ¿Qué vende el hombre?

⊕ B. Study the dialogue thoroughly. Then, following the example given, make complete sentences of the word groups. Use the words in the order given and make any changes or additions necessary to form a complete sentence.

   (Nosotros)/aprender/hablar/español. / *Aprendemos a hablar español.*

1.   Alumno/vivir/en/casa/grande.
2.   ¿Por qué/escribir/Ud./carta/todos/días?
3.   (Ellos)/leer/y/estudiar/en casa.
4.   Mi hermana/estar/Nueva York. ¿Dónde/vivir/tú?

LECCIÓN TRES

Basic Words and Expressions

a veces at times
comprender to understand
¿Cuántos? How many?
enseñar to teach, show
hay que + *inf.* It is necessary + *inf.*

mirar to look (at)
olvidar to forget
recibir to receive
ser to be
trabajar to work

el amigo friend
el examen examination
la familia family
el médico doctor
la medicina medicine
la nota grade
la televisión television
la universidad university

la verdad truth

bonito pretty
cansado tired
contento happy
difícil difficult
enfermo sick
fácil easy
feliz (*pl.* **felices**) happy
feo ugly
joven young
malo bad
mismo same
triste sad

de of, from
para in order to, for
también also
tu your (*fam., sing.*)

Pronunciation

Spanish vowels are short, pure sounds with no "glide" or final drawl as often occurs in English.

a   Similar to the English *a* in *ha!* and *aha!*
       la casa, la carta, la hermana, la nota

e   Approximately the sound between the *a* in *mate* and the *e* in *met*.
       mesa, pero, señor, señorita

i   Similar to the *ee* in *seek*.
       amigo, difícil, bonito, recibir

o   Similar to the *o* in *open*.
       joven, malo, nota, como

u   Similar to the *oo* in *boot*.
       universidad, tú, pluma, puro.

Basic Patterns

1. **Somos amigos y estamos en la misma clase.**
    We are friends and we are in the same class.
2. **El hombre no es viejo, pero está enfermo.**
    The man is not old, but he is sick.
3. **Mañana estudiamos en casa de Juan.**
    Tomorrow we'll study at John's house.
4. **Pedro es médico y es de México.**
    Peter is a doctor and he is from Mexico.
5. **Juan es el hermano de María.**
    John is Mary's brother.
6. **La casa de Juan es grande.**
    John's house is large.
7. **Hablo con mi padre mañana.**
    I'll speak with my father tomorrow.
8. **La hermana de Juan es de Nueva York.**
    John's sister is from New York.
9. **¿Olvidas el examen de mañana?**
    Are you forgetting tomorrow's exam?
10. **Hay que estudiar para aprender.**
    It's necessary to study in order to learn.

Drills

Present Indicative of SER

Repeat the model sentences and then change according to the cues.

1. Yo no soy médico.
   (*tú, él, nosotros, ellos, Uds., Pablo, yo*)
2. Yo no soy un médico bueno.
   (*mi padre, tú, nosotros, ellos, yo, Ud.*)

Uses of SER and ESTAR

Repeat the model sentences and then change according to the cues.

1. Yo soy médico, pero no estoy contento.
   (*Juan, tú, ellos, Ud., yo, nosotros, él*)
2. María es bonita, pero está enferma.
   (*yo, Elena, Uds., tú, nosotros, Ud., la señorita*)
3. El libro es de Juan, pero está en la clase.
   (*la pluma, las cartas, la silla, la mesa, los libros*)
4. Pedro es de México, pero está aquí.
   (*tú, ellos, Ud., yo, él, nosotros, Uds.*)

Make short sentences using the words given and a form of **ser** or **estar**.

casa/bonita, lección/difícil, Pablo/contento, María/triste, yo/cansado, nosotros/aquí, mesa/de Juan, hombre/viejo, ellos/enfermos, lección/interesante

⊕ Translate the following.

1. We are friends.
2. He is here.
3. She is happy.
4. He is a good doctor.
5. We are tired.
6. My brother is from New York.
7. Where is the television?
8. The chairs are beautiful.
9. We are happy.
10. Mary is young and pretty.

Discussion

Present Indicative of SER

Ser is conjugated as follows.

ser (to be)

soy I am	**somos** we are
eres you (*fam., sing.*) are	
es he, she, it is; you (*formal, sing.*) are	**son** they, you (*formal, pl.*) are

Uses of SER and ESTAR

There are two Spanish verbs to express the English *to be*. Each has a particular usage and each expresses a different concept.

Estar is used to express: (1) location or position

Juan está en Nueva York.	John is in New York.
Las sillas están en la clase.	The chairs are in the class.

(2) the present condition of a person or thing. This condition is more or less temporary and is judged to be different from the normal state or condition. Some common adjectives from this lesson which are normally used with **estar** are: **triste, enfermo, contento.***

Estoy cansado y triste.	(*Neither is the normal condition of the individual and thus* **estar** *is used.*)
Estamos contentos.	(*Note that the adjective is plural to agree with the subject.*)

Ser is used to express: (1) an innate or relatively permanent characteristic of a person or thing.

El hombre es viejo.	The man is old.
La mujer es fea.	The woman is ugly.
Soy médico.**	I am a doctor.

(2) other concepts expressing ownership, origin or material and which incorporate the word **de**. The word **de** may be considered a marker which in most cases demands the use of **ser**.

La casa es de María.	The house is Mary's. (*see following discussion*)
Somos de México.	We are from Mexico.

---

* **Contento** is used with **estar** to indicate a state. **Feliz** is normally used with **ser** to indicate a characteristic:

María está contenta hoy.	Mary is happy today.
María es muy feliz.	Mary is very happy. (*by nature, characteristically*)

** After **ser** the indefinite article is omitted before unmodified nouns denoting occupation, nationality or religion. When the noun is modified, the article is used.

Soy un médico bueno. I am a good doctor.

Possession with DE

Translate the following.

John's house, the Spanish lesson, Elena's father, the family's table, my brother's restaurant, the Spanish class, the woman's letters, the students' books, the students' class, my friend's grades

Plural of Adjectives Ending in Consonants

Read the following sentences and change all parts to the plural.

1. Ella es muy joven.
2. La lección es difícil.
3. Soy muy feliz.
4. La clase es muy fácil.
5. El alumno español está aquí.

Present Tense with Future Meaning

⊕ Read the following sentences, translating the English into Spanish.

1. *I'll read* el libro mañana.
2. *I'll study* la lección mañana.
3. *We'll buy* la tienda mañana.
4. *They will write* la carta mañana.
5. *You will enter* la clase mañana.

Cardinal Numbers (1-10)

1. Write the following numbers: 1, 8, 6, 5, 9, 10, 4, 7, 3, 2, 6, 5, 7, 10, 4.
2. Count from 1 to 10 forward and then backward.

Possession with DE

Possession is expressed with **de** + noun.

los hermanos de María Mary's brothers
el amigo de él (ella) His (her) friend
La casa es de Juan. The house is John's.

Plural of Adjectives Ending in Consonants

For adjectives ending in a consonant, add **es** to form the plural.

joven **jóvenes**   **fácil** **fáciles**

For adjectives ending in **z,** change the **z** to **c** and add **es.**

feliz **felices**

Present Tense with Future Meaning

Often the present tense is used to express intended future action.

Mañana estudiamos. Tomorrow we'll study.
Leo el libro mañana. I'll read the book tomorrow.

Cardinal Numbers (1–10)

1	uno (un), una	6	seis
2	dos	7	siete
3	tres	8	ocho
4	cuatro	9	nueve
5	cinco	10	diez

The number *one* agrees in gender with the noun that follows. Before a masculine noun it contracts to **un.** All other cardinal numbers are invariable.

un libro   **cinco libros**
una casa **cinco casas**

Combined Exercises

A. Repeat the models and then change according to the cues.

1. Mi madre comprende el español.
    (tú, ella, nosotros, ellos, yo)
2. A veces Pablo olvida los libros.
    (yo, mi hermano y yo, Uds., él, tú)
3. Miro la televisión todos los días.
    (Juan, tú, las dos amigas, nosotros, yo)
4. Recibimos cartas de la señorita García.
    (yo, Ud., tú, ellos, nosotros)

B. Read each sentence aloud, changing all parts from plural to singular.

1. Los hermanos trabajan en la tienda y están muy contentos. 2. Las lecciones son fáciles, pero los exámenes son difíciles. 3. Compramos medicina cuando estamos enfermos. 4. Comprenden las lecciones, pero olvidan los libros. 5. Abrimos los libros para leer.

⊕ C. Write and be prepared to recite the following orally.

three pretty girls, one difficult lesson, seven old men, six easy classes, two sad students, ten good books, one good restaurant, four tired doctors, five small tables, eight large stores, nine hard tests, one happy man

D. Repeat the model sentence; then, using **ser** and **estar,** change according to the cues.

La señorita es bonita.
(cansada, enferma, fea, contenta, bonita, triste)

E. Write answers to the following questions and be prepared to give them orally.

1. ¿Hay un examen hoy en la clase de español? 2. ¿Cómo se llama Ud.? 3. ¿Recibe Ud. malas notas? 4. ¿Olvida Ud. los libros a veces? 5. ¿Estás cansada hoy? 6. ¿Comprenden Uds. la lección de hoy? 7. ¿Cuántos libros necesitas para la clase de español? 8. ¿Cómo están Uds.? 9. ¿Hay que olvidar para comprender?

⊕ F. Write the following sentences in Spanish.

1. We receive ten letters every day. 2. We are friends and are in the same class. 3. We work in the same restaurant. 4. You *(fam., sing.)* forget to open the bookstore at times. 5. They don't understand the lesson. 6. We are reading a sad book. 7. The exam is John's, but he is not here. 8. You *(formal, pl.)* are students, but I am a doctor. 9. Tomorrow I'll study at John's house. 10. The men are old, but they are not sick. 11. The class is easy, but it's necessary to study. 12. We are from Mexico, but we are happy here. 13. Mary's brother is a good doctor. 14. The lessons are hard, but they are interesting. 15. It's necessary to work in order to live. 16. I'm tired today, but I'll work tomorrow. 17. She is also buying one table and four chairs. 18. There are seven students in class and eight at home. 19. Where are Mary's brothers?

Reading and Conversation

La Familia

María y Elena son amigas y están en la misma clase de español. A veces estudian las lecciones en casa de María. La familia de Elena es muy grande y no es fácil estudiar en casa.

Elena   Mañana es día de clase. ¿Comprendes la lección de español? Es difícil, ¿no?

María   Estamos en la lección tres, ¿verdad? No, no es muy difícil, pero hay que estudiar mucho para comprender.

Elena   Sí, pero es difícil estudiar en mi casa. Mi familia es muy grande y la casa es pequeña.

María   ¿Cuántas personas hay en tu familia? En mi familia somos cuatro, mi madre, mi padre, mi hermano y yo.

Elena   En mi familia somos diez, cinco hermanos y tres hermanas. Es una familia grande, pero somos muy felices. Mi madre trabaja mucho, pero está contenta con la familia.

María   ¿Dónde trabaja tu padre?

Elena   Es médico. También enseña medicina en la universidad.

María   ¡La universidad! ¡Ay, Elena! ¿Olvidas que estamos aquí para estudiar el español?

Elena   No, pero estoy cansada. ¿Por qué no miramos la televisión?

A la mañana siguiente* las dos amigas entran en la clase de español. Hay un examen y reciben notas muy malas.

Dialogue Practice

A. Prepare oral responses to the following.

1.   ¿Dónde estudian las dos señoritas?
2.   ¿Cómo es la familia de María? ¿y la familia de Elena?
3.   ¿Cuántos hay en la familia de Elena?
4.   ¿Dónde enseña el padre de Elena?
5.   ¿Qué miran las señoritas?
6.   ¿Qué reciben en el examen?

⊕ B. Rewrite the paragraph, based on the dialogue, filling in the blanks.

Hoy nosotros _____ en la lección tres. No es muy _____ pero hay _____ estudiar todos los _____. No miramos la _____ porque mañana _____ un examen.

C. Pretend you are speaking to a friend, Cecilia, and express the following to her in Spanish:

1. Her sister and you are in the same class.   2. Your father is a doctor.
3. Your family is very large, four brothers and one sister.   4. Sometimes you and she study at Mary's house.   5. Your house is very small.

* **A la mañana siguiente** The next morning

LECCIÓN CUATRO

Basic Words and Expressions

¿**Cómo se llama él (ella)?** What is his (her) name?

¡**Dios mío!** Oh my goodness!

El (Ella) se llama ... His (Her) name is ...

No es para tanto. It's not all that important.

¿**Qué pasa?** What's happening? (What's going on?)

Vamos. Let's go.

correr to run
esperar to wait (for), hope
ir to go
tener to have
venir to come

el banco bank
la carne meat
la comida meal, food
la cosa thing
el director director
el hijo son
la hija daughter
la legumbre vegetable
la luz (*pl.* **luces**) light
la mamá mother
el mercado market

la muchacha girl
el muchacho boy
la novia sweetheart (*f.*)
el novio sweetheart (*m.*)
los padres parents
el pan bread
el papá father
la puerta door
la sirvienta maid, servant
la sopa soup
la tarde afternoon

alguno some
rico rich
simpático nice

a to, at
además besides
además de in addition to
ahora now
ahora mismo right now
algo something
hasta until
más more
mientras while
tarde late
ya already, now

28

Pronunciation

rr
initial r
When the letter **r** is the first letter of a word, it has the same sound as the double **r (rr)**. This sound is more strongly trilled than the single **r** and is produced by placing the tongue on the gum ridge just behind the upper front teeth. When air is blown out between the gum ridge and teeth, it produces a flap or vibration of the tongue against the gum ridge. The proper tongue position is obtained by saying the English word *had* and holding the tongue in the position of the final *d*.

> rico, recibir, rojo (*red*), restaurante,
> correr, perro (*dog*), carro (*car, cart*)

Poor pronunciation of this sound is one of the most obvious speech problems a student can have. It is so obvious to a native speaker that it gives the impression of a very "thick accent" although all other sounds may be pronounced correctly. For this reason, pay special attention to the laboratory exercises and practice them until mastered.

Basic Patterns

1.	**Mi libro es viejo.**	My book is old.
2.	**Su libro y sus cartas están aquí.**	His book and his letters are here.
3.	**No tengo legumbres para la sopa.**	I don't have any vegetables for the soup.
4.	**Tengo que esperar aquí.**	I have to wait here.
5.	**Voy a la tienda para comprar pan.**	I am going to the store to buy bread.
6.	**Vamos a estudiar aquí.**	We are going to study here.
7.	**Yo voy al mercado pero él viene del banco.**	I am going to the market, but he is coming from the bank.

Drills

Possessive Adjectives

Repeat the models and make all changes necessitated by the cues.

1. Mi libro es viejo.
   (*su, nuestros, tus, mis, nuestro, sus, mi*)
2. Su padre trabaja aquí.
   (*mis, tu, nuestros, sus, tus, su, nuestro*)
3. Su libro y sus cartas están aquí. (Substitute for both poss. adjs.)
   (*mi, tu, nuestro, su, tu, mis, nuestros*)

⊕ Provide the necessary possessive adjectives.

my amigos, *his* médico, *our* universidad, *their* exámenes, *her* cartas, *my* medicina, *your (formal)* pluma, *his* padres, *their* silla, *our* alumnos, *your (formal)* mesa, *your (fam.)* tienda, *their* hermano, *our* libro, *her* novio

Write the following using **su(s).** Then write each phrase a second time using the clarification.

her sweethearts, his house, their father, his son, your (*sing.*) door, your (*pl.*) door, his vegetables, her soup, your (*sing.*) maids, their parents

Present Indicative of TENER and VENIR

Repeat the model sentences and then change according to the cues.

1. No tengo legumbres para la sopa.
   (*tú, él, Uds., yo, ella, nosotros, Ud., ellos*)
2. Vengo aquí para estudiar.
   (*él, Ud., tú, yo, nosotros, ellos, Uds., ella*)

Discussion

Possessive Adjectives

The possessive adjectives are

mi	my	**mis**	my
tu	your (*fam., sing.*)	**tus**	your (*fam., pl.*)
su	his, her, their, your, its (*formal, sing.*)	**sus**	his, her, their, your, its (*formal, pl.*)
nuestro (a)	our	**nuestros (as)**	our

Like all adjectives, possessive adjectives agree in number with the noun they modify. Thus, **s** is added when the noun is plural.

mi padre	my father	**mis padres**	my parents
tu puerta	your door	**tus puertas**	your doors
su libro	his book	**sus libros**	his books
su libro	your book	**sus libros**	your books
nuestra casa	our house	**nuestras casas**	our houses
su casa	their house	**sus casas**	their houses

The word **su(s)** has a variety of possible meanings, but the meaning intended by the speaker is usually clear from context. If clarification is needed, **su(s)** may be replaced by **el . . . de**, or **la . . . de** and the appropriate subject pronoun.

su libro	**el libro de él (ella, Ud., Uds., ellos)**
su tienda	**la tienda de él (ella, Ud., Uds., ellos)**
sus amigos	**los amigos de él (ella, Ud., Uds., ellos)**
sus casas	**las casas de él (ella, Ud., Uds., ellos)**

Present Indicative of TENER and VENIR

The verbs **tener** and **venir** are irregular, but they both follow the same pattern. They are conjugated as follows.

tener (to have)   **venir** (to come)

tengo	tenemos	vengo	venimos
tienes		vienes	
tiene	tienen	viene	vienen

TENER QUE + *Infinitive*

Repeat the model sentence and then change according to the cues.

    Tengo que esperar aquí.
    (*él, nosotros, yo, Ud., tú, ella*)

⊕ Write the Spanish for the following sentences.

1. I have to study.
2. He has to go.
3. We have to run.
4. I have to live.
5. They have to come.
6. You (*fam., sing.*) have to open the door.
7. You (*formal, sing.*) have to prepare the meal.
8. He has to have the medicine.

Present Indicative of IR (to go)

Repeat the models and then change according to the cues.

1. Voy a la tienda para comprar unas cosas.
   (*nosotros, tú, Pedro, Uds., ella, yo, Ud.*)
2. Vamos a estudiar aquí mañana.
   (*tú, Elena, nosotros, ella, Uds., Ud., yo*)
3. Aprendo a hablar español.
   (*Ud., ellas, nosotros, tú, yo, él, Uds.*)

Contractions AL and DEL

Read the model sentences and then substitute according to the cues.

1. Voy al mercado.
   (*clase, tiendas, médico, universidad, restaurantes, banco*)
2. Venimos del restaurante.
   (*clase, banco, tiendas, bancos, mercado, restaurante*)
3. La casa es del muchacho.
   (*muchacha, hijo, señora, hijos, señorita, señor*)

TENER QUE + *Infinitive*

When the verb **tener** is followed by **que** and an infinitive, it expresses obligation or necessity.

> **Tengo que estudiar.** I have to study.
> **El tiene que comer ahora.** He has to eat now.

Present Indicative of IR (to go)

The verb **ir** is irregular and is conjugated as follows.

ir (to go)

voy	**vamos**
vas	
va	**van**

Ir, venir and other verbs of motion are followed by the preposition **a** before an infinitive. **Aprender** also requires **a** before an infinitive. Other verbs of the same type will be given in later lessons.

> **Voy a hablar.** I am going to talk.
> **Vienen a estudiar.** They are coming to study.
> **Aprende a leer.** He is learning to read.

The expression **vamos** may also mean *let's go.*

> **Vamos ahora.** Let's go now.

Contractions AL and DEL

The words **a el** and **de el** are contracted in Spanish to form the words **al** and **del.**

> **Voy al mercado.** I am going to the market.
> **Vengo del mercado.** I am coming from the market.
> **El libro es del muchacho.** The book belongs to the boy.

Combined Exercises

A. Repeat the models and substitute the cues.

1. Corro a casa y escribo la lección.
    (*nosotros, sus alumnos, mi hija, tus padres, yo, tú*)
2. Voy a comprar pan ahora mismo.
    (*tú, su sirvienta, Ud., nosotros, yo, mis amigos*)
3. Viene del banco. Es rico y simpático.
    (*tú, mi amigo y yo, el novio, yo, ellos, ella*)
4. Sus cartas son interesantes. Están aquí.
    (*su, mis, tu, nuestras, mi, sus, nuestra*)

B. Read each sentence aloud changing the subject and the verb from singular to plural.

1. La sirvienta espera en el mercado.   2. Tengo que aprender en la universidad.   3. Yo tengo el libro y la pluma.   4. El hijo del hombre va al mercado.   5. Además, mi hijo está aquí.   6. La luz viene de la tienda grande.

C. Express the left column in English without referring to the translation. Then cover the Spanish and express the English phrase in Spanish. Repeat until you make no mistakes.

1.	más cosas	*more things*
2.	unas cosas	*some things*
3.	algo	*something*
4.	algo más	*something more*
5.	ahora mismo	*right now*
6.	además	*besides*
7.	además de la carne	*besides the meat*
8.	algo además de carne	*something besides meat*
9.	Tenemos algo además de carne.	*We have something besides meat.*
10.	ya	*already*
11.	ya tengo	*I already have*
12.	Ya tengo pan.	*I already have bread.*
13.	Ya es tarde.	*It's already late.*
14.	a la puerta	*at the door*
15.	Ya está a la puerta.	*He's already at the door.*
16.	mientras	*while*
17.	mientras vamos	*while we go*
18.	mientras él espera	*while he waits*
19.	mientras corren	*while they are running*
20.	mientras tenemos luz	*while we have light*
21.	¿Qué pasa aquí?	*What's going on here?*
22.	¡Dios mío!	*My goodness!*
23.	No es para tanto.	*It's not all that important.*
24.	¡Vamos!	*Let's go!*
25.	¡Vamos al banco!	*Let's go to the bank!*
26.	¡Vamos al mercado!	*Let's go to the market!*
27.	¿Cómo se llama Ud.?	*What's your name?*
28.	Me llamo Carlos.	*My name is Carlos.*

29.	¿Cómo se llama él?	*What's his name?*
30.	El se llama Carlos.	*His name is Carlos.*
31.	¿Cómo se llama ella?	*What's her name?*
32.	Ella se llama Ana.	*Her name is Ana.*

D. Write answers to the following questions and be prepared to recite them orally.

1. ¿Tienes que estudiar para aprender el español? 2. ¿A veces corre Ud. a las clases? 3. ¿Es rico(a) su novio(a)? ¿Es simpático(a)? 4. ¿Esperan Uds. un examen ahora mismo? 5. ¿Cómo se llama su padre?

⊕ E. Write the following sentences in Spanish.

1. We have meat, soup and vegetables, but there's no bread.
2. She is running to the store to buy some things.
3. They are coming right now, but it's already late.
4. She is waiting for her meal.
5. His name is John, but he's not very nice.
6. Their class is large, but their lessons are easy.
7. In addition to his two sisters, he has seven brothers.
8. Our parents are waiting at the door.
9. I am going to write a letter while there is light.
10. We come to our Spanish class every day.

Reading and Conversation

Preparando* la Comida

María, su madre, la Sra. de Valdez, y Pilar, la sirvienta, hablan de la comida que van a preparar más tarde.

Sra. Pilar, tenemos que preparar una comida para seis. Elena y su novio vienen a comer con nosotros.

Pilar No hay mucho de comer en casa, señora. Tengo que comprar unas cosas.

María Yo voy al mercado mientras Uds. preparan la comida. ¿Qué necesitan?

Pilar Ya tengo carne, pero necesito pan y también legumbres para la sopa.

María Voy ahora mismo. Ya es tarde y tengo que ir a muchas tiendas para comprar todas las cosas.

Sra. No tienes que correr. No vienen hasta la tarde.

. . .

Pilar La comida ya está en la mesa, señora. ¿Algo más necesita?

Sra. Gracias, Pilar, tenemos que esperar ahora. María, ¿cómo se llama el novio de Elena?

* **Preparando** preparing

María	Se llama Carlos. Sus padres son muy ricos.
Sra.	¿Carlos Benítez? ¿Es hijo del director del banco? ¡Dios mío! ¡Pilar! ¡Nuestra vajilla* especial!
María	No es para tanto, mamá. Carlos es muy simpático y además ya están a la puerta. ¡Pilar! ¿Vas a abrir la puerta?
Pilar	¿Qué pasa, señora? No hay luz aquí.
Sra.	¡Dios mío! ¿Cómo vamos a comer?
María	¿Vamos a un restaurante, mamá?

Dialogue Practice

A. Prepare oral responses to the following questions.

1. ¿Qué tienen que preparar Pilar y la Sra.?
2. ¿A dónde va María?
3. ¿Qué necesita Pilar del mercado?
4. ¿Cómo se llama el novio de Elena?
5. ¿Cómo es Carlos?
6. ¿A dónde van a comer?

⊕ B. Using the dialogue as a model, make complete sentences of the following. Use the words in the order given and make any changes or additions necessary to form complete sentences.

1. Yo/ir/mercado/porque/tener que/comprar/unas/cosas
2. Carlos/ser/simpático/y/estar/a la puerta
3. Elena y/amigo/venir/comer/nosotros
4. Tú/tener/carne/pero/necesitar/legumbres/para/sopa

---

* **Vajilla** dishes

36

LECCIÓN CINCO

Basic Words and Expressions

A propósito ... By the way ...
¿A qué hora ...? At what time ...?
¿Cuándo? When?
¡Qué va! Nonsense! On the contrary!
¿Quién? Who?

caer to fall
cenar to have dinner
hacer to do, make
llegar to arrive
ocupar to occupy
pasar to pass, spend (time)
poner to put
salir to leave, go out, come out
traer to bring

el aeropuerto airport
el año year
el avión airplane
el calor warmth, heat
la ciudad city
el cuarto room, quarter
el dormitorio bedroom
el frío cold

el hambre hunger
la maleta suitcase
el mes month
la noche night
el país country, nation
la razón reason
la sed thirst
la semana week
el sueño sleep
las vacaciones vacation (*normally plural in Spanish*)

amable nice
otro another, other

allí there
casi almost
después de after
media half
nunca never
o or
porque because
siempre always
sobre on, about

Basic Patterns

1.	¿Qué hora es?	What time is it?
2.	Son las dos y veinte.	It's twenty past two. (2:20)
3.	Son las tres menos cinco.	It's five minutes to three. (2:55)
4.	María siempre llega a las dos.	Mary always arrives at two.
5.	Tengo frío.	I am cold.
6.	Juan nunca tiene calor.	John is never warm.
7.	Tengo hambre pero no tengo sed.	I'm hungry but I'm not thirsty.
8.	¿Tiene Ud. sueño?	Are you sleepy?
9.	¿Cuántos años tiene Ud.?	How old are you?
10.	Tengo diecinueve (años).	I am nineteen (years old).

Drills

Cardinal Numbers (11–30)

1. Count from 11 to 20.
2. Count from 21 to 30.
⊕ 3. Write the following numbers: 11, 14, 15, 16, 20, 28, 30.
⊕ 4. Read the following sentences aloud: Necesitamos 21 libros más. Necesitamos 21 casas más.

Telling Time

Answer the question as shown in the example, using the hours indicated.

¿Qué hora es? 2:00 / *Son las dos.*
1:00, 3:00, 5:10, 7:25, 9:40, 11:55, 2:15 A.M., 4:30 P.M.

Answer the following questions orally, as shown in the example.

¿A qué hora llega María? ¿A las dos? / *Sí. Llega a las dos.*
1. ¿A qué hora sale Juan? ¿A las ocho y cuarto?
2. ¿A qué hora traen la comida? ¿A las nueve y cuarto?
3. ¿Cuándo llegan a la clase? ¿A las ocho y media?
4. ¿Cuándo recibimos las notas? ¿A la una?

Now provide responses for the above questions and change the time to fifteen minutes later.

¿A qué hora llega María? A las dos? / *No. Llega a las dos y cuarto.*

Discussion

Cardinal Numbers (11–30)

11	once	16	dieciséis	21	veintiuno*	26	veintiséis
12	doce	17	diecisiete	22	veintidós	27	veintisiete
13	trece	18	dieciocho	23	veintitrés	28	veintiocho
14	catorce	19	diecinueve	24	veinticuatro	29	veintinueve
15	quince	20	veinte	25	veinticinco	30	treinta

Telling Time

It is one o'clock is expressed as follows.

> **Es la una.**

All other hours of the day are plural.

> **Son las dos (las tres, las cuatro, etc.).**

Time from the hour up to, and including, the half-hour is expressed by stating the hour, followed by **y** and the number of minutes.

> **Es la una y diez.**   It is 1:10.   **Son las dos y siete.**   It is 2:07.

Time beyond the half-hour to the next hour is expressed by stating the following hour, followed by **menos** and the number of minutes.

> **Son las dos menos diez.**   It is 1:50.   **Son las dos menos veinte.**   It is 1:40.

The quarter-hour is expressed by **cuarto,** the half-hour by **media.**

> **Son las nueve y cuarto.**   It is 9:15.
> **Son las diez y media.**   It is 10:30.
> **Son las ocho menos cuarto.**   It is 7:45.

A.M. is expressed by **de la mañana.** P.M. until approximately six o'clock is expressed by **de la tarde.** P.M. after six is **de la noche.**

> **Son las diez y cinco de la mañana.**   It's 10:05 A.M.
> **Son las once y diez de la noche.**   It's 11:10 P.M.

The letter **a** is equivalent to the English *at* when expressing the time at which an action takes place.

> **Juan llega a la una.**   John arrives at one.
> **Siempre salen a las once.**   They always leave at eleven.

When no specific hour is expressed, *in the morning, in the afternoon,* and *in the evening* become **por la mañana, por la tarde,** and **por la noche.**

---

* Remember that the number *one* becomes **una** before a feminine noun. Before a masculine noun it contracts to **un:**

> **veintiún libros**   **veintiuna casas**

More Idioms with TENER

Answer affirmatively the following questions.

¿Tiene Ud. hambre? / *Sí, siempre tengo hambre.*

1. ¿Tiene Ud. frío?
2. ¿Tiene Ud. sed?
3. ¿Tienen mucho sueño?
4. ¿Tenemos mucha suerte?
5. ¿Tiene Ud. mucho calor?
6. ¿Tenemos razón?

Now answer the above questions in the negative.

¿Tiene Ud. hambre? / *No, nunca tengo hambre.*

Answer the following questions using the ages indicated.

¿Cuántos años tiene Ud? **(19)** / *Tengo diecinueve.*

1. ¿Cuántos años tiene su amigo? *(20)*
2. ¿Cuántos años tiene su hermano? *(28)*

Present Indicative of PONER, HACER, SALIR, CAER, TRAER

Repeat the models and then change according to the cues.

1. María pone los libros en la mesa.
   (*mis amigos, yo, Juan y Teresa, tú, nosotros*)
2. Mi madre hace pan en casa.
   (*yo, sus amigos, nosotros, tú, María*)
3. Roberto siempre sale a las dos.
   (*yo, ellos, María y yo, tú, Ricardo*)
4. El libro cae de la mesa.
   (*la pluma, los libros, el pan, la carne, las cartas*)
5. Trae la sopa y la carne a la mesa.
   (*nosotros, yo, tú, la señora, las señoritas*)

More Idioms with TENER

Many nouns can be used with **tener** to form idiomatic expressions. Following are some of the most common.

tener (mucho) frío	to be (very) cold (a person)
tener (mucho) calor	to be (very) warm (a person)
tener (mucha) hambre	to be (very) hungry
tener (mucha) sed	to be (very) thirsty
tener (mucho) sueño	to be (very) sleepy
tener (mucha) suerte	to be (very) lucky
no tener suerte	to be unlucky
tener razón	to be right
no tener razón	to be wrong
tener . . . años	to be . . . years old

Present Indicative of PONER, HACER, SALIR, CAER, TRAER

These verbs are irregular only in the first person singular.

poner (to put, place)   **hacer** (to make, do)   **salir** (to leave, go out)

pongo	ponemos		hago	hacemos		salgo	salimos
pones			haces			sales	
pone	ponen		hace	hacen		sale	salen

caer (to fall)   **traer** (to bring)

caigo	caemos		traigo	traemos
caes			traes	
cae	caen		trae	traen

Combined Exercises

A. Substitute the cues in the model sentences.

1. A propósito, María no viene porque tiene frío.
   (yo, Juan y Alberto, tú, Ud., mis amigos)
2. Los dos muchachos no van al aeropuerto porque tienen sueño.
   (María, nosotros, tú, yo, Ud., mis amigos)
3. Siempre traen algo cuando vienen a Madrid.
   (yo, tú, María, Juan y yo, ellos, Ud.)

B. Answer orally with a complete sentence, as shown in the example.

¿A qué hora llega Ud. a Madrid? (2:15 P.M.) / *Llego a Madrid a las dos*
y cuarto de la tarde.

1. ¿A qué hora trae Ud. las cartas? (9:20 A.M.)
2. ¿A qué hora hace Ud. el pan? (6:00 A.M.)
3. ¿A qué hora sale Ud. para su país? (11:30 P.M.)
4. ¿A qué hora pone Ud. los libros en la mesa? (7.45 A.M.)

C. Prepare an oral response in Spanish for each of the following.

1. ¿Qué hora es? 2. ¿Cuántos años tiene Ud.? 3. ¿Cuántos años tiene su amigo? 4. ¿Tiene Ud. frío ahora? ¿calor? ¿sed? 5. ¿Qué hace Ud. cuando tiene mucha hambre? 6. ¿Siempre tiene Ud. razón? 7. ¿Cuántos años tienen sus hermanos? 8. ¿A qué hora sale Ud. para su casa? 9. ¿Qué trae Ud. a la clase de español? 10. ¿Qué va a hacer después de la clase?

⊕ D. Write the following in Spanish.

22 large planes, 16 small suitcases, 13 nice men, his bedroom, their country, your vacation, to the airport, in the suitcase, from the room, from the rooms

E. Express the Spanish words in English without referring to the translation. Then cover the Spanish and translate the English phrase without referring to the Spanish. Repeat until you make no mistakes.

1.	a las ocho	*at eight o'clock*
2.	Llego a las ocho.	*I arrive at eight o'clock.*
3.	Salgo a las ocho.	*I leave at eight o'clock.*
4.	Sale a las ocho en punto.	*He is leaving at eight sharp.*
5.	Salimos a las ocho y media.	*We are leaving at 8:30.*
6.	Salen a la una.	*They are leaving at 1:00.*
7.	Vienen a la una.	*They are coming at 1:00.*
8.	hasta la una	*until 1:00*
9.	casi las dos	*almost 2:00*
10.	Son casi las dos.	*It is almost 2:00.*
11.	Es casi la una.	*It is almost 1:00.*

⊕ F. Write the following sentences in Spanish.

1. He is arriving at 6:30 in order to have dinner with us.
2. By the way, at what time does the airplane leave?
3. He never spends his vacation there.
4. They have almost twenty-five letters.
5. I am going to bring books or pens.
6. We are going to spend a week in Toledo and a month in Madrid.
7. We have to leave now because it's 11:00 P.M. and I am sleepy.
8. I am bringing a book about Mexico to the class.
9. In my house we never have dinner until very late.
10. The book falls from the table.

Reading and Conversation

En Casa de Antonio

José Mora, joven mexicano, llega a Madrid en avión a las nueve de la noche. Va a pasar un mes de vacaciones con su amigo, Antonio Rodríguez. Los dos muchachos son jóvenes; tienen dieciocho o diecinueve años. Antonio espera el avión en el aeropuerto, y los dos salen en taxi para la casa de Antonio.

José	Ahora llegamos. ¿Dónde pongo las maletas?
Antonio	Aquí, en el cuarto de mi hermano Felipe que trabaja en otra ciudad y no vive en casa ahora. Tú vas a ocupar su dormitorio.
José	¡Muy bien! Tengo suerte; es un cuarto muy bonito. A propósito, ¿qué hora es? ¿Es muy tarde?
Antonio	No, son las diez. ¿Tienes hambre?
José	Sí, pero es muy tarde para cenar, ¿no?
Antonio	¡Qué va! Aquí en la capital casi nunca cenamos hasta las nueve y media o las diez.
José	Ah, sí, tienes razón, todo es diferente en Madrid.
Antonio	Bueno, ¿qué hacemos mañana? ¿Vamos a Toledo o pasamos el día aquí?
José	¿Por qué no pasamos el día en Madrid? Necesito comprar unas cosas para mis amigos de México. Y, a propósito, traigo algo de allí para tu mamá.
Antonio	Eres muy amable; mamá va a estar muy contenta. ¿Qué traes?
José	Es un libro muy interesante sobre la comida de mi país. Y hablando de comida*, ¿cuándo vamos a comer? Tengo mucha hambre.
Antonio	Ahora mismo, amigo, ahora mismo. Vamos.

Mientras cenan José habla con los padres de Antonio sobre México y sobre sus amigos de allí. Después de la comida, José escribe una carta a sus padres y Antonio lee y mira la televisión hasta muy tarde.

---

* hablando de comida speaking of food

Dialogue Practice

A. Prepare oral responses to the following questions.

1. ¿En qué llega José Mora a Madrid?
2. ¿A qué hora llega?
3. ¿En qué salen los dos muchachos para la casa de Antonio?
4. ¿Qué trae José para la madre de Antonio?
5. ¿Qué hace José después de la comida?
6. ¿Qué hace Antonio después de la comida?

⊕ B. Using the dialogue as a model, copy the following sentences and fill in the blanks.

1. José pone las _____ en el cuarto de Felipe.
2. José _____ un libro muy interesante _____ la comida.
3. José necesita _____ unas cosas para _____ amigos.
4. José _____ suerte porque el cuarto _____ bonito.
5. Los dos muchachos _____ jóvenes. _____ dieciocho o diecinueve
    _____.

⊕ C. Rewrite the last paragraph of the dialogue, changing the verbs from third person singular **(él)** to first person singular **(yo).**

REPASO (1-5)

⊕ A. Ask the following questions in Spanish and then answer them in Spanish.

1. Ask your friend how he is. Tell him you are fine.   2. Ask how everyone is. Tell him you are all fine.   3. Ask him if he is in the Spanish class. Tell him you are not.   4. Ask if he studies at home. Tell him you study at home every day.   5. Ask him how many chairs are in the class. Tell him there are twenty-six chairs and a table.

⊕ B. Make complete sentences of the following.

1.   (Nosotros)/abrir/tienda/ocho/de la mañana.
2.   Pedro/ser/médico/pero/estar/enfermo.
3.   Lecciones/ser/difícil/pero/clase/ser/fácil.
4.   Ella/venir/de/mercado/ahora mismo.

C. Answer the questions in Spanish.

1. ¿Cómo se llama Ud.?   2. ¿Cómo se llama su padre?   3. ¿Dónde aprendes a leer y escribir?   4. ¿Lees un libro todos los días?   5. ¿Siempre recibes notas buenas?   6. ¿Estás cansado hoy?   7. ¿Tienen Uds. que leer mucho en la clase de español?   8. ¿Quién abre la puerta de la clase?   9. ¿Cuántos años tienes?   10. ¿Qué hora es?

D. The sentences which will be read to you are based on the first dialogues. If the sentence makes sense, mark it true; if not, mark it false. If you miss more than two items, go back and review the appropriate dialogue.

E. A short passage from the dialogue of Lesson IV will be read to you. Write the passage without referring to your books and then check what you have written against the appropriate lines of the dialogue. If you have too much trouble, you should review the dialogue.

⊕ F. Translate the following sentences into Spanish.

1.   The tables and chairs are in the store.
2.   They study all day.
3.   Do you (fam., sing.) live here?
4.   Why do you (fam., sing.) open the store every day?
5.   She is tired today, but she's not sick.
6.   John's father is a student, but he's not very young.
7.   He already has something besides bread.
8.   She runs to the store to buy something besides bread.
9.   They spend the day in Madrid.
10.   It's almost 7:15 and I'm already sleepy.

Recommended Readings from Appendix

La Ciudad de México Se Hunde and *Stalin y el Oro de España.*

ESPAÑA

MAR CANTABRICO

F R A N C I A

La Coruña
GALICIA
● Santiago
ASTURIAS
● Oviedo
Santander ●
PROVINCIAS
VASCONGADAS
● Bilbao
Pamplona ●
P I R I N E O S
NAVARRA
ANDORRA
● León
Burgos ●
Río Miño
LEON
CASTILLA
LA VIEJA
Valladolid ●
Río Duero
Zaragoza ●
ARAGON
CATALUÑA
Brava
Barcelona ●
Costa
Salamanca ●
Segovia ●
E   S   Ñ   A
P
● Alcalá de
Henares
● Madrid
Río Tajo
Toledo ●
CASTILLA
LA NUEVA
VALENCIA
L A   M A N C H A
Valencia ●
ISLAS BALEARES
EXTREMADURA
Río Guadiana
Río Júcar
● Lisboa
P O R T U G A L
MURCIA
Córdoba ●
Río Guadalquivir
Murcia ●
● Sevilla
Granada ●
ANDALUCIA
M E D I T E R R A N E O
Cádiz ●
Málaga ● *Costa del Sol*
*Estrecho
de Gibraltar*
M A R
*O C E A N O
A T L A N T I C O*
A R G E L I A
M A R R U E C O S
A F R I C A   D E L   N O R T E

Windmills in
La Mancha, south
of Madrid.

Sidewalk café
in Barcelona.

Typical street in Palma de Mallorca,
Balearic Islands. Mallorca is one of the
most popular tourist areas in
western Europe.

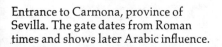

Entrance to Carmona, province of
Sevilla. The gate dates from Roman
times and shows later Arabic influence.

Village square
in southeastern Spain.

Building in Barcelona illustrating the unique
architectural style of Antonio Gaudí.

Private homes on Ibiza, one of the Balearic Islands,
showing the typical architectural style of the region.

The Alcázar, in Segovia, a favorite residence of Spanish sovereigns in the fifteenth century.

View of Avila in central Spain.

LECCIÓN
DE PRONUNCIACIÓN

The correlation between your ability to pronounce Spanish sounds and your overall success in the language is evident. This chapter is designed to aid you in mastering the sounds which are most different from English and is supplemented by taped explanations and drills, which should be studied thoroughly in the language laboratory or with a tape recorder.

Sounds of Spanish

Spanish pronunciation is relatively simple for two reasons: (1) many sounds approximate or are identical to English sounds, and (2) Spanish is very consistent in that most Spanish letters represent only one sound. There are very few exceptions to this rule which need concern you in your first year. If you relax and imitate, these sounds should not be difficult.

Part 1 *Vowels*

Contrary to English, where vowels may represent a variety of sounds, Spanish vowels represent one sound. Listen to the drills and imitate as closely as possible.

a   ba, da, fa, la, ma, na, pa, ca, ta
    paso, pan, asta, casa, mas, la, las, nota, da, mamá

e   be, de, fe, le, me, ne, pe, se, te
    mesa, en, veces, fea, esta, lema, tema, pelo, tela, meses, pesa

i   bi, di, fi, li, mi, ni, pi, si, ti
    día, bien, vivir, tienda, familia, medicina, difícil, también

o   bo, fo, lo, mo, no, po, so, to
    bonito, sopa, cosa, comida banco, mío, nota, contento, feo, como

u   bu, fu, lu, mu, nu, pu, su, tu
    luces, nunca, mucho, buscar, luego, muy, universal

y   muy, estoy, soy

A. Repeat the following.

    paso, peso, piso, poso, puso   nata, neta, nita, nota, nuta
    masa, mesa, misa, mosa, musa   lama, lema, lima, loma, luma

B. Repeat the following, being careful to note the contrasting sounds.

e — a		o — a (final)		e — a (final)	
mesa	masa	chicos	chicas	meses	mesas
peso	paso	picos	picas	mires	miras
tesa	tasa	miro	mira	cenen	cenan
plena	plana	míos	mías	baten	batan
neta	nata	muchos	muchas	españoles	españolas

a — u		i — e		o — u	
macho	mucho	piso	peso	poso	puso
paso	puso	misa	mesa	mosa	musa
masa	musa	lima	lema	bosque	busque

C. Repeat the following Spanish sentences.

1.	¿Cómo estás?	*How are you?*
2.	Estoy bien.	*I am fine.*
3.	¿Están aquí?	*Are they here?*
4.	Los alumnos están en la clase.	*The students are in the class.*

D. *Quiz.* Identify the vowel sounds. Identify first vowel. Identify last vowel.

Part 2 *Consonants*

h   In Spanish the **h** is *always* silent.
   hay, hoy, hasta, habla, hola

ll   Similar to the *y* in *yes.*
   llama, llamo, silla, sillas, ella, ellos

ñ   Similar to the *ny* in *canyon.*
   España, español, mañana, sueño, dueño, año, piña, otoño, uña

d   Similar to the *th* in *they;* harder when in initial position.
   adiós, ustedes, cada, estudio, usted, todo, día, de, donde

A. Repeat the following words.

1. silla   2. sueño   3. cada   4. llama   5. todos   6. español   7. ella   8. dueño
9. ellos   10. España   11. de   12. mañana   13. adiós   14. año   15. ustedes
16. sillas   17. estudio   18. piña   19. donde   20. otoño   21. día

B. *Quiz.* The preceding list will be read again in a different order. Identify the sounds (**ll, ñ, d**) represented in each word. Repeat until you make no mistakes.

b   The letters *b* and *v* are pronounced the same in Spanish. They are similar to the English *b* but the lips do not close. When these letters appear as the first letter in a word, the sound is slightly harder; the lips close slightly.
   nuevo, vivo, bueno, vaso, abro, novio, avión, lobo, nabo

j An aspirated sound similar to, but stronger than the *h* in *Hi!* Close off the air with the back of the tongue.

   viejo, joven, hijo, hijas, junta, fija, jota, paja

A. Repeat.

1. nuevo   2. hijo   3. joven   4. novio   5. paja

B. Repeat.

1. silla   2. jota   3. vaso   4. ellos   5. sueño   6. año   7. ella   8. vivo   9. hijo
10. adiós   11. avión   12. todo   13. español   14. junta   15. cada

C. Repeat the Spanish sentences.

1.	¿Cómo se llama Ud.?	*What is your name?*
2.	Me llamo Juan.	*My name is John.*
3.	Los jóvenes son novios.	*The young people are sweethearts.*
4.	El señor es viejo.	*The man is old.*
5.	Hablo español cada día.	*I speak Spanish each day.*

D. *Quiz.* The preceding list will be read in different order. Identify the sounds **(ll, d, ñ, b, j)** represented by each word. Repeat until you make no mistakes.

Part 3

r Pronounced much like the *d* in English *ladder*. The tip of the tongue touches the roof of the mouth just behind the upper front teeth. Compare the diagrams.

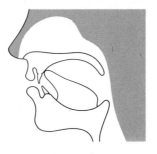 

Spanish **r**   English **r**

   pero, para, ahora, puro, fruta, fresca, padre, señor, señoras, señoritas, estar, hablar, libro, carta, mujer, mejor

rr Several vibrations or flaps of the tongue in same position as for the single
initial r **r** *(see diagram)*. When the single **r** is the first letter of a word, it has the same sound as the double **r.**

   rico, recibir, rojo, correr, perro, carro, rosa, raro, barra, corro

A. Repeat.

1. rico 2. perro 3. libro 4. hablar 5. pero 6. carro 7. padre 8. rojo
9. carta 10. rosa

B. Repeat.

1. Mi mujer es rica. 2. El perro corre mucho. 3. La fruta es fresca.

C. *Quiz.* The preceding list will be read again in different order. Identify the
sound (**r** or **rr**) represented by each word.

g   The sound of Spanish **g** varies according to the letter which follows. It is
pronounced like Spanish **j** when used before **i** and **e**.
   gente, **g**ira, **g**eneral, **g**imo

When followed by **a, o,** or **u,** the Spanish **g** is similar to but somewhat
softer than the English *g*. The letter **u** is silent following **g.**
   pon**g**o, **g**anga, si**g**o, se**g**uida, lle**g**o, lue**g**o

c   The letter **c** also varies according to the letter which follows. **C** before **i**
and **e** is like the English *s*.
   cenar, **c**era, **c**ine, ve**c**es

C before **a, o,** or **u** is like *k* but somewhat softer. Double **c** is like *x*.
   casa, es**c**ribir, **c**omer, **c**omo, **c**on, le**cc**ión

u   The letter **u** is silent when following **g** and **q.**
   parq**u**e, seg**u**ida, q**u**e, por q**u**é, peq**u**eño, lleg**u**é

z   This letter is pronounced like the English *s*.
   lu**z**, ve**z**, **z**umo, ca**z**a

A. Repeat.

1. gente 2. sigo 3. cena 4. vez 5. como 6. general 7. ganga 8. seguida
9. porque 10. luz 11. gira 12. pongo 13. cine 14. casa 15. parque

B. *Quiz.* This time you will be asked to read the above list. When you hear the
number, pronounce the corresponding word into the microphone. Then
listen for the correct pronunciation and repeat.

Accentuation and Stress

Spanish words generally have only one strong syllable and a succession of weak
syllables. The rules for this stress are relatively simple.

Stress falls on the next to the last syllable if the word ends in a vowel, an *n* or
an *s*.
   casa, **to**do, her**ma**no, **hom**bre, intere**san**te, fa**mi**lia, en**fer**mo, con**ten**to,
se**ño**res, **jo**ven, e**xa**men

Note that no vowel is slurred over and that each is pronounced clearly, although
the next to the last receives the stress.

54

Stress falls on the last syllable for words ending in consonants other than *n* and *s*.

usted, hablar, preparar, entrar, ciudad, mitad, español, feliz

Words that are exceptions to these rules have a written accent to show the variation.

difícil, está, librería, inglés, médico, fácil, también

A few words carry an accent to distinguish them from other words which are spelled the same. All question-asking words carry written accents.

¿cómo? how?   **como** since

Note carefully the pronunciation of the following words which contain combinations of vowels.

luego, bueno, bien, adiós, tienda, viejo, gracias, leer, caer

A. Repeat.

1. casa   2. familia   3. está   4. usted   5. ustedes   6. preparar   7. inglés
8. están   9. contento   10. joven   11. luego   12. médico   13. interesante
14. tienda   15. gracias

B. *Quiz*. This time you will be asked to read the above list. When you hear the number, pronounce the corresponding word into the microphone. Then listen for the correct pronunciation and repeat.

LECCIÓN SEIS

Basic Words and Expressions

¿**Cuánto (a)?** How much?
¿**Cuántos (as)?** How many?
por favor please

caminar to walk
conocer to know (be acquainted with)
creer to believe
dar to give
llamar to call
oír to hear
parecer to seem, appear
saber to know (a fact)
terminar to end
tomar to have (food or drink), take
visitar to visit
ver to see

la calle street
el camarero waiter
la biblioteca library
el centro downtown, center
la ciudad city
el ecuador equator
la estación season (of year)
el este east

el estudiante student
el hombre man
el invierno winter
el lago lake
la montaña mountain
el norte north
el oeste west
el otoño fall, autumn
la primavera spring
el refresco cold drink, refreshment
el ruido noise
el sol sun
el sur south
el tiempo weather, time
el trabajo work
el verano summer
el viento wind

poco little (in amount)
en seguida immediately
hoy today
por through, along, by, for
que that
solo alone (*adj.*)
sólo only (*adv.*)

Basic Patterns

1. **Juan no olvida a sus amigos.**   John doesn't forget his friends.
2. **Conozco a María, pero no sé cuántos años tiene.**   I know Mary, but I don't know how old she is.
3. **Al entrar en la clase, siempre habla con los alumnos.**   On entering (when he enters) the class, he always speaks with the students.
4. **Es un buen hombre.**   He is a good man.
5. **¿Qué tiempo hace hoy?**   What's the weather today?
6. **Hace buen (mal) tiempo.**   It is good (bad) weather.
7. **Hace frío en el invierno.**   It is cold in winter.

Drills

Personal A

Substitute the objects provided and determine whether the personal **a** is required.

1. Juan no olvida a su amigo.
   (*libro, madre, clase, padres, pluma*)
2. Voy a esperar a Roberto.
   (*la carta, el avión, el amigo de Roberto, la comida, el padre de Juan*)
3. Tengo dos amigos.
   (*un libro interesante, un novio, tres hermanas, una casa nueva*)

Present Indicative of CONOCER, SABER, PARECER, VER, DAR, OÍR

Repeat the model sentences, then substitute the indicated cues.

1. Conozco a la hermana de Juan.
   (*él, nosotros, tú, yo, ellos, Ud.*)
2. Saben que nuestros amigos vienen mañana.
   (*yo, María, tú, Juan y yo, Ud., ellos*)
3. Felipe no parece mexicano.
   (*yo, tú, Juan y Alberto, Ud., María, nosotros*)
4. María no ve a la sirvienta.
   (*yo, él, mis hermanos, nosotros, tú, Ud.*)
5. Siempre da cosas a los niños.
   (*yo, Juan y yo, tú, ellos, Ud., Teresa*)
6. Oigo el ruido del avión.
   (*María, mis amigos, tú, Roberto y yo, Ud., yo*)

SABER and CONOCER

Prepare oral responses in Spanish to the following questions as illustrated in the example.

> **¿Conoce Ud. a mi hermana?** / *No, no conozco a su hermana.*
> **¿Sabe Ud. cuántos años tiene?** / *No, no sé cuántos años tiene.*

1. ¿Conoce Ud. al señor Morales?
   ¿Sabe Ud. dónde vive?
2. ¿Conoce Ud. al alumno español?
   ¿Sabe Ud. cuándo llega?
3. ¿Conoce Ud. las calles de Madrid?
   ¿Sabe Ud. que vivo en una de las calles principales?

Repeat the model sentences, then substitute the cues using either **saber** or **conocer.** Do not change the subject. Include personal **a** where required.

1. Conozco la ciudad.
   (*su hermana, que Juan llega hoy, hablar español, la calle donde viven*)
2. Ustedes saben escribir una carta interesante.
   (*el amigo de Juan, que el avión llega tarde, hacer el trabajo*)

Discussion

Personal A

When the direct object of a verb, other than **tener,** is a noun which stands for a definite person, the letter **a** must appear before the noun. Used in this way, **a** has no translation; it serves merely to indicate that the noun which follows is the object of the verb, not the subject. However, no personal **a** is required after the verb **tener.**

No comprendo a Juan.	I don't understand John.
Tengo que esperar a mis amigos.	I have to wait for my friends.
Tiene una hermana hermosa.	He has a beautiful sister.

Present Indicative of CONOCER, SABER, PARECER, VER, DAR, OÍR

Except for **oír,** all these verbs are irregular only in the first person.

conocer (to know, be acquainted with)		saber (to know a fact)	
conozco	conocemos	sé	sabemos
conoces		sabes	
conoce	conocen	sabe	saben

parecer (to seem, appear)		ver (to see)		dar (to give)		oír (to hear)		
parezco	parecemos	veo	vemos	doy	damos	oigo	oímos	*(note accent)*
pareces		ves		das		oyes		
parece	parecen	ve	ven	da	dan	oye	oyen	

SABER and CONOCER

Saber means *to know* in the sense of knowing a fact or knowing how to do something.

Saben que vivimos aquí.	They know that we live here.
Sabe hablar español.	He knows how to speak Spanish.

Conocer means *to know* in the sense of being acquainted with or familiar with a person or thing.

Conozco a su amigo.	I know your friend.
Conoce Madrid.	He knows Madrid.
Conoce las calles de la ciudad.	He knows the streets of the city.

AL + *Infinitive*

Substitute the infinitives provided. Make no other changes.

1. Al entrar en la clase habla con los alumnos.
   (*salir de, llegar a, terminar*)
2. Siempre estoy contento al ver a mi novia.
   (*escribir, mirar, llamar*)

Shortening of Adjectives BUENO and MALO

⊕ Supply the proper form of the adjectives in parentheses.

1. Es un (*bueno*) hombre.
2. Son (*bueno*) muchachas.
3. Es una (*malo*) cosa.
4. Es un (*malo*) día.
5. Son (*bueno*) amigos.

Weather Expressions

Prepare oral responses to the following.

1. ¿Qué tiempo hace hoy?
2. ¿Qué tiempo hace aquí en el verano? ¿En el invierno? ¿En el otoño?
3. ¿Hace calor hoy?
4. ¿Hace mucho viento aquí en la primavera?
5. ¿Hace mucho sol hoy?
6. ¿Hace mal tiempo hoy?

AL + *Infinitive*

Al plus the infinitive expresses two simultaneous actions and is equivalent to the rather literary *on doing something,* for example, *On arriving at the university, I always speak with John.* More common English equivalents are *when I arrive* or *as soon as I arrive.*

Tiene que hablar con el profesor al llegar.	You have to talk with the teacher on arriving (as soon as you arrive, when you arrive).
Al salir, siempre va a la biblioteca.	On leaving (as soon as he leaves, when he leaves), he always goes to the library.

Shortening of Adjectives BUENO and MALO

These two adjectives may be placed before or after the noun. When placed before a masculine singular noun, they drop the final **o.**

un buen muchacho	un muchacho bueno
dos buenos muchachos	dos muchachos buenos
un mal hombre	un hombre malo
una mala idea	una idea mala

Weather Expressions

Most weather expressions use **hacer.**

¿Qué tiempo hace?	How is the weather? (What's it like out?)
Hace buen tiempo.	The weather is good. (It's a nice day.)
Hace mal tiempo.	It's a bad day.
Hace (mucho) frío.	It is (very) cold.
No hace frío.	It's not cold.
Hace (mucho) calor.	It's (very) warm.
Hace (poco) viento.	It's (not very) windy.
Hace (poco) sol.	It's (not very) sunny.

Because **frío, calor, viento,** and **sol** are nouns, they are modified by the adjectives **mucho** and **poco.**

Combined Exercises

A. Substitute the cues for the first verb only in 1, 2, and 3, but for both verbs in 4 and 5.

1. Yo veo que los estudiantes caminan por las calles hoy.
   (*nosotros, Juan, tú, ellos, Ud.*)
2. Sabemos que Tomás siempre toma un refresco al llegar.
   (*yo, ellos, María, tú, Ud., Juan y yo*)
3. Yo sólo doy trabajo a mis estudiantes en el invierno.
   (*Ud., el señor Bellido, nosotros, ellos, tú*)
4. Juan oye poco ruido cuando visita Buenos Aires.
   (*yo, nosotros, Rafael, tú, Ud., ellos*)
5. No conozco al camarero, pero sé que trabaja en el centro.
   (*Teresa, tú, ellos, nosotros, yo, Ud.*)

B. Write answers to the following questions and be prepared to answer them orally without referring to your notes.

1. ¿Conoce Ud. un buen restaurante aquí en la ciudad? 2. ¿A qué hora entra Ud. en la clase de español? 3. ¿Va Ud. en seguida a la biblioteca al terminar su trabajo en su cuarto? 4. ¿Va Ud. a las montañas del norte en el verano? 5. ¿En qué parte del país vive Ud.? ¿Hace mucho frío allí en el invierno? 6. ¿Cuánto trabajo tiene Ud. para mañana? ¿Hay mucho trabajo en su clase de español? 7. ¿Sabe Ud. cuántas estaciones del año hay? ¿Cuántas hay? 8. ¿Conoce Ud. a la novia de mi hermano? 9. ¿Estudia Ud. mucho o poco cuando hace mal tiempo? 10. ¿Hay mucho ruido en su cuarto cuando Ud. tiene que estudiar?

C. Express the Spanish sentences in English without referring to the translation. Then cover the Spanish and translate the English into Spanish. Repeat until you make no mistakes.

1.	Hace frío.	*It's cold.*
2.	Tengo frío.	*I am cold.*
3.	Tengo mucho frío.	*I am very cold.*
4.	Tengo mucho calor.	*I am very warm.*
5.	Hace mucho calor.	*It's very warm.*
6.	Hace viento.	*It's windy.*
7.	Hace sol.	*It's sunny.*
8.	¿Qué tiempo hace?	*How's the weather?*
9.	Conozco a María.	*I know Mary.*
10.	Conozco las montañas.	*I know the mountains.*
11.	El sabe que hace frío.	*He knows it's cold.*
12.	Yo sé cuántos años tengo.	*I know how old I am.*
13.	Conoce a los estudiantes.	*He knows the students.*
14.	Sabemos que es otoño.	*We know that it's autumn.*

⊕ D. Write the following sentences in Spanish.

1. I know that it is cold in Madrid in the winter.
2. I go immediately to my room when I finish (on finishing) my work.
3. It is always warm in the south in the summer.
4. It is very windy in the spring in my country.
5. The four seasons of the year are: spring, summer, fall, and winter.

6.   In the countries south of (to the south of) the equator the weather is not always good.
7.   What's it like out today? (What's the weather today?) It's very sunny.
8.   I'm hungry; I'm going to call the waiter. What are you going to have? Meat and vegetables, please.
9.   I don't know your sister well, but she seems very nice.

Reading and Conversation

En la Argentina*

Tomás Galán, español y estudiante de la Universidad de Madrid, visita a un amigo, Rafael Mendoza, en Buenos Aires. Es un día de verano y hace mucho calor. Los dos muchachos caminan por las calles del centro de la ciudad, y al pasar por un café, entran para tomar un refresco y hablar.

Rafael   Bueno, Tomás, tengo sed. Voy a llamar al camarero. ¿Qué vas a tomar?

Tomás   Una Coca-Cola, por favor. Y tú, ¿qué tomas?

Rafael   Una Coca también. (*Al camarero:*) Dos Cocas, por favor.

Camarero   En seguida, señor.

Tomás   ¿Sabes, Rafael, que es difícil creer que ahora en mi país es invierno, y aquí en la Argentina* estamos en verano?

Rafael   Es muy natural, porque como tú bien sabes estamos al sur del ecuador y aquí las estaciones del año son diferentes. Cuando hace frío en tu país aquí hace calor. Pero no hay que hablar del tiempo. Tú sólo vas a estar aquí un mes y tienes que visitar muchas partes del país. ¿Conoces la ciudad de Bariloche?

Tomás   No, no conozco la ciudad. Sólo sé que está en el suroeste en una región que tiene muchos lagos y montañas. Es una ciudad muy grande, ¿no?

Rafael   ¡Qué va! Es pequeña y muy tranquila, no como Buenos Aires o las ciudades grandes donde siempre hay mucho ruido en el centro. Además, Bariloche es una de las regiones más hermosas de la Argentina. Mis amigos pasan las vacaciones allí casi todos los años y cuando escriben, siempre hablan de los lagos tranquilos y de las montañas hermosas.

Tomás   Muy interesante. Parece que voy a tener que visitar Bariloche.

Rafael   Bueno, Tomás, veo que son las siete y tengo que ir a casa para comer y después preparar un trabajo para una de mis clases. Mañana hablamos más sobre otras regiones interesantes de mi país.

Al salir del café, Rafael va a su casa para comer a las siete y media, y Tomás camina por las calles para conocer el centro de la ciudad.

---

* The names of certain countries require the definite article.

Dialogue Practice

A. Prepare oral responses to the following questions.

1. ¿Qué tiempo hace cuando los dos muchachos caminan por las calles?
2. ¿En dónde entran los dos y qué toman?
3. ¿Cómo es la región de Bariloche?
4. ¿A qué hora tiene que comer Rafael?
5. Cuando hace frío en el país de Tomás, ¿qué tiempo hace en la Argentina?
6. ¿Cuánto tiempo va a pasar Tomás en la Argentina?
7. ¿Dónde está la ciudad de Bariloche?
8. ¿Qué hace Rafael al salir del café?

⊕ B. Using the dialogue as a model, rewrite the following and change the verbs from third person singular and plural to first person singular and plural.

Tomás visita a su amigo Rafael. Ellos caminan por las calles del centro y entran en un café. Tomás tiene sed y llama al camarero. Los dos toman Coca-Cola y hablan de las estaciones. Tomás sólo va a estar un mes allí y tiene que visitar muchas regiones del país. No conoce la ciudad de Bariloche pero sabe que es muy bonita. Después de tomar las Cocas, salen del café.

LECCIÓN SIETE

Basic Words and Expressions

comenzar a + *inf.* to begin + *inf.*
fin de semana weekend
¡Hola! Hello! Hi!
Mucho gusto. Glad to meet you (much pleasure).
al fin at last
tener prisa to be in a hurry
¡Vaya! Well! For goodness sake!

buscar to look for
comenzar (ie) to begin
costar (ue) to cost
decir to say, tell
llevar to carry, wear
llover (ue) to rain
nevar (ie) to snow
pedir (i) to ask for
perder (ie) to lose, miss
poder (ue) to be able
presentar to present
querer (ie) to wish, want, love
volver (ue) to return

el autobús bus
la chica girl

el chico boy
el cielo sky
la esquina corner
el forastero stranger, foreigner
la manzana apple, city block
el mundo world
el número number
el pariente relative
el parque park
la peseta unit of currency (*Spain*)
el policía policeman

cerca close, near
desde from, since
entonces then
hacia toward
maldito cursed, blasted
mejor better, best
nada nothing
nadie no one
pronto soon
pues well
si if
varios several

Basic Patterns

1.	**Juan comienza a caminar hacia el parque.**	John begins to walk toward the park.
2.	**Quiero tomar el autobús aquí, pero no sé el número.**	I want to take the bus here, but I don't know the number.
3.	**Juan no tiene cuatro pesetas y las pide a un forastero.**	John doesn't have four pesetas and he asks a stranger for them.
4.	**El forastero dice, "Vuelva a casa si no las tiene."**	The stranger says, "Go back home if you don't have them."
5.	**El autobús me lleva al parque.**	The bus takes me to the park.
6.	**No hable Ud. tanto.**	Don't talk so much. (*sing.*)
7.	**No hablen Uds. tanto.**	Don't talk so much. (*pl.*)
8.	**No tengo prisa. Hoy no llueve.**	I'm not in a hurry. It won't rain today.

Drills

Present Indicative of Stem-Changing Verbs

Repeat the model sentences and then substitute the cues.

1. Juan comienza a caminar por las calles.
   (*tú, yo, él, nosotros, ellos, Ud.*)
2. Siempre pierdo el autobús.
   (*tú, nosotros, él, ellos, yo, Uds.*)
3. El chico quiere volver ahora.
   (*yo, nosotros, tú, Ud., mis parientes, ella*)
4. En invierno no podemos hacer nada.
   (*yo, tú, el hombre, nuestros padres, nosotros, ellos*)
5. Vuelvo al parque en seguida.
   (*tú, varias personas, nosotros, nadie, los estudiantes*)
6. Pido carne y sopa para la comida.
   (*los chicos, tú, nosotros, yo, nadie, el camarero*)
7. El forastero dice que ya son las ocho.
   (*yo, tú, nosotros, la chica, yo, mis parientes*)

⊕ Give the Spanish orally.

It costs, I say, we lose, they begin, it rains, you eat (*formal, sing.*), we can, they cost, we want, he asks for, we return, they lose, we say, you look for (*fam., sing.*), they carry, I present, he returns, I can, it snows, we begin

⊕ Read and then change the verbs to the plural.

1. Quiero tomar el autobús aquí, pero no sé el número.
2. El no dice nada porque no puede.
3. Tengo que volver ahora, pero no quiero.

Double Negative

⊕ Express the following sentences in Spanish.

1. He is not buying anything.
2. He can't do anything.
3. They don't say anything.
4. He doesn't study anything.
5. She doesn't forget anyone.

Discussion

Present Indicative of Stem-Changing Verbs

(e–ie) In the present tense, the **e** of the stem of some verbs regularly changes to **ie**. Note that this occurs in all forms except the first person plural **(nosotros)**.

comenzar (to begin)		perder (to lose, miss)		querer (to want, love)	
comienzo	comenzamos	pierdo	perdemos	quiero	queremos
comienzas		pierdes		quieres	
comienza	comienzan	pierde	pierden	quiere	quieren

The verb **nevar** (*to snow*) is of the same type, but is used only in the third person singular, **nieva** (*It is snowing*).

(o–ue) Change the **o** of the stem to **ue** in all forms except the first person plural **(nosotros)**.

poder (to be able)		volver (to return)	
puedo	podemos	vuelvo	volvemos
puedes		vuelves	
puede	pueden	vuelve	vuelven

The verbs **costar** (*to cost*) and **llover** (*to rain*) are of the same type. However, **costar** is usually used only in the third person singular and plural (**cuesta** and **cuestan**), and **llover** is used only in the third person singular **(llueve)**.

(e–i) Change the **e** of the stem to **i** in all forms except the first person plural **(nosotros)**. Note that **decir** is also irregular in the first person singular.

pedir (to ask for)		decir (to say, tell)	
pido	pedimos	digo	decimos
pides		dices	
pide	piden	dice	dicen

Stem-changing verbs will be indicated in the vocabulary of each lesson as they appear. They will be followed by the indication: **(ie)**, **(ue)**, **(i)**.

Double Negative

Contrary to English usage, two negative words are often used in the same sentence to express negation in Spanish.

No veo nada.	I don't see anything.
No esperan a nadie.	They don't wait for anyone.
No voy nunca.	I never go.

Formal Commands

Form singular commands of the following verbs. Then repeat, forming plural commands.

hablar / *Hable Ud., Hablen Uds.*

aprender, comer, escribir, tener, hacer, traer, oír, volver, saber, llevar, dar, ir, estar, ser, decir, leer, olvidar, terminar, poner, pedir

Express the following in Spanish, first in the singular and then in the plural.

Don't open. / *No abra Ud., No abran Uds.*

Don't buy, Don't speak, Don't read, Don't look at, Don't come, Don't return, Don't give, Don't wear, Don't leave, Don't eat, Don't forget, Don't be **(ser),** Don't be **(estar),** Don't ask for, Don't lose, Don't go, Don't say, Don't work, Don't fall.

Direct Object Pronouns

Read each sentence aloud and then substitute the appropriate pronoun for the italicized object.

Abro *la puerta* **/** *La* **abro.**

1. Paco no abre *la puerta.*
2. Busco *a mis padres.*
3. Pide *una sopa con legumbres.*
4. Pone *muchas cosas* en la mesa.
5. Trae *a su novia* a casa.
6. Pierdo *mis libros.*
7. El quiere *a los chicos.*
8. Olvido *la manzana.*
9. Traigo *a mis parientes.*
10. Visita *a su hermano.*
11. El autobús lleva *a Juan.*
12. Ponemos *la silla* cerca de la mesa.

⊕ Express the following in Spanish.

1. I know it.
2. I know him.
3. We have it.
4. He believes me.
5. They are visiting us.
6. You (*fam., sing.*) know me.
7. They don't understand me.
8. They are selling them (*refreshments*).
9. They don't see us.
10. I am bringing it (*table*).
11. They are looking at her.
12. She doesn't see them (*boys*).
13. We don't hear you (*m., sing.*)
14. He knows me.
15. I am beginning it (*lesson*).

Formal Commands

The affirmative command of regular verbs is formed by adding the following endings to the stem of the first person singular of the present indicative.

hablar/habl *o*	volver/vuelv *o*	venir/veng *o*
habl *e* Ud. ⎫ speak habl *en* Uds. ⎭	vuelv *a* Ud. ⎫ return vuelv *an* Uds. ⎭	veng *a* Ud. ⎫ come veng *an* Uds. ⎭

The negative command is formed by placing the word **no** before the affirmative form. Note that **Ud.** and **Uds.** are regularly used with commands although their use is not required.

no hable **Ud.** ⎫ don't   **no vuelva** **Ud.** ⎫ don't   **no venga** **Ud.** ⎫ don't
no hablen Uds. ⎭ speak   **no vuelvan Uds.** ⎭ return   **no vengan Uds.** ⎭ come

The following verbs add the above endings to different stems and must be memorized.

dar	ir	saber
dé Ud. ⎫ give . . . den Uds. ⎭	vaya Ud. ⎫ go . . . vayan Uds. ⎭	sepa Ud. ⎫ know . . . sepan Uds. ⎭

ser	estar
sea Ud. ⎫ be . . . sean Uds. ⎭	esté Ud. ⎫ be . . . estén Uds. ⎭

Direct Object Pronouns

The direct object pronouns are

me	me	**nos**	us
te	you (*fam., sing.*)		
le*	him, you (*formal, sing., m.*)	**los**	them (*m.*), you (*formal, pl., m.*)
la	her, it (*f.*), you (*formal, sing., f.*)	**las**	them (*f.*), you (*formal, pl., f.*)
lo	it (*m.*)		

Normally, the direct object pronouns are placed before the verb. In a negative sentence the **no** must precede the object pronoun.

Pido una silla. I ask for a chair.   **La pido.** I ask for it.

Pierdo mis libros. I lose my books.   **Los pierdo.** I lose them.

El me busca.	He is looking for me.	**El no me busca.**	He is not looking for me.
Nos esperan.	They're waiting for us.	**No nos esperan.**	They're not waiting for us.

Note that the verbs **buscar, esperar, pedir** do not require the preposition *for* because it is included in the meaning of the verb. Another verb of this type is **mirar** (*to look at*).

---

* Many native speakers, particularly those in Spanish America, prefer to use **lo** instead of **le** to express **him** or **you** (formal). For simplicity at this level, only the **le** form will be used here.

Combined Exercises

A. Express the following Spanish phrases and sentences in English without referring to the translation. Then cover the Spanish and express the English in Spanish. Repeat until you make no mistakes.

1.	en la esquina	*on the corner*
2.	El autobús está en la esquina.	*The bus is at the corner.*
3.	El forastero está en la esquina.	*The stranger is at the corner.*
4.	Los chicos están en la esquina.	*The boys are at the corner.*
5.	Varios chicos están en la esquina.	*Several boys are at the corner.*
6.	Varios policías están en la esquina.	*Several policemen are at the corner.*
7.	hacia nosotros	*toward us*
8.	Vienen hacia nosotros.	*They come toward us.*
9.	Nuestros parientes vuelven.	*Our relatives return.*
10.	Nuestros parientes están cerca.	*Our relatives are nearby.*
11.	Nadie está cerca.	*No one is near.*
12.	El mundo es grande.	*The world is large.*
13.	El mundo es pequeño.	*The world is small.*
14.	El parque está cerca.	*The park is near.*
15.	varias manzanas	*several blocks*
16.	Camino varias manzanas.	*I walk several blocks.*
17.	Comienzo a caminar varias manzanas.	*I begin to walk several blocks.*
18.	el número de manzanas	*the number of blocks*
18.	No sé el número de manzanas.	*I don't know the number of blocks.*
20.	Cuestan dos pesetas.	*They cost two pesetas.*
21.	Cuesta dos pesetas.	*It costs two pesetas.*
22.	Pierdo las pesetas.	*I lose the pesetas.*
23.	Las busco.	*I look for them.*

B. Substitute the cues.

1. El policía vuelve por fin.
   (*los policías, tú, nosotros*)
2. ¡Vaya! Qué suerte tengo yo. La chica me quiere.
   (*tú, Pedro, Ud.*)
3. El autobús los lleva al parque.
   (*nos, las, le, te, me, la*)
4. Me espera en el centro de la ciudad.
   (*la, me, te, le, las, nos*)

⊕ C. Translate the following.

1. I always lose it (*book*).   2. She loves me.   3. He asks for them (*chairs*).
4. The bus takes them (*girls*).   5. They wear them (*things*).   6. They are
looking for us.   7. I believe you (*m.*).   8. They always put it (*pen*) here.
9. We make them (*houses*).   10. She forgets me.

D. Answer the questions in Spanish.

1. ¿Nieva hoy en tu país?   2. ¿Pueden Uds. preparar la lección?   3. ¿Cuántas
pesetas cuesta una manzana?   4. ¿Traen Uds. los libros cada día?   5. ¿Tienes

suerte todos los días?   6. ¿En qué estación del año estamos?   7. ¿Qué tiempo hace hoy?   8. ¿Quiere Ud. ser camarero? ¿policía?   10. ¿Le cuesta mucho ir a las montañas?

⊕ E. Translate these sentences.

1. I am looking for my books. I don't have them.   2. I have a girl friend now, and I love her very much.   3. I need vegetables, and I always buy them downtown.   4. Go (*pl., formal*) on the bus. It takes you to the park. 5. Run (*formal, sing.*), don't walk. Leave the store and don't return. 6. Don't (*formal, sing.*) say anything else. I believe you.

⊕ F. Read the sentence, filling in the proper form of **ser** and **estar.**

1.   Ellos _____ mis parientes y _____ allí.
2.   Mi hermano _____ policía pero yo no _____ nadie.
3.   Todos los autobuses _____ grandes y varios _____ en la esquina.
4.   La chica _____ muy fea y además _____ enferma.
5.   Nosotros _____ en el norte del país y las montañas _____ bonitas.

Reading and Conversation

En el Retiro*

José Mora, el joven mexicano, sale de casa a las diez de la mañana y comienza a caminar por las calles de Madrid. Su amigo Antonio le espera en el Retiro a las doce, y José le busca allí. Al caminar varias manzanas, quiere tomar el autobús, pero no sabe el número y habla con un policía que está en la esquina.

José   Por favor, señor, un amigo me espera en el Retiro y soy forastero. ¿Sabe Ud. el número del autobús que va al Retiro?

Policía   No, el número no lo sé, y además, para llegar al Retiro es mejor tomar el Metro.** Espere Ud. en esta esquina y puede tomar el autobús hasta la Puerta del Sol.† Desde allí el Metro le lleva al Retiro.

José   Muchas gracias, aquí viene el autobús. A propósito, ¿cuánto cuesta?

Policía   Cuatro pesetas, pero corra o lo pierde. No esperan a nadie.

. . .

José llega por fin al Retiro. Su amigo y dos chicas le esperan allí. Cuando los ve, comienza a correr hacia ellos.

Antonio   ¡Hola amigo! Al fin llegas. Te quiero presentar a dos amigas, Elena Callas y María Tudela.

José   Mucho gusto, señoritas. María, ¿eres pariente del señor Alonso de Tudela, el famoso médico?

* **Retiro**   the central park of Madrid
** **Metro**   the Madrid subway
† **La Puerta del Sol**   the central plaza of Madrid

María	Sí, es mi padre. El y mi madre están en el parque también. Venimos aquí todos los fines de semana.
José	¡Vaya! ¡Ya conozco a tu padre! Eres de México entonces. El y mi padre son muy amigos.
María	Pues, vengan con nosotras y pueden hablar con él.
Antonio	Sí . . . pero . . . y después nosotros, digo, nosotros cuatro, podemos tomar un refresco aquí cerca, ¿verdad?
María	Sí, si es que no llueve. Miren el cielo.
Antonio	(*a José*) Sí, en seguida va a llover. Maldita la suerte que tengo yo con las chicas.

Dialogue Practice

A. Prepare oral responses to the following questions.

1. ¿A qué hora sale José de la casa?
2. ¿A qué hora le espera Antonio? ¿Dónde le espera?
3. ¿Dónde está el policía?
4. ¿Cuánto cuesta el autobús?
5. ¿Qué hace José cuando ve a sus amigos?
6. ¿Cómo se llaman las dos chicas?
7. ¿Cuándo vienen María y sus padres al parque?
8. ¿Qué quiere hacer Antonio?
9. ¿Qué tiempo hace?
10. ¿Tiene suerte Antonio con las chicas?

LECCIÓN OCHO

Basic Words and Expressions

Lo siento (mucho). I am (very) sorry.
¿Qué tal? How are you? How goes it?
¿Qué hay de nuevo? What's new?
muchas veces often, many times
en malas condiciones in bad condition
de todos modos anyhow, at any rate

andar to run (machinery)
arrancar to start (machinery)
arreglar to repair, arrange
consumir to consume, use
dormir (ue) to sleep
encontrar (ue) to meet, find
exagerar to exaggerate
funcionar to function, work
mostrar (ue) to show
pensar (ie) to think
pensar + inf. to intend + inf.
preferir (ie) to prefer
responder to respond, answer
sentir (ie) to feel, regret
tratar (de) to try (to)

el asiento seat
el automóvil automobile
el coche car, automobile
el defecto defect
el desastre disaster
el freno brake
la ganga bargain
la importancia importance
el modelo model, make
la ventaja advantage
el viaje trip

estupendo stupendous, wonderful
magnífico great, magnificent

mil thousand
mucho much
muchos many
lejos distant, far away
sin without
como like, as
conmigo with me
contigo with you (fam.)

Basic Patterns

1. **Habla español, amigo.** — Speak Spanish, friend.
2. **Ven a las siete, Teresa.** — Come at seven, Theresa.
3. **Le hablo todos los días.** — I speak to him every day.
4. **Cómpralas hoy, Juan.** — Buy them today, John.
5. **Me los vende.** — He is selling them to me.
6. **Se los vende (a él).** — He is selling them to him.
7. **Quiere vendérselos (a ella).** — He wants to sell them to her.

Drills

Familiar Commands: Affirmative

Repeat the statement, then form a familiar affirmative command as shown.

María habla español. / *María, habla español.*

1. Roberto estudia la lección.
2. Juan compra el coche.
3. Pablo cierra la puerta.
4. María vende los libros.
5. Eduardo vuelve tarde.
6. José espera a Antonio.
7. Tomás come en casa.

Form commands as above, using the irregular verbs provided.

Juan sale temprano. / *Juan, sal temprano.*

1. Rafael pone el libro aquí.
2. Juan viene conmigo.
3. Roberto hace el trabajo.
4. María dice la verdad.
5. Pablo va al parque.
6. Teresa es buena.
7. José sale con María.

Indirect Object Pronouns

Read each sentence aloud, then substitute the appropriate pronoun for the italicized object.

Juan escribe *a sus amigos.* / **Juan** *les* **escribe.**

1. Hablo *a Roberto* todos los días.
2. Digo la verdad *a mi madre.*
3. Damos el libro *a los niños.*
4. Venden el coche *a mi amigo.*
5. María dice algo interesante *a sus amigas.*

Answer the following questions as though they were directed to you. (Decide whether the answer should be singular or plural from the sense of the question.)

¿Quién les habla en español? / *El profesor nos habla en español.*

1. ¿Quién les dice que el examen es fácil?
2. ¿Quién le da notas muy buenas?
3. ¿Quién les parece muy simpático?
4. ¿Quién le habla todos los días?
5. ¿Quién le escribe cartas?

Discussion

Familiar Commands: Affirmative

In the affirmative singular, most commands take the same verb form as the third person singular of the present indicative.

Habla español, Juan.	Speak Spanish, John.
Estudia la lección.	Study the lesson.
Vuelve conmigo.	Go back with me.

The most common exceptions to the above rule are the following.

poner/pon	hacer/haz
salir/sal	decir/di
tener/ten	ir/ve
venir/ven	ser/sé

Ven aquí, amigo.	Come here, friend.
Pon el libro en la mesa.	Put the book on the table.
Di la verdad, niño.	Tell the truth, child.

In Spain, separate forms are used for plural familiar commands and these will be presented in the Verb Appendix. In Spanish America, the **ustedes** form is used for both formal and familiar plural commands in the affirmative and negative.

Formal	*Familiar*
Hablen Uds. español, señores.	**Hablen español, niños.**
No hablen Uds. español, señores.	**No hablen español, niños.**
Vengan Uds. aquí, señores.	**Vengan aquí, niños.**
No vengan Uds. aquí, señores.	**No vengan aquí, niños.**

Indirect Object Pronouns

The indirect object pronouns are

me	to me	**nos**	to us
te	to you (*fam., sing.*)		
le	to him, to her, to you (*formal, sing.*)	**les**	to them, to you (*formal, pl.*)

Like direct object pronouns, they are normally placed before the conjugated verb.

Juan me escribe una carta.	John is writing a letter to me.
No les da el libro.	He is not giving them the book.

Position of Direct and Indirect Object Pronouns

Read each sentence aloud and then substitute the appropriate pronoun (direct or indirect) for the italicized object.

> **Juan quiere ver *la casa*. / Juan quiere ver*la*.**
> **Venda Ud. su coche *a María*. / Vénda*le* su coche.**

1. No quiero comprar *los refrescos*.
2. Quiero hablar *a los niños*.
3. No pueden vender *su casa*.
4. María piensa buscar *el coche*.

5. Venda Ud. su casa *al Sr. López*.
6. Tengo que terminar *el libro* hoy.
7. Traiga Ud. *el dinero* mañana.
8. Abran Uds. *los libros*.

Follow the instructions given for the drill above. Note that in this drill you will be using the direct and indirect object pronouns together.

> **María me vende *el coche*. / María me *lo* vende.**
> **Juan quiere venderme *la casa*. / Juan quiere vendér*mela*.**
> **Tráiganme *el dinero* hoy. / Tráiganme*lo* hoy.**

1. Quiero decirte *la verdad*.
2. Juan piensa darme *las mesas*.
3. Sr. García, deme *la pluma*.
4. Mamá, pásame *la carne*, por favor.

5. ¿Quién nos escribe *las cartas?*
6. Roberto te da *el dinero*.
7. María nos vende *la casa*.
8. Juan me da *las sillas*.

Continue as in the above drills. Note that here both object pronouns are in the third person, and **se** must replace the indirect.

> **Le doy *el libro*. / Se *lo* doy.**
> **Les traigo *pan*. / Se *lo* traigo.**

1. Le paso *la carne*.
2. Les escribo *la carta*.
3. Le vendo *el coche*.
4. Le damos *los libros*.
5. Les digo *la verdad*.

6. Le muestra *el automóvil*.
7. Quiero darle *los libros*.
8. Pienso decirles *la verdad*.
9. No puedo traerle *las sillas*.
10. Sr. López, páseles *la sopa*, por favor.

Provide clarification for the italicized indirect objects.

> **Le da el libro *a Juan*. / Le da el libro *a él*.**
> **Se lo da *a los alumnos*. / Se lo da *a ellos*.**

1. Les vendo el coche *a los dos muchachos*.
2. Se los damos *a Teresa*.
3. Se lo doy *a mis amigos*.
4. Le escribo *a Roberto*.

Position of Direct and Indirect Object Pronouns

As you have already learned in Lessons 7 and 8, direct and indirect object pronouns are normally placed before a conjugated verb.

María lo compra.	Mary is buying it (*the book*).
No lo compre, Sr. Mora.	Don't buy it, Mr. Mora.
El señor Mora me habla.	Mr. Mora is speaking to me.

However, they follow and are attached to infinitives and affirmative commands.

El señor Mora quiere hablarme.	Mr. Mora wants to talk to me.
Hábleme, Sr. Mora.*	Speak to me, Mr. Mora.

When indirect and direct object pronouns are used together, the indirect comes first.

María me lo vende.	Mary is selling it (*the book*) to me.
Quieren vendérmela.**	They want to sell it (*the house*) to me.
Véndamela, señor.*	Sell it (*the house*) to me, sir.

When both object pronouns are in the third person (when both begin with the letter *l*) the indirect object (**le** or **les**) changes to **se.**

Escribo la carta a Juan.	I am writing the letter to John.
Le escribo la carta.	I am writing the letter to him.
Se la escribo.	I am writing it to him.
Quiero dar el libro a Pepe.	I want to give the book to Joe.
Quiero darlo a Pepe.	I want to give it to Joe.
Quiero dárselo.	I want to give it to him.

In many cases the meaning of the indirect object pronoun is not clear. For clarification or emphasis use the appropriate prepositional pronoun.

Le da el dinero.	He is giving the money to you. (*Or* to him, to her)
Le da el dinero a él.	(Here no doubt remains.)
Se lo da.	He is giving it to you. (*Or* to him, to her, to you, to them)
Se lo da a él.	(Here no doubt remains.)
Te da el dinero a ti, no a ella.	(Here emphasis is provided.)

---

* If the original stress changes when one or two object pronouns are added to a regular affirmative command, place an accent where the stress fell before the pronouns were added.
** When two object pronouns are added to an infinitive, place an accent where the stress fell before the pronouns were added.

Combined Exercises

A. Express the following Spanish phrases and sentences in English without referring to the translation. Then cover the Spanish and express the English phrases and sentences. Repeat until you make no mistakes.

1.	en malas condiciones	*in bad condition*
2.	El coche está en malas condiciones.	*The car is in bad condition.*
3.	El automóvil está en malas condiciones.	*The automobile is in bad condition.*
4.	Los frenos están en malas condiciones.	*The brakes are in bad condition.*
5.	Los asientos están en malas condiciones.	*The seats are in bad condition.*
6.	de todos modos	*anyhow*
7.	De todos modos el coche es estupendo.	*Anyhow, the car is stupendous.*
8.	De todos modos el coche es magnífico.	*Anyhow, the car is great (magnificent).*
9.	De todos modos el coche es una ganga.	*Anyhow, the car is a bargain.*
10.	De todos modos el coche tiene ventajas.	*Anyhow, the car has advantages.*
11.	De todos modos el coche no es viejo.	*Anyhow, the car is not old.*
12.	De todos modos el coche no tiene defectos.	*Anyhow, the car has no defects.*
13.	De todos modos el coche consume poca gasolina.	*Anyhow, the car uses little gasoline.*
14.	muchas veces	*often*
15.	Muchas veces el coche no anda bien.	*Often the car doesn't run well.*
16.	Muchas veces el coche no arranca bien.	*Often the car doesn't start well.*
17.	Muchas veces los frenos no funcionan bien.	*Often the brakes don't work well.*
18.	Muchas veces tratan de arreglar el coche.	*Often they try to repair the car.*

B. Substitute the cues.

1. Enrique muestra el coche al muchacho.
   (*yo, ellos, tú, ella, nosotros, Uds.*)
2. El señor López piensa salir mañana.
   (*yo, tú, ella, nosotros, Uds., ellos*)
3. Lo siento mucho.
   (*Juan, tú, Uds., nosotros, ellas*)
4. En los viajes, muchas veces duermo en el coche.
   (*ella, nosotros, tú, Uds., Juan*)
5. Siempre la encontramos en casa.
   (*yo, tú, ellos, ella, Uds.*)
6. Prefiero tomar el autobús.
   (*él, tú, nosotros, ellos, Uds.*)

C. Repeat the statement, then substitute the appropriate pronouns for the italicized objects.

> **Doy** *el libro a Juan.* / *Se lo doy.*

1. Digo *la verdad a María.*   2. El director escribe *cartas a los alumnos.*   3. Juan vende *el coche a Enrique.*   4. La madre lee *el libro a los niños.*   5. Elena quiere dar *pan a los niños.*   6. Mi padre puede escribir *la carta a su amigo.*   7. Roberto piensa mostrar *el coche al muchacho.*

⊕ D. Translate. Where a first name appears, use the familiar form of *you*; where a title appears, use the formal.

1. Don't exaggerate, Mr. García.   2. Sell the car, John; sell it to me.   3. Put the book here, Mary.   4. Leave now, Robert.   5. Come here, Mary. Be good. 6. Do the work now, Mr. Mora; don't do it tomorrow.   7. I want to buy the chair, Mr. López; sell it to me.   8. How are you? What's new?   9. He is coming with me. Mary is going with you (*fam.*).   10. He lives far away, but he brings me many books.

⊕ E. Answer in Spanish.

1. ¿Qué tal?
2. ¿En qué condiciones está su coche?
3. ¿Anda bien su coche? ¿Consume mucha gasolina?
4. ¿Cuántos asientos tiene?
5. ¿Qué modelo es?
6. ¿Funcionan bien los frenos?
7. ¿Duerme Ud. en el coche a veces?
8. ¿Piensa venderlo? ¿Es una ganga?
9. ¿Piensa Ud. visitar a sus padres mañana?

Reading and Conversation

El Automóvil (Primera Parte)

Juan Benavides, joven español, tiene un automóvil que quiere vender. Es un coche Ford, modelo sesenta*, que está en muy malas condiciones. Al salir de** la universidad Juan encuentra a Enrique Morales y le habla sobre las ventajas de su automóvil.

Juan Hola, Enrique. ¿Qué tal?

Enrique Bien, gracias, Juan. ¿Qué hay de nuevo? Me dicen que vas a vender tu coche.

Juan Sí. Es un coche estupendo y no quiero venderlo, pero mi padre me dice que si recibo malas notas en mis clases no puedo tener coche. Y tú sabes que mis notas son un desastre.

---

* **sesenta** sixty
** When stating the place or object from which one leaves, **de** must be used.

Enrique	¿Por qué no me lo vendes a mí? Pienso comprar un coche porque vivo lejos de la universidad y no hay autobús. ¿Quieres mostrármelo? *(Los dos muchachos van a ver el auto.)*
Juan	Aquí está. Es muy bonito, ¿verdad? Míralo y dime si no es un coche magnífico.
Enrique	Me parece un poco viejo. ¿Qué modelo es?
Juan	Es del año sesenta,* pero todo funciona muy bien.
Enrique	Pero, Juan, no puedo abrir la puerta para ver mejor el interior.
Juan	Bueno, es un pequeño defecto sin importancia. Entra por la otra.
Enrique	¡Hombre! Veo que los frenos están muy malos.
Juan	Amigo, no tiene importancia. Con poco dinero puedes arreglarlos. Mira los asientos; son muy grandes. En los viajes muchas veces duermo en el coche.
Enrique	¡En los viajes! Me parece que con los frenos que tiene el coche, no puedes salir de la ciudad.
Juan	Tu exageras. Tiene unos defectos pero el motor es estupendo. Anda bien y consume muy poca gasolina. *(Enrique trata de arrancar el motor pero no responde.)*
Enrique	Juan, ¡ya sé por qué no consume mucha gasolina!
Juan	No sé qué pasa. Casi siempre arranca muy bien. Pero de todos modos es una ganga. Solo pido treinta mil pesetas.** A propósito, hay muchos que quieren comprarlo, pero prefiero vendérselo a un amigo.
Enrique	Me parece que si lo vendes, pierdes al amigo porque el coche, como tus notas, es un desastre.

Dialogue Practice

A. Prepare oral responses to the following questions.

1. ¿En qué condiciones está el coche de Juan?
2. ¿Dónde encuentra Juan a Enrique?
3. ¿Son buenas las notas de Juan?
4. ¿Por qué Enrique no puede ver bien el interior del coche?
5. ¿Cómo están los frenos?
6. ¿Qué hace Juan muchas veces?
7. ¿Cuánto pide Juan por el coche?

* **sesenta** sixty
** Approximately $525 U.S.

LECCIÓN NUEVE

Basic Words and Expressions

acabar de + *inf.* to have just done
something
al fin at last
costarle a uno trabajo to be a lot of work
el año pasado last year
salir caro to be expensive

el lápiz (*pl.* **lápices**) the pencil
la mitad half
la película film, moving picture
el problema problem
la prima cousin (*f.*)
el primo cousin (*m.*)

conducir to drive
despertarse (ie) to wake up
lavarse to wash oneself
levantarse to get up
llevarse to take away, carry off
negar (ie) to deny, refuse
pagar to pay
regresar to return
sentarse (ie) to sit down

alguno some, someone
aquel that (over there) (*m.*)
caro expensive
ese that (*m.*)
este this (*m.*)
otro another
primero first
propio own
suficiente sufficient

anoche last night
anteayer day before yesterday
ayer yesterday
el anuncio the advertisement
el campo the country
el cine movie
el dinero money

afortunadamente fortunately
aunque although
bastante enough, rather
demasiado too, too much
temprano early
todavía still, yet

Basic Patterns

1. **Compré un coche anteayer.** I bought a car the day before yesterday.
2. **Don Lucas fue a México.** Don Lucas went to Mexico.
3. **Este libro y esa pluma son rojos.** This book and that pen are red.
4. **Paco se lava todos los días.** Paco washes (himself) every day.
5. **Yo me lavo todos los días.** I wash (myself) every day.
6. **El se levanta temprano.** He gets up early.
7. **Ellos se levantan temprano.** They get up early.
8. **Yo me levanto temprano.** I get up early.
9. **Levántese temprano.** Get up early.
10. **Quiero levantarme temprano.** I want to get up early.

Drills

Preterite Indicative of Regular Verbs

Repeat the model sentences and substitute the cues.

1. Compré un coche anteayer.
   (*tú, él, nosotros, ellos, Paco, yo, Uds.*)
2. Volvimos muy tarde anoche.
   (*yo, él, tú, nosotros, Uds., Ud., ella*)
3. Pedro escribió la lección tres veces.
   (*ellos, el estudiante, tú, nosotros, Ud., yo, Uds.*)

Read aloud and change to the preterite.

1. Acabo de estudiar la lección.
2. Regreso a las ocho de la noche.
3. Mi padre me lo niega.
4. Aprendes a escribir.
5. Perdemos el lápiz.
6. Responden en español.
7. Recibo una carta de mi primo.
8. Vivimos en una ciudad grande.
9. Pedro sale de casa.
10. Consume poca gasolina.

Irregular Preterite of SER and IR

Repeat the model sentences and substitute the cues.

1. Don Lucas fue médico.
   (*yo, ellos, tú, él, nosotros, Ud.*)
2. Yo fui a México el año pasado.
   (*él, nosotros, ellos, yo, los amigos, ella*)

Demonstrative Adjectives

⊕ Read in Spanish using the correct form of the three demonstrative adjectives with each noun.

> libro / *este libro, ese libro, aquel libro.*
>
> ciudad, avión, hombres, lecciones, luz, coche, carta, anuncios, chico, tienda

Repeat the model sentences and substitute the cues.

1. Esta carne es buena.
   (*asiento, calle, comida, estudiantes, legumbres*)
2. Compré ese coche ayer.
   (*pluma, pan, modelos, medicina, manzanas, legumbres, avión*)
3. Aquella casa es grande.
   (*coche, ciudad, cine, silla, mercados, autobús*)

Discussion

Preterite Indicative of Regular Verbs

The preterite, or simple past tense, of regular verbs is formed by adding the following endings to the stem. It is translated *I spoke, you spoke,* etc.

hablar		comer		vivir	
habl *é*	habl *amos*	com *í*	com *imos*	viv *í*	viv *imos*
habl *aste*		com *iste*		viv *iste*	
habl *ó*	habl *aron*	com *ió*	com *ieron*	viv *ió*	viv *ieron*

There are no stem-changing verbs in the preterite except for certain **-ir** verbs which will be presented later.

Irregular Preterite of SER and IR

ser		ir	
fui	fuimos	fui	fuimos
fuiste		fuiste	
fue	fueron	fue	fueron

These two verbs have identical forms in the preterite tense. Any confusion in meaning is usually made clear by the context.

Demonstrative Adjectives

Demonstratives, as all adjectives, agree in number and gender with the nouns they modify.

Masculine	*Feminine*		*Masculine*	*Feminine*	
este	**esta**	this	**estos**	**estas**	these
ese	**esa**	that	**esos**	**esas**	those
aquel	**aquella**	that	**aquellos**	**aquellas**	those

este libro y esta pluma	this book and this pen
esos coches y esas chicas	those cars and those girls
ese hombre y aquellas chicas	that man (close by) and those girls (far away)

Both **ese** and **aquel** mean *that.* The distinction in Spanish is one of distance: **ese** is used for things relatively close at hand; **aquel** for things which are distant.

Ese coche es nuevo.	That car is new. (*It is near to the speakers.*)
Aquel coche es nuevo.	That car is new. (*It is far from the speakers.*)

Demonstrative Pronouns

⊕ Replace the italicized words with a demonstrative pronoun.

1. Prefiero *esta casa*.
2. Quiero ver *aquellos mercados*.
3. *Esa comida* es buena.
4. *Ese lago* es grande.
5. Voy a leer *estos libros, esas lecciones* y *aquellos anuncios*.

Demonstrative Pronouns

A demonstrative pronoun is used in place of a noun. It differs from the demonstrative adjective only in that it carries an accent.

Masculine	*Feminine*			*Masculine*	*Feminine*	
éste	**ésta**	this (one)		**éstos**	**éstas**	these
ése	**ésa**	that (one)		**ésos**	**ésas**	those
aquél	**aquélla**	that (one)		**aquéllos**	**aquéllas**	those

No quiero éstos. Quiero ésos.   I don't want these. I want those.

PROCESION SIN PASOS

Reflexive Pronouns

Repeat the model sentences and substitute the cues.

1. Paco se lava todos los días.
   (*yo, él, nosotros, Ud., ellos, tú, Uds.*)
2. Paco se lavó ayer.
   (*yo, nosotros, Ud., él, ellos, Uds., tú*)
3. Pablo se levanta temprano.
   (*tú, ellos, nosotros, yo, Ud., Uds., ella*)
4. Ellos se sentaron a la mesa.
   (*nosotros, él, tú, yo, Ud., Uds.*)
5. Prefiero levantarme ahora.
   (*Paco, nosotros, él, tú, yo, ellos, Ud.*)

Make the following commands negative.

Duérmase ahora. Váyase. Levántese Ud. Lávense Uds. Siéntese Ud. Póngaselo. Siéntense Uds. Despiértese Ud.

Change to the preterite.

1. Juanito se levanta a las ocho.
2. Yo me voy de esta ciudad.
3. Paco se lleva una mesa y dos sillas.
4. Nos sentamos en esta silla.
5. Te despiertas muy temprano.

⊕ Write in Spanish.

1. I want to wash myself.
2. He has to get up.
3. We have to wake up.
4. Get up.
5. They are going to sit down.
6. You (*fam., sing.*) prefer to go away.
7. He wants to go to sleep.
8. Don't sit down there.

Reflexive Pronouns

The reflexive pronouns are

me	myself		**nos**	ourselves
te	yourself (*fam., sing.*)			
se	himself, herself, itself, yourself		**se**	themselves, yourselves

The reflexive pronouns follow the same rules for placement as all other object pronouns. They usually precede the verb, but follow and are attached to affirmative commands and infinitives.

Statements

me lavo	I wash myself	**nos lavamos**	we wash ourselves
te lavas	you wash yourself		
él se lava	he washes himself	**ellos se lavan**	they (*m.*) wash themselves
ella se lava	she washes herself	**ellas se lavan**	they (*f.*) wash themselves
Ud. se lava	you wash yourself	**Uds. se lavan**	you wash yourselves

Commands

lávese Ud.	wash yourself	**no se lave Ud.**	don't wash yourself
lávense Uds.	wash yourselves	**no se laven Uds.**	don't wash yourselves
lávate	wash yourself (*fam., sing.*)		

Infinitives

quiero lavarme	I want to wash myself	**queremos lavarnos**	we want to wash ourselves
quieres lavarte	you (*fam., sing.*) want to wash yourself		
quiere lavarse	he, she, it wants to wash himself (herself, itself); you (*formal, sing.*) want to wash yourself	**quieren lavarse**	they want to wash themselves; you (*formal, pl.*) want to wash yourselves

Many verbs change their meanings when used with reflexive pronouns. Here are some you have already studied.

dormir	to sleep	**dormirse**	to fall asleep
ir	to go	**irse**	to go away
llamar	to call	**llamarse**	to be named (call oneself)
llevar	to carry, wear	**llevarse**	to carry off, obtain
poner	to put	**ponerse**	to put on, become

These are some common reflexive verbs.

levantarse	to get up
sentarse (ie)	to sit down
despertarse (ie)	to wake up

Pedro se duerme a las ocho.	Peter goes to sleep at 8 o'clock.
Nos levantamos temprano.	We got up early.
Siéntese.	Sit down.
No se levante ahora.	Don't get up now.
Quiero sentarme aquí.	I want to sit down here.

Combined Exercises

A. Substitute the cues in the model sentences.

1. Felipe acaba de regresar.
   (*yo, ellos, Ud., nosotros, tú, ella, yo*)
2. Esta lección me cuesta trabajo.
   (*viaje, problema, exámenes, problemas*)
3. El viaje me salió caro.
   (*cine, anuncio, comidas, casa, refrescos*)
4. Juan me lo vendió anteayer.
   (*él, tú, ellos, ella*)
5. Me llevé una ganga.
   (*tú, él, nosotros, Uds., yo, Pablo, ellos*)

B. Answer the questions in Spanish.

1. ¿Compraste un coche ayer?   2. ¿Sabe Ud. conducir?   3. ¿Adónde fue Ud. el fin de semana pasado?   4. ¿Llovió hoy?   5. ¿Te cuesta trabajo hablar español?   6. ¿Fuiste al cine la semana pasada?   7. ¿A qué hora salió Ud. de clase ayer?   8. ¿Sabes algo de automóviles?   9. ¿A qué hora te levantaste esta mañana?   10. ¿Quieres levantarte más temprano mañana?

⊕ C. Translate.

1. I wake up at eight o'clock, but I don't get up until nine o'clock.
2. Wake up (*fam., sing.*) now.
3. Why did you (*formal, sing.*) sit down there?
4. He went into a restaurant and ate a lot.
5. They went to the country but the trip was expensive.
6. That car (over there) runs rather well, but this one runs better.
7. They missed half of that picture.
8. How wonderful to have your own car!
9. We want to get up early in order to go downtown.
10. He studied the lesson, but he didn't learn it.

⊕ D. Review. Translate the following sentences into Spanish.

1. Put (*fam., sing.*) it (*the book*) on the table and come here.
2. Tell (*fam., sing.*) me the truth.
3. He wants to give it (*f.*) to me.
4. She wants to give it (*m.*) to them.
5. The car cost him a lot, but he bought it.
6. He sold it (*m.*) to us.
7. Come (*formal, sing.*) and I'll take you to see a movie.
8. I visited them last year.
9. Don't (*formal, sing.*) study today. You can do it tomorrow.
10. At last he bought me a car.

Reading and Conversation

El Automóvil (Segunda Parte)

Enrique Morales acaba de comprar el coche de Juan. Al llegar a la universidad encuentra a sus amigos Antonio y María.

Antonio ¡Hola, Enrique! Me dicen que compraste un coche.

Enrique Sí, me lo vendió anteayer Juan Benavides. Trató de vendérmelo por treinta mil pesetas pero al fin me lo llevé por veinte mil.

María ¡Parece estupendo! Te llevaste una ganga si pagaste solo veinte mil. El año pasado le* pedí un coche a mi padre pero me lo negó.

Antonio Pero, ¿qué quieres, María? Si todavía no sabes conducir . . . Aprende primero en el coche de Enrique y luego puedes pedírselo a tu padre otra vez. A propósito, Enrique, ¿anda bien el coche?

Enrique Bastante bien ahora. Ayer llevé a varios amigos al campo y al regresar el motor no arrancó. Afortunadamente Jorge, mi primo, sabe algo de automóviles y lo arregló, aunque le costó mucho trabajo y volvimos a casa muy tarde.

María Pero, ¡qué estupendo tener tu propio coche y poder salir de la ciudad los fines de semana!

Enrique Sí, pero el viaje me salió bastante caro y ahora no tengo dinero para gasolina. ¿Y Uds.? ¿Fueron al cine anoche?

Antonio Sí, pero como llovió mucho y llegamos tarde, perdimos casi la mitad de la película.

María Es que los cines comienzan demasiado temprano. Si tienes clases hasta las nueve y media y si después quieres cenar, no hay tiempo suficiente para llegar al cine a las once.

Antonio Es verdad, pero si uno va en coche como hacen algunos, no hay problema.

Enrique No lo crean, amigos. Con estos coches viejos, siempre hay problemas.

Dialogue Practice

A. Prepare oral responses to the following questions.

1. ¿Qué acaba de hacer Enrique?
2. ¿Cuánto le costó el coche? ¿Quién arregló el coche?
3. ¿Quién no sabe conducir?
4. ¿Adónde llevó Enrique a sus amigos?
5. ¿Adónde fueron Antonio y María anoche?
6. ¿Por qué perdieron la mitad de la película?

---

* Although not absolutely required, in common usage an indirect pronoun is included when the noun which is the indirect object is a person.

⊕ B. Using the dialogue as a model, make complete sentences in the preterite.

1. Anoche/(yo)/despertarme/diez/noche.
2. El/levantarse/cansado/y/lavarse.
3. Llover/mucho/y/(nosotros)/perder/mitad/la película.
4. Cine/comenzar temprano/y/(nosotros)/llegar tarde.
5. (Tú)/llevar/amigos/campo/y/volver/tarde.

⊕ C. Using the dialogue as a model, rewrite the following paragraph, changing all verbs to the preterite.

Enrique Morales le compra un coche nuevo a Juan Benavides. Se lleva una ganga porque paga sólo veinte mil. Jorge arregla el motor aunque le cuesta mucho trabajo. Por fin todos salen de la ciudad.

LECCIÓN DIEZ

Basic Words and Expressions

estar de mal (buen) humor to be in a bad (good) mood
hoy día nowadays

acercarse (a) to draw near (to)
aconsejar to advise
bailar to dance
bajar to go down, lower
bajar (de) to get off, get out (of) (a vehicle)
calmarse to calm down
cantar to sing
cuidar to care for, tend
desear to desire, want
encantar to charm, enchant
gritar to shout
insistir en to insist
mandar to order
permitir to permit, allow
practicar to practice
rogar (ue) to beg

el barrio district, neighborhood

la canción song
la esposa wife
el esposo husband
la estación station
el extranjero foreigner
el huésped guest, lodger
el inglés English, Englishman
la locura madness, insanity
el periódico newspaper
la revista magazine
el sitio place
el sueldo salary

alto tall, loud
bajo low, short
delgado thin
ésta the latter (f.)
éste the latter (m.)
extranjero foreign
gordo fat
lejano distant
moreno dark, brunette
rubio blond

Basic Patterns

1. **Quiero que Ud. hable español.** — I want you to speak Spanish.
2. **Insisto en que Juan salga ahora.** — I insist that John leave now.
3. **Prefiero que no duerma aquí.** — I prefer that you don't sleep here.
4. **Te digo que vayas ahora.** — I am telling you to go now.
5. **Vamos a comer.** — Let's eat.
6. **Comamos.** — Let's eat.
7. **Vamos a levantarnos.** — Let's get up.
8. **Levantémonos.** — Let's get up.
9. **No nos levantemos.** — Let's not get up.

Drills

Present Subjunctive of Regular Verbs

⊕ Give the proper form of the present subjunctive.

1. (yo) abrir, admitir, andar, aprender, arreglar, caminar
2. (tú) cenar, comer, comprar, comprender, correr, escribir
3. (Juan) esperar, estudiar, hablar, leer, llamar, mirar
4. (nosotros) olvidar, pasar, presentar, recibir, regresar
5. (ellos) responder, terminar, tomar, trabajar, vivir

Subjunctive After Verbs of Persuasion

Change the second verb according to the cue.

1. Quiero que *Ud.* hable español.
   (*tú, ellos, nosotros, Juan*)
2. Insisto en que *María* salga.
   (*ellos, Ud., tú, nosotros*)
3. Roberto pide que *tú* no bailes.
   (*ella, yo, nosotros, ellos*)
4. Prefiero que *Uds.* lo compren.
   (*tú, Ud., nosotros, ellas*)
5. Mi padre no permite que *yo* trabaje.
   (*ellos, nosotros, tú, Ud.*)

Repeat the following sentences. Then say them again, beginning with the expressions in parentheses and changing the verb from the indicative to subjunctive.

1. Carlos termina el trabajo ahora.
   (*Quiero que, Deseo que, Prefiero que*)
2. Alicia no canta en casa.
   (*Insisto en que, Ruego que, Pido que*)
3. Felipe vive con sus amigos.
   (*Permito que, Mando que, Aconsejo que*)

Repeat the following sentences. Then say them again, making the indirect object pronoun agree with the objects in parentheses. The subjunctive verb will also agree.

Me manda que estudie más. ⎰ *Le manda que estudie más.*
(a usted, a nosotros) ⎱ *Nos manda que estudiemos más.*

1. Me pide que no coma mucho.
   (*a Ud., a nosotros, a ti, a ellos*)
2. Les ruega que no griten.
   (*a mí, a Ud., a ti, a ellas*)

Discussion

Present Subjunctive of Regular Verbs

The present subjunctive of regular verbs is formed by adding the following endings to the stem of the first person singular of the present indicative.

hablar/habl-*o*	comer/com-*o*	vivir/viv-*o*
habl *e* habl *emos*	com *a* com *amos*	viv *a* viv *amos*
habl *es*	com *as*	viv *as*
habl *e* habl *en*	com *a* com *an*	viv *a* viv *an*

Note that all commands in Lessons 7 and 8 are subjunctive forms. The only exception is the familiar affirmative command.

Habla español, Juan. Speak Spanish, John.
Come el pan, niño. Eat the bread, child.

Subjunctive After Verbs of Persuasion

In Spanish the subjunctive mood is used to express various attitudes. In this lesson it is used to indicate persuasion or influence on another subject. Following are verbs most commonly used to express this attitude.

querer (ie)	to want, wish	**aconsejar**	to advise
desear	to desire, wish, want	**insistir en**	to insist
decir	to tell, say	**mandar**	to order
pedir (i)	to request, ask for	**permitir**	to permit
preferir (ie)	to prefer	**rogar (ue)**	to beg, request

Quiero que Ud. escriba una carta. I want you to write a letter.
Quiero escribir una carta. I want to write a letter. (*No second subject, therefore, no subjunctive*)

Le aconsejo que estudie. I advise you to study.
Me manda que salga. He orders me to leave.
Te ruego que no grites. I beg you not to shout.

Note that **que** must introduce the subjunctive.

Present Subjunctive of Stem-Changing Verbs

⊕ Give the proper form of the present subjunctive.

1. (*yo*) perder, poder, querer, volver, pedir
2. (*tú*) dormir, encontrar, mostrar, pensar, preferir
3. (*él*) sentir, despertarse, sentarse, dormir
4. (*nosotros*) perder, poder, sentir, dormir, pedir
5. (*ellos*) volver, pedir, mostrar, sentarse, perder

⊕ Supply the proper form of the infinitives in parentheses.

1. Prefiero que Ud. no (*dormir*) aquí.
2. No quiero que María (*perder*) el dinero.
3. El profesor nos aconseja que (*pensar*).
4. Prefiero (*volver*) ahora.
5. El señor no quiere que nosotros (*pedir*) más sueldo.
6. El profesor insiste en que nosotros no (*dormir*) en la clase.
7. No quieren que los huéspedes (*sentarse*) en esta silla.
8. Nos aconseja que no (*volver*) a este barrio.
9. Mi madre prefiere que nosotros no (*pedir*) nada.
10. Quiere que Uds. (*despertarse*) temprano.

Present Subjunctive of Irregular Verbs

Change according to the example.

Juan está aquí.   (*Quiero que*) / *Quiero que Juan esté aquí.*
Mi hijo es médico. (*Insisto en que*) / *Insisto en que mi hijo sea médico.*

1. Los alumnos saben la lección.   (*Insisto en que*)
2. Mi esposa va al banco.   (*No permito que*)
3. El extranjero me da el libro.   (*Desean que*)
4. Vamos al cine mañana.   (*Mis amigos quieren que*)
5. Van al parque mañana.   (*Quieren*)
6. Eres un hombre bueno.   (*Te aconsejo que*)
7. Están aquí todos los días.   (*Quiero que*)
8. María no sabe la verdad.   (*Prefiero que*)
9. Mis amigos están en la estación.   (*Mando que*)
10. Le damos más sueldo.   (*Aconsejan que*)

Present Subjunctive of Stem-Changing Verbs

In the subjunctive, **-ar** and **-er** stem-changing verbs undergo the same change in the stem as in the present indicative.

perder (ie) (to lose)		**pensar (ie)** (to think)	
pierda	perdamos	piense	pensemos
pierdas		pienses	
pierda	pierdan	piense	piensen

Certain **-ir** verbs change in the first person plural as well as in the other forms.

sentir (ie) (to feel)		**dormir (ue)** (to sleep)		**pedir (i)** (to ask for)	
sienta	sintamos	duerma	durmamos	pida	pidamos
sientas		duermas		pidas	
sienta	sientan	duerma	duerman	pida	pidan

Present Subjunctive of Irregular Verbs

The following irregular verbs add endings to stems other than the first person singular. They must be memorized.

dar		estar		ser	
dé	demos	esté	estemos	sea	seamos
des		estés		seas	
dé	den	esté	estén	sea	sean

saber		ir	
sepa	sepamos	vaya	vayamos
sepas		vayas	
sepa	sepan	vaya	vayan

Subjunctive for *Let's*

Express the following first person plural commands a second way, as shown by the examples.

Vamos a comer. / *Comamos.*
Vamos a venderlo. / *Vendámoslo.*
Vamos a lavarnos. / *Lavémonos.*

1. Vamos a bailar.
2. Vamos a leer.
3. Vamos a escribir.
4. Vamos a comprarlo.
5. Vamos a estudiarlo.

⊕
6. Vamos a levantarnos.
7. Vamos a sentarnos.
8. Vamos a trabajar.
9. Vamos a hacerlo.
10. Vamos a salir.
11. Vamos a traerlo.

Form negative first person plural commands (*Let's not . . .*) as shown by the examples.

Vamos a bailar. / *No, no bailemos ahora.*
Vamos a comprarlo. / *No, no lo compremos ahora.*
Vamos a levantarnos. / *No, no nos levantemos ahora.*

1. Vamos a leer.
2. Vamos a escribir.
3. Vamos a estudiarlo.
4. Vamos a sentarnos.
5. Vamos a comer.

⊕
6. Vamos a venderlo.
7. Vamos a lavarnos.
8. Vamos a trabajar.
9. Vamos a salir.
10. Vamos a hacerlo.
11. Vamos a traerlo.

Familiar Commands: Negative

Repeat the statement, then form a negative familiar command as shown.

María habla español. / *María, no hables español.*

1. Roberto estudia la lección.
2. Juan compra el coche.
3. Pablo cierra la puerta.
4. María pierde sus libros.
5. Eduardo vuelve tarde.
6. José espera a Antonio.
7. Tomás come en casa.
8. Rafael pone el libro aquí.
9. Juan viene conmigo.
10. Roberto hace el trabajo.
11. María dice la verdad.
12. Pablo va al parque.
13. Teresa es buena.
14. José sale con María.

⊕ Now say the following familiar and formal commands in Spanish. Assume that where a first name is used the familiar command would be appropriate; where a title appears, use the formal command.

1. John, study.
2. Robert, don't speak.
3. Mr. Mora, don't work.
4. Mr. Mora, don't leave.
5. Mary, leave.
6. Pepe, come here.
7. Children, eat.
8. Mr. López, don't read.

Subjunctive for *Let's*

To express the equivalent of the English *let's,* use (1) **Vamos a** + *infinitive*

Vamos a estudiar.	Let's study.
Vamos a levantarnos.	Let's get up.
Vamos a comprarlo.	Let's buy it.

or (2) the first person plural of the subjunctive.

Comamos.	Let's eat.
Comprémoslo.	Let's buy it.
Levantémonos.	Let's get up.

Note that when object pronouns or reflexive pronouns are added to the affirmative command a written accent is required on the stressed syllable. Note also that with reflexive verbs the final **s** is dropped before adding **nos.**

levantemos + nos: levantémonos

Let's not can be expressed only with the first person plural of the subjunctive. Since the command is negative, any object pronouns or reflexive pronouns must precede the verb.

No comamos.	Let's not eat.
No lo compremos.	Let's not buy it.
No nos levantemos.	Let's not get up.

Familiar Commands: Negative

In the negative singular, the familiar command is the same as the formal singular command (*see p. 69*), but the letter **s** is added.

No hables inglés, Juan.	Don't speak English, John.
No estudies hoy.	Don't study today.
No vengas conmigo.	Don't come with me.

Remember that we are expressing *all* plural commands, including familiar, with the formal command forms (*see p. 69*).

Señores, hablen español.	Gentlemen, speak Spanish.
Niños, hablen español.	Children, speak Spanish.

Combined Exercises

A. Assume that the following questions are directed to you, so answer in the first person. You may choose either verb for your answer.

¿Quiere que Juan trabaje ahora o prefiere que hable con las chicas? /
Quiero que Juan trabaje ahora.
¿Quiere que estudiemos la lección o prefiere que vayamos al cine? /
Prefiero que vayamos al cine.

1. ¿Quiere que salgamos ahora o prefiere que esperemos a Juan?   2. ¿Desea que yo cante o prefiere que no haga nada?   3. ¿Quiere que yo traiga el libro o prefiere que se lo dé a María?   4. ¿Desea que yo trabaje ahora o prefiere que espere hasta mañana?   5. ¿Deseas trabajar ahora o prefieres esperar hasta mañana?   6. ¿Quiere que yo esté aquí mañana o prefiere que vaya a otro sitio?   7. ¿Quiere que yo sea médico o prefiere que trabaje en un banco?

B. Assume that the following questions are directed to you. Be prepared to answer them orally in the affirmative or negative without referring to your notes.

¿Quiere que yo hable inglés con el extranjero? / *Sí, quiero que Ud.*
hable inglés con el extranjero.
¿Nos manda que vengamos mañana? / *No, no les mando que vengan*
mañana.

1. ¿Quiere que yo compre un periódico?   2. ¿Quieres comprar un periódico? 3. ¿Desea que leamos la revista ahora?   4. ¿Me aconseja que baje del coche?   5. ¿Insiste en que salgamos mañana?   6. ¿Insiste Ud. en salir manana?   7. ¿Me manda que cante una canción?   8. ¿Nos dice que pongamos los libros aquí?   9. ¿Me permite que traiga los refrescos? 10. ¿Prefiere que yo vuelva temprano?   11. ¿Quiere que durmamos aquí? 12. ¿Desea que yo me despierte temprano?

C. Say the following in the preterite.

1. El inglés se acerca a mi esposa.   2. Mi esposa va a otro sitio.   3. Yo no vivo en este barrio.   4. Los huéspedes comen aquí muchas veces.   5. Hablan con un señor alto y rubio.   6. Un señor bajo y moreno baja del coche. 7. Dos señoras delgadas cuidan a los niños.   8. Cuando vamos a México practicamos el español.   9. Soy huésped de este hotel.   10. Compro periódicos y revistas en la ciudad.

⊕ D. Write in Spanish.

1. Let's dance.   (*Write two ways.*)
2. Don't leave this neighborhood, John.
3. Let's get up now.   (*Write two ways.*)
4. Don't shout, Mary.
5. Theresa and Mary are here; the latter is rather fat.
6. Mary and John are foreigners; the latter is from Mexico.
7. I want to go, but I don't want them to go.
8. Let's not get up early tomorrow.
9. Give me the newspaper, John (*fam.*); don't give it to him.
10. Put the magazine here, Mary (*fam.*); don't put it on the table.

11. Sit down here, Robert (*fam.*); don't sit there.
12. Bring it to me, Mr. Robles (*formal*); don't give it to them.
13. I want to buy this book, that magazine and those newspapers.
14. He wants me to live in this neighborhood.
15. They tell us to study every day.

E. Review. Change from the affirmative familiar command to the negative familiar command.

1. Carlos, escríbemelo.   2. Juan, dímelo.   3. Ana, ven ahora mismo.
4. Tomas, hazlo en seguida.   5. María, ve al mercado.

Reading and Conversation

Un Padre Español

En casa de la familia Alvarez. El señor Alvarez lee el periódico. La señora habla con Margarita, señorita de unos diecinueve años, sobre los planes de ésta para el verano.

Sra. A. Margarita, te aconsejo que no hables con tu padre ahora. Volvió muy cansado de la oficina y está de mal humor.

Margarita Parece que siempre está de mal humor. De todos modos, yo no puedo esperar; tengo que hablarle ahora. (*Se acerca a su padre.*) Papá, tengo una oportunidad estupenda para el verano. Buscan chicas para trabajar en un hotel del Parque Nacional. El trabajo es cuidar a los niños de los huéspedes extranjeros—y tú sabes que me encantan los niños. También, va a ser una buena oportunidad para practicar mi inglés. Nos dan habitación y comida y también un pequeño sueldo. Oh, papá, ¿puedo ir?

Sr. A. ¡Qué locura! No permito que vayas a un sitio tan* lejano y tan solitario. Es ridículo. Además, una chica de buena familia no hace esta clase de trabajo.

Sra. A. Pero, Juan, cálmate. No es para tanto. Hoy día muchas jóvenes de buena familia trabajan.

Sr. A. (*En una voz muy alta*) Mujer, no me hables más. Yo no voy a permitir que Margarita trabaje entre extranjeros. Quiero que esté aquí en Santiago con nosotros.

Margarita Papá, te ruego que no grites.

Sr. A. No me digas que no grite. En esta casa mando yo, y si quiero gritar, grito.

Sra. A. Ven, Margarita. Es imposible hablar con tu padre esta noche. Esperemos hasta mañana.

* **tan** so

Dialogue Practice

A. Prepare oral responses to the following questions.

1. ¿Qué hace el Sr. Alvarez?
2. ¿Qué hace la Sra. Alvarez?
3. ¿De qué humor está el Sr. Alvarez?
4. ¿Qué trabajo quiere hacer Margarita?
5. Si su padre permite que vaya, ¿qué va a practicar Margarita?
6. ¿Les dan a las chicas mucho sueldo?
7. ¿Qué hacen hoy día muchas jóvenes de buena familia?
8. ¿Por qué no quiere el padre que Margarita trabaje en el Parque Nacional?
9. ¿Dónde quiere el padre que Margarita pase el verano?
10. ¿Cuándo van a hablar con el padre?

⊕ B. Using the dialogue as a model, write the following in Spanish.

Mrs. Alvarez advises Margarita not to talk with her father now because he is in a bad mood. But Margarita can't wait; she has to talk to him now. They are looking for girls to care for children at a hotel in the National Park. She loves children and they are giving room and board and a small salary. Her father won't permit her to go to a place so far away. He wants her to be in Santiago this summer. Margarita and her mother are going to wait until tomorrow to talk to him.

REPASO (6-10)

⊕ A. Using the dialogue of Lesson Seven as a model, write a short dialogue on the following.

1. You ask a policeman the number of the bus that goes to the Retiro.   2. He tells you that it is number 12, but the Metro is better.   3. You ask him how much the bus costs.   4. He says that it costs four pesetas but to run because it's going to rain.   5. Thank him and say that you will wait on the corner.

⊕ B. Make complete sentences of the following.

1. (Yo)/tener hambre/y/ir/llamar/camarero.
2. Juan/comenzar/caminar/hacia/parque.
3. Siempre/(nosotros)/encontrarla/en casa.
4. (Yo)/querer/levantarse/para/ir/centro.
5. El/querer/que yo/venderle/coche.

C. Answer the questions in Spanish.

1. ¿Me mandas que traiga refrescos ahora?   2. ¿Prefiere Ud. que vuelvan temprano?   3. ¿Te costó trabajo arreglar el coche?   4. ¿Quieres ser camarero? 5. ¿Hay mucho ruido aquí?

D. These sentences are based on the dialogues in Lessons Six through Ten. If the sentence makes sense, mark it true; if not, mark it false. If you miss more than two items, go back and review the appropriate dialogue.

E. The dictation is taken from the dialogue of Lesson Eight. Write the Spanish without referring to your books and then check what you have written against the appropriate lines of the dialogue.

⊕ F. Translate the following.

1. In winter we can't do anything.
2. Several policemen are on the corner.
3. The park is far, but the bus costs 14 pesetas.
4. I don't know Madrid very well, but I know it's cold today.
5. The car runs well, but the brakes don't work.
6. The advantage is that I can sleep in the car.
7. Do (*fam., sing.*) the work now, John; don't do it tomorrow.
8. We woke up at nine and got up at ten.
9. Let's get up late tomorrow.
10. They want me to work at home.
11. Sell it to me; don't sell it to him. (*fam.*)
12. Don't leave until seven and don't run. (*fam.*)

Recommended Readings from Appendix

Bosquejo de México and **Observaciones sobre Latinoamérica.**

MÉXICO

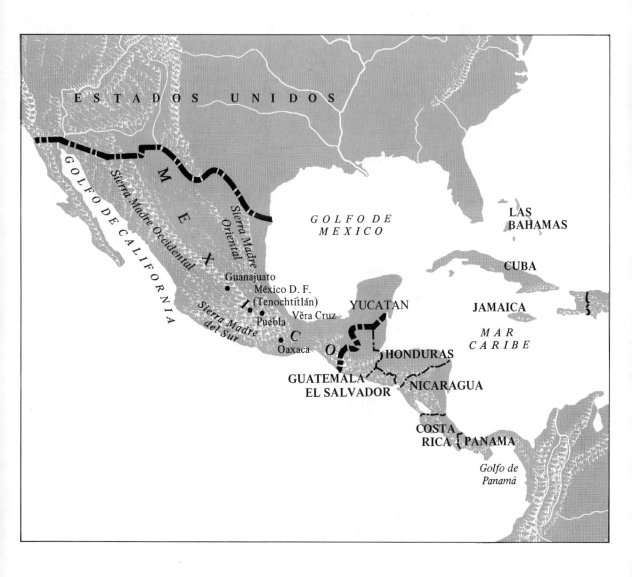

Pyramid of the Moon at Teotihuacán, an ancient ceremonial city only thirty miles from Mexico City.

Stone carving from the Aztec culture. Many such relics were found during excavation for Mexico City's new subway system.

The Pyramid of the Sun, Teotihuacán.

Open-air section of the market
"La Libertad" in Guadalajara.

The old San Angel
section of Mexico City.

Rope tricks at the "charreada" *(rodeo)*.

1300 year-old Mayan murals from the province of Chiapas in Southern Mexico.

Taxco, a silver-mining center, is also the residence of many writers and artists.

La corrida de toros *(bullfight)*.

View of Acapulco.

Mayan ruins on the Yucatan Penninsula.

LECCIÓN ONCE

Basic Words and Expressions

de repente suddenly
de veras certainly, truly
insistir en + *inf.* to insist upon something
¿Para qué? Why? For what reason?
tal vez perhaps

andar to walk
ayudar to help
charlar to chat
conseguir (i) to obtain, get
corresponder to suit, fit, correspond
cruzar to cross
decidir to decide
ganar to earn, win
importar to be important
invitar to invite
nacer to be born
pasearse to take a walk
saludar to greet

la acera sidewalk
la avenida avenue
la cuenta bill
la dirección address
la fecha date
el kilómetro kilometer, (⅝ mile)
el Ministerio government department
la niña girl
el niño boy
la preparación preparation
el pueblo small town
la siesta afternoon nap
la tontería silliness, stupid thing

caro expensive
educado educated

acá here
actualmente at the present time
durante during
naturalmente naturally

Basic Patterns

1.	**Juan anduvo toda la noche.**	John walked all night long.
2.	**Hace una hora que leo.**	I have been reading for an hour.
3.	**Juan lo hizo rápidamente.**	John did it rapidly.
4.	**María llega el lunes.**	Mary is arriving on Monday.
5.	**Viernes, primero de junio.**	Friday, the first of June.
6.	**Lunes, cuatro de julio.**	Monday, the fourth of July.

Drills

Preterite Indicative of Irregular Verbs

Repeat the model sentences and then subsitute the cues.

1. Juan anduvo toda la noche.
   (*yo, nosotros, él, tú, ellos, Juan y yo*)
2. Martín estuvo enfermo ayer.
   (*María, yo, ellos, nosotros, tú, mi amigo*)
3. Tuvimos un examen en la clase de español.
   (*yo, ellas, nosotros, él, tú, mis amigos*)
4. La madre de Elena hizo la comida.
   (*tú, yo, nosotros, él, ellos, Juan*)
5. Quise buscarte pero no pude.
   (*él, nosotros, ellos, yo, Juan*)
6. Vino en autobús y trajo al niño.
   (*yo, tú, nosotros, ellos, Ud., Juan y Pedro*)
7. Rafael no dijo la verdad.
   (*yo, Ud., nosotros, ellos, tú*)
8. Condujimos con mucho cuidado.
   (*ellos, Uds., nosotros, Ud., tú*)
9. Puse la cuenta en la mesa.
   (*él, nosotros, Ud., yo, tú*)
10. No supimos la dirección de la casa.
    (*Ud., él, Uds., nosotros, tú, ellos*)

Be able to change the following sentences to the preterite orally.

1. María anda por las calles.
2. Traen mucho dinero.
3. ¿Por qué no me lo dices?
4. Muchos vienen al pueblo.
5. ¿Sabes la verdad?
6. No quieres invitarme a tu casa.
7. ¿Dónde lo pones?
8. No podemos ganar mucho dinero.
9. El hace muchas tonterías.
10. Tienes que pagar la cuenta.
11. Estoy siempre de buen humor.

Discussion

Preterite Indicative of Irregular Verbs

Note that all the following verbs have irregular stems in the preterite tense. You will have to memorize them. The preterite endings for these verbs are also irregular, but the entire group uses the same endings. However, the third person singular of **hacer** is **hizo.**

andar/anduv-		tener/tuv-		venir/vin-	
anduv *e*	anduv *imos*	tuv *e*	tuv *imos*	vin *e*	vin *imos*
anduv *iste*		tuv *iste*		vin *iste*	
anduv *o*	anduv *ieron*	tuv *o*	tuv *ieron*	vin *o*	vin *ieron*

estar/estuv-
___
hacer/hic- (*but:* hizo)
poder/pud-
poner/pus-
querer/quis-
saber/sup-

The verbs **decir, traer, conducir,** however, add **-eron** to the third person plural.

decir/dij-		traer/traj-		conducir/conduj-	
dij *e*	dij *imos*	traj *e*	traj *imos*	conduj *e*	conduj *imos*
dij *iste*		traj *iste*		conduj *iste*	
dij *o*	dij *eron*	traj *o*	traj *eron*	conduj *o*	conduj *eron*

A few of these verbs have special meanings in the preterite tense. **Querer** means *to try* when used in the affirmative and *to refuse* when used in the negative. **Saber** may mean *to find out.* **Poder** means *to succeed* in the affirmative and *to fail* in the negative. **Tener** means *to get or receive,* **conocer** means *to meet.*

Quise estudiar pero no pude.	I tried to study, but I couldn't.
Le conocí ayer.	I met him yesterday.
Supe la verdad.	I found out the truth.
Tuve una carta de mi amigo.	I got a letter from my friend.
Pablo no quiso ir.	Paul refused to go.

Time Expressions with HACER

Say the following in Spanish.

1. I have been reading for an hour.
2. They have been here for two weeks.
3. We haven't seen her for a month.

Answer the questions in Spanish.

1. ¿Cuánto tiempo hace que vives aquí?
2. ¿Cuánto tiempo hace que charlamos?
3. ¿Cuánto tiempo hace que estás enfermo?
4. ¿Cuánto tiempo hace que estudian?

Formation of Adverbs

⊕ Translate and then substitute the other adverbs.

1. He did it rapidly.   (*carefully, perfectly*)
2. He drove perfectly.   (*easily, rapidly, with difficulty*)
3. They wrote clearly.   (*naturally, perfectly, carefully*)
4. I spoke to him respectfully.   (*nicely, clearly*)
5. He walked rapidly.   (*naturally, carefully, with difficulty*)

Time Expressions with HACER

To express duration of action, Spanish uses a grammatical construction different from English.

> *English:* I have been here for a year.
> *Spanish:* **It makes a year that I am here.**
> *English:* He has been studying for an hour.
> *Spanish:* **It makes an hour that he is studying.**

The Spanish construction is: **Hace** + *time* + **que** + *present tense.*

Hace dos horas que estudio.	I have been studying for two hours.
Hace un año que está aquí.	He has been here for a year.
Hace mucho tiempo que viven aquí.	They have been living here for a long time.

The question form is: **¿Cuánto tiempo** + **hace** + **que** + *present tense?*

¿Cuánto tiempo hace que estudias español?	How long have you been studying Spanish?

Formation of Adverbs

English adverbs in *-ly* are usually formed in Spanish by adding **-mente** to the feminine singular of the adjective.

perfecto	perfectamente	fácil	fácilmente
exacto	exactamente	amable	amablemente
claro	claramente	probable	probablemente
rápido	rápidamente	natural	naturalmente

Sometimes **con** + *noun* is used in Spanish for the English *-ly*.

con cuidado	carefully	**con respeto**	respectfully

Likewise *with* + *noun* is sometimes used in English where **-mente** is used in Spanish.

difícilmente   with difficulty

Days of the Week

⊕ Translate into Spanish.

1. He is arriving on Monday.
2. We study on Sundays.
3. Saturday is a holiday.
4. There is no school on Tuesday.
5. Tomorrow is Thursday.
6. We had class on Wednesday.

Months of the Year

⊕ Translate the following dates.

1. Friday, the first of June.
2. Monday, the fourth of July.
3. Saturday, the tenth of August.
4. Tuesday, the 26th of May.
5. Wednesday, the first of January.
6. Thursday, the 13th of February.
7. Sunday, the 12th of November.
8. Wednesday, the 11th of September.
9. Let's go on the 21st of December.
10. What's the date? It's the tenth of June.

Days of the Week

el lunes	Monday
el martes	Tuesday
el miércoles	Wednesday
el jueves	Thursday
el viernes	Friday
el sábado	Saturday
el domingo	Sunday

The definite article is used with the days of the week except after the verb **ser**. The English *on* is expressed in Spanish by the definite article.

Hoy es lunes.	Today is Monday.
Vamos los viernes.	We go on Fridays.
El llega el martes.	He arrives on Tuesday.
El sábado es día de fiesta.	Saturday is a holiday.

Months of the Year

enero	January	**julio**	July
febrero	February	**agosto**	August
marzo	March	**septiembre**	September
abril	April	**octubre**	October
mayo	May	**noviembre**	November
junio	June	**diciembre**	December

To ask the date in Spanish, the following expression is used.

¿Cuál es la fecha?

Regular cardinal numbers (**dos, tres, cuatro,** etc.) are used to give the day of the month except the first (**primero**).

Lunes, primero de julio.	Monday, the first of July.
Martes, dos de julio.	Tuesday, the second of July.
Jueves, quince de agosto.	Thursday, the 15th of August.

Combined Exercises

A. Express the Spanish in English without referring to the translations. Then cover the Spanish and translate the English into Spanish. Repeat until you make no mistakes.

1.	Insisto.	*I insist.*
2.	Insisto en ayudar.	*I insist on helping.*
3.	Insisto en ganar.	*I insist on winning.*
4.	Insisto en pagar.	*I insist on paying.*
5.	Insisto en invitarle.	*I insist on inviting him.*
6.	Pienso.	*I think.*
7.	Pienso pagar la cuenta.	*I intend to pay the bill.*
8.	Pienso invitar a mis amigos.	*I intend to invite my friends.*
9.	Pienso cruzar la calle.	*I intend to cross the street.*
10.	Pienso charlar con mis amigos.	*I intend to chat with my friends.*
11.	Pienso conseguir buenas notas.	*I intend to get good grades.*
12.	Pienso tomar una siesta.	*I intend to take a siesta.*
13.	¿Para qué son los amigos?	*What are friends for?*
14.	¿Para qué son los niños?	*What are children for?*
15.	¿Para qué son las siestas?	*What are siestas for?*
16.	¿Para qué pagamos las cuentas?	*Why are we paying the bills?*
17.	¿Para qué charlan?	*Why are they chatting?*
18.	Decidió ayer.	*He decided yesterday.*
19.	De repente decidió.	*He suddenly decided.*
20.	Tal vez decidió.	*Perhaps he decided.*
21.	De veras decidió.	*He truly decided.*

B. Answer the questions in Spanish.

1. ¿Quisiste pagar la cuenta o no tuviste dinero?   2. ¿Anduvieron a mi casa o condujeron el coche?   3. ¿Dijo Ud. la verdad o hizo Ud. una tontería? 4. ¿Estuviste en el pueblo ayer o viniste a la ciudad?   5. ¿Cruzaron los niños a la otra acera o no pudieron?   6. ¿Le pagaste el dinero o no quisiste hacerlo?   7. ¿Lo pusiste allí o lo trajiste aquí?

C. Be able to answer the following orally.

1. ¿En qué fecha nació Ud.?   2. ¿Cuál es la fecha de hoy?   3. ¿Cuánto tiempo hace que estás en la universidad?   4. ¿Condujo Ud. su coche a la universidad?   5. ¿Piensan Uds. estudiar español mañana?   6. ¿Viniste a clase durante la noche?   7. ¿Trajeron Uds. los libros a casa?   8. ¿Insistieron Uds. en conseguir buenas notas?   9. ¿Actualmente estudias mucho?   10. ¿Tal vez naciste en octubre?

D. Change the following to the preterite orally.

1. Mis amigos conducen con mucho cuidado.   2. Piensan venir pero no pueden.   3. Está enfermo todo el día.   4. Los hombres respetables pagan las cuentas.   5. Durante la siesta Pablo no puede charlar.   6. Trabaja en el Ministerio pero no gana mucho.   7. Su casa está a dos kilómetros de aquí. 8. Mi esposo quiere ser un hombre respetable.   9. Naturalmente no dice tonterías.   10. La vida es muy cara en los pueblos y muchos vienen a la ciudad.

⊕ E. Translate into Spanish.

1. I tried to study, but I couldn't.
2. I was born on December 21st, but my wife was born on January first.
3. He insisted on paying all his bills on Saturdays.
4. On Tuesday he came to the house and told us the truth.
5. I have been thinking for an hour, and naturally, I still don't know the date.
6. What is the date? Today is Friday, the ninth of April.
7. Did you really (truly) make that meal? I tried to do it, but I couldn't.
8. Do you always have to win? No, it's not important to me.
9. Suddenly my wife said to me that she didn't bring any money.
10. He drove rapidly, but he couldn't see clearly.
11. I met him in the movies.
12. How long have you been here? I have been in the city for three days.

⊕ F. Review. Translate the sentences.

1. They want me to go to the movies.
2. He advises me to sit down.
3. I want her to leave.
4. Let's leave now. No, I want you to wait.
5. I prefer that you not sleep in class.
6. Get up early. I never get up early.
7. Mr. Mora, come here; don't leave.
8. Juanito, come here; don't leave.
9. Give it to me. Don't give it to her.
10. I am paying it (bill).

Reading and Conversation

Dos Amigos

Juan García nació en el pueblo de San Juan, a cuarenta kilómetros de la ciudad de México, pero vive y trabaja actualmente en México. Después de comer y durante la hora de la siesta, decide pasearse por el Paseo de la Reforma.* De repente ve a un viejo amigo, Pepe Morales, de San Juan y le grita:

Juan ¡Pepe! ¡Oye, Pepe! ¡Hombre, ven acá! ¡Soy yo, Juan!

(Pepe está en la otra acera y al oír a su amigo, cruza la calle y le saluda.)

Juan ¡Pepe! Por Dios, hombre, ¿tú aquí en la ciudad? ¿Cuándo llegaste? ¿Qué haces aquí, amigo?

Pepe Hace tres días que estoy aquí. Vine en autobús el martes pasado para buscar trabajo.

Juan ¿Quieres trabajo? ¿Por qué no me lo dijiste antes de venir? ¿Para qué son los amigos? Tal vez puedo ayudarte.

Pepe Tus padres me dieron tu dirección pero la perdí. Quise buscarte pero no pude. La ciudad es muy grande, no como San Juan.

* **Paseo de la Reforma** central thoroughfare of Mexico City

Juan	Bueno, no importa. Ya que estás aquí, vamos a encontrarte algo. Entremos en este café para tomar algo y hablar. La esposa y los niños, ¿los trajiste a México también?
Pepe	No, no pude traérmelos. Pienso conseguir trabajo antes. Tú sabes que la vida aquí es cara.
Juan	¿Qué clase de trabajo quieres? Eres un hombre bien educado y naturalmente tiene que corresponder a tu preparación.
Pepe	De veras, no me importa mucho. En el pueblo casi no hay trabajo estos días y hay que hacer algo para ganarse la vida.
Juan	Amigo, no me digas tonterías. Mis amigos no tienen que trabajar con las manos.* Tengo amigos en el Ministerio. Mañana vamos allí.

Después de tomar los refrescos y charlar durante media hora, los dos amigos se levantan para salir. Juan quiere pagar la cuenta pero Pepe, aunque no tiene mucho dinero, insiste en invitar a Juan.

Dialogue Practice

A. Prepare oral responses to the following questions.

1. ¿Dónde nació Juan? ¿Dónde vive actualmente?
2. ¿Qué decide hacer Juan durante la siesta?
3. ¿Cuánto tiempo hace que Pepe está en la ciudad?
4. ¿Por qué no dijo nada a Juan antes de venir?
5. ¿Trajo Pepe a su esposa y a sus niños también? ¿Por qué?
6. ¿Qué clase de trabajo quiere Pepe?
7. ¿A dónde van los dos amigos mañana?
8. ¿Qué hacen los dos amigos?
9. ¿Quién paga la cuenta?

---

* Juan's remarks regarding manual labor reflect an attitude which is still observable in some areas of Latin America.

LECCIÓN DOCE

Basic Words and Expressions

acordarse (de) (ue) to remember
al lado (de) alongside (of), beside
camino a on the way to
delante (de) in front (of)
detrás (de) in back (of), behind
es lástima it's a shame, pity
los tiempos pasados the old days, days
  gone by
¿Por dónde se va . . . ? How do you get
  to . . . ?
tener ganas (de) to feel like

alegrarse (de) to be glad
casarse (con) to get married (to)
cobrar to charge, collect
esperar to hope, wait for
merendar (ie) to have an afternoon
  snack, picnic
nadar to swim
preguntar to ask
preocuparse (de) to worry (about)
sentir (ie), (i) to be sorry
sorprender to surprise
subir to go up
temer to be afraid, fear

el abrigo overcoat
el ascensor elevator
la boda wedding
la camisa shirt
la corbata tie
el cura priest
el despacho office
la época epoch, period
la fortuna fortune
la juventud youth
el matrimonio marriage, married couple
la noticia news
los pantalones trousers
el piso apartment, floor
el puesto job, position
el río river
el sombrero hat
el traje suit
el traje de baño bathing suit
el vestido dress
el zapato shoe

divertido amusing
quinto fifth
último last

Basic Patterns

1. **Este libro es mío; el suyo está en casa.**
   This book is mine; yours is at home.
2. **Estas cartas son suyas; las de ella están en la mesa.**
   These letters are his; hers are on the table.
3. **Me alegro de que salga.**
   I am happy that he is leaving.
4. **Espero que escriba mañana.**
   I hope that he will write tomorrow.
5. **Espero escribir mañana.**
   I hope to write tomorrow.
6. **La casa era muy grande.**
   The house was very large.
7. **Iba allí todos los días.**
   I used to go there every day.
8. **Juan comía cuando entré.**
   John was eating when I entered.

Drills

Possessive Pronouns

Replace the words in italics with possessive pronouns.

1. Tu camisa y *mi camisa.*
2. Mi despacho y *tu despacho.*
3. Mi corbata y *su corbata.*
4. Su vestido y *nuestro vestido.*
5. Sus corbatas y *nuestras corbatas.*
6. Mi abrigo no es tan bonito como *su abrigo.*
7. Su matrimonio no es tan feliz como *mi matrimonio.*
8. Nuestros zapatos no son tan grandes como *tus zapatos.*
9. Este piso no es tan grande como *nuestro piso.*

⊕ Restate the following sentences, clarifying the exact meaning of the third person forms **el suyo, los suyos,** etc.

Mi corbata y la suya (*his*). / *Mi corbata y la de él.*

1. Mi abrigo no es tan bonito como el suyo (*hers*).
2. Este ascensor no sube tan rápidamente como el suyo (*yours*).
3. Nuestra casa está al lado de la suya (*yours*).
4. Estos zapatos son más bonitos que los suyos (*theirs*).
5. Nuestra casa está detrás de la suya (*theirs*).

Subjunctive after Verbs or Expressions of Emotion

Change according to the example.

Juan está aquí.   (*Me alegro de que*) / *Me alegro de que Juan esté aquí.*

1. Felipe se casa con María mañana.   (*Siento que*)
2. No me cobran mucho dinero.   (*Espero que*)
3. Los niños no hablan español.   (*Teme que*)
4. No podemos subir en el ascensor.   (*Es lástima que*)
5. Ella nos invita a la fiesta.   (*Se alegran de que*)

Repeat the following sentences. Then say them again, beginning with the cues and changing the verb from the indicative to the subjunctive.

1. Carlos termina el trabajo ahora.
   (*Se alegra de que, Es lástima que, Teme que*)
2. Los niños no nadan en el invierno.
   (*Nos alegramos de que, Esperamos que, Sentimos que*)
3. Vivimos en el quinto piso de ese edificio.
   (*Se alegran de que, Esperan que*)

Discussion

Possessive Pronouns

The possessive pronouns are

el mío, la mía
los míos, las mías } mine

el tuyo, la tuya
los tuyos, las tuyas } yours *(fam.)*

el suyo, la suya
los suyos, las suyas } his, hers, yours *(formal)*, theirs

el nuestro, la nuestra
los nuestros, las nuestras } ours

They must agree in number and gender with the object possessed, *not* with the possessor.

El padre de Juan está en
  México, pero el mío está en casa.   John's father is in Mexico, but mine is at home.

Los zapatos de Juan son grandes,
  pero los suyos son más grandes.   John's shoes are big, but hers are bigger.

The definite article is normally omitted after **ser.**

Esta casa es suya.   This house is his.

The third person forms **suyo, suyos,** etc., may be clarified by a prepositional phrase, **de Ud., de él, de ella,** etc.

Tengo mis cartas y las de él.   I have my letters and his.

Tengo nuestros libros y los de usted.   I have our books and yours.

Subjunctive after Verbs or Expressions of Emotion

As is the case with verbs of persuasion *(see page 93)*, the subjunctive is used also after verbs or expressions of emotion. Here are some of the more common verbs and expressions.

alegrarse de	to be happy	**temer**	to be afraid
sentir (ie), (i)	to be sorry	**es lástima**	it's a shame, pity
esperar	to hope		

Remember that there must be a change of subject in order to use the subjunctive, if not, the infinitive is used.

Me alegro de que Juan esté aquí.   I am happy John is here.

Me alegro de estar aquí.   I am happy to be here. (*Note that the infinitive is used when there is no change of subject.*)

Es lástima que no trabajen.   It's a shame that they don't work.

Espero que salgan mañana.   I hope they will leave tomorrow. (*Note that the present subjunctive can express the future tense in English.*)

Imperfect Indicative of Regular and Irregular Verbs

Repeat the model sentences and substitute the cues.

1. Juan nadaba mucho en aquellos tiempos.
   (*tú, él, nosotros, ellos, Paco, yo, Uds.*)
2. Volvíamos muy tarde.
   (*yo, él, tú, nosotros, Uds., Ud., ella*)
3. Pedro escribía muchas cartas.
   (*ellos, el alumno, tú, nosotros, Ud., yo, Uds.*)

Substitute the cues which apply to both verbs.

1. Cuando yo era joven, veía muchas películas.
   (*ellos, nosotros, yo, tú, Juan, ella*)
2. Cuando estaban en Madrid, iban al Prado todos los días.
   (*yo, ellos, ella, tú, nosotros, Juan*)

Distinctions Between Preterite and Imperfect Usage

Substitute the subjects for the first verb only.

1. Yo nadaba en el río cuando llegó el policía.
   (*ellos, nosotros, tú, Juan, mis amigos*)
2. Vivíamos en el quinto piso cuando Juan vino a Madrid.
   (*yo, ella, tú, los muchachos, Ud.*)
3. Mientras Juan estaba en la ciudad, María compró un abrigo nuevo.
   (*ellos, yo, tú, ella, nosotros, mis amigos*)

⊕ Give the proper form of the infinitives in parentheses, using either the preterite or imperfect.

1. Juan (*comer*) cuando yo (*entrar*).
2. María (*ser*) muy joven cuando (*casarse*) con Roberto.
3. Mi padre (*nacer*) en México.
4. Mi esposo (*pagar*) la última cuenta esta tarde.
5. La casa (*ser*) muy grande.
6. Cuando yo (*ser*) joven, (*vivir*) al lado de la biblioteca.

Imperfect Indicative of Regular and Irregular Verbs

This tense is formed by adding the following endings to the stem of the verb. Note that the endings for **-er** and **-ir** verbs are the same. The imperfect may be translated three different ways: *I was talking, I used to talk, I talked*, etc. The third way implies a repeated action, as *I talked Spanish every day.* (**Hablaba español todos los días.**)

hablar/habl-		vender/vend-		vivir/viv-	
habl *aba*	habl *ábamos*	vend *ía*	vend *íamos*	viv *ía*	viv *íamos*
habl *abas*		vend *ías*		viv *ías*	
habl *aba*	habl *aban*	vend *ía*	vend *ían*	viv *ía*	viv *ían*

Only three verbs are irregular in the imperfect.

ser		ir		ver	
era	éramos	iba	íbamos	veía	veíamos
eras		ibas		veías	
era	eran	iba	iban	veía	veían

Distinctions Between Preterite and Imperfect Usage

As was illustrated in Lesson 9, the preterite is used to narrate completed action.

Roberto vendió el coche.	Robert sold the car.
Vivimos veinte años en Lima.	We lived in Lima twenty years.
Llegaron a las nueve.	They arrived at nine.

The imperfect is a descriptive tense and does not express completed action. It is used (1) to describe a situation or state in the past

La casa era muy grande.	The house was very large.
María quería ir al cine.	Mary wanted to go to the movies.
Hacía frío.	It was cold out.

or (2) to express what happened habitually or repeatedly in the past.

Comía allí todos los días.	He ate (used to eat) there every day.
Siempre visitaba a mis amigos cuando iba a Madrid.	I always visited (used to visit) my friends when I went (used to go) to Madrid.

When the imperfect and the preterite are used in the same sentence, the imperfect describes the situation or action *already* existing when another act took place. This act, which breaks in on the situation or action already existing, is expressed by the preterite.

Juan comía cuando entré.	John was eating when I entered.
Eran las seis cuando llegaron.	It was six o'clock when they arrived.
Mientras hablaba, mi amigo salió.	While I was talking, my friend left.

Combined Exercises

A. Translate the Spanish into English without referring to the translation. Then cover the Spanish and translate the English into Spanish.

1.	camino a	*on the way to*
2.	Camino al mercado, vimos a Juan.	*On the way to the market, we saw John.*
3.	Camino a la tienda, perdió el dinero.	*On the way to the store, he lost the money.*
4.	Camino al banco, saludó a sus amigos.	*On the way to the bank, he greeted his friends.*
5.	acordarse (de)	*to remember*
6.	Me acuerdo de eso.	*I remember that.*
7.	Me acuerdo de Juan.	*I remember John.*
8.	No se acuerda de María.	*He doesn't remember Mary.*
9.	¿Te acuerdas de mí?	*Do you remember me?*
10.	merendar	*to have an afternoon snack, to picnic*
11.	No quiero merendar ahora.	*I don't want to have an afternoon snack now.*
12.	Prefiero merendar a las cinco.	*I prefer to have an afternoon snack at five.*
13.	Merendamos todos los días.	*We have an afternoon snack every day.*
14.	tener ganas de	*to feel like*
15.	Tengo ganas de nadar hoy.	*I feel like swimming today.*
16.	No tiene ganas de esperar.	*He doesn't feel like waiting.*
17.	No tienen muchas ganas de comer.	*They don't feel much like eating.*

⊕ B. Write the following in Spanish. (Remember that when you use possessive pronouns the article is normally omitted after **ser**).

1. This book is mine. Where is yours?   2. These trousers are his. Mine are on the chair.   3. Where are the bathing suits? Yours is here and hers (*clarify*) is there.   4. I am happy that she's getting married, but I am sorry that she's not marrying Robert.   5. It's a shame that the children can't swim in the river.   6. I hope that he will leave today.   7. I hope to leave today. 8. I am afraid that she will speak with my father.   9. I am afraid to speak with my father.   10. I am happy that I am in this class. (I am happy to be in this class.)

C. Following the example given, ask directions to the places listed.

el banco / *¿Por dónde se va al banco?*
la biblioteca, el aeropuerto, el cine Rex, la clase de español

D. Answer in Spanish.

1. ¿Está tu casa al lado de la biblioteca o detrás de la tienda?   2. Cuando estás en casa, ¿te acuerdas de tus amigos de la universidad?   3. ¿Quiere Ud. que yo le escriba una carta?   4. ¿Cobran mucho dinero por la comida aquí en la universidad?   5. ¿Es divertida la vida de estudiante?
6. ¿Prefieres vivir en un piso en la ciudad o en una casa de campo?   7. ¿Te

alegras de que tu novio(a) venga a verte hoy?   8. ¿A qué hora vino Ud.
a la clase hoy, y qué trajo?   9. ¿Tuvo que andar a este edificio o vino
en coche?   10. ¿Le sorprendió el examen que tuvimos hoy?   11. ¿Qué otras
cosas puedes comprar en una tienda que vende trajes?

⊕ E. Review. Translate.

1. I want you to be here at six.
2. He prefers that I give you the money.
3. They insist that their son be a doctor.
4. We advise that you go there tomorrow.
5. I request that you know this lesson well.
6. We went there yesterday.
7. He said that he put the book on the table.
8. He was here two hours this morning, and afterward he had to leave.
9. They brought the money when they came.
10. I tried to leave, but I couldn't.
11. He walked all day.
12. We learned (found out) that he did it.

F. After reading all the following sentences, change the verbs in the present
tense to the appropriate past tense, either preterite or imperfect. Note that
the sentences narrate a brief story.

1. Dos amigos van al Ministerio a buscar trabajo.
2. De camino, hablan de su juventud.
3. Uno de ellos dice que el día de su boda,
4. el cura llega tarde.
5. El otro dice que en los días de mucho calor,
6. nada en el río detrás de su casa.
7. Todavía hablan cuando llegan al Ministerio.
8. Entran en el edificio,
9. y preguntan por dónde se va al despacho del Sr. Guzmán.
10. Buscan un ascensor
11. y suben al quinto piso
12. donde los espera Felipe Guzmán.

Reading and Conversation

Camino al Ministerio

Los dos amigos, Juan García y Pepe Morales se encontraron en la ciudad de
México, y ahora van al Ministerio a buscarle trabajo a Pepe. Juan tiene amigos
que van a ayudarle a encontrar un puesto. Camino al Ministerio, hablan de
su juventud y de los tiempos pasados en San Juan.

Juan Tú no sabes cuánto me alegro de que estés aquí en la capital. Hace
diez años que no nos vemos, ¿verdad?

Pepe Sí, hombre. Si no me acuerdo mal, creo que la última vez que te vi fue
el día de tu boda, cuando te casaste con Pilar.

Juan	Ay, ¡qué día! El cura que venía de otro pueblo llegó muy tarde y Pilar y yo creíamos que no iba a llegar nunca. ¿Y te acuerdas de aquella casa al lado de la tuya, donde yo vivía con mis padres? Nos divertíamos mucho allí, ¿verdad?
Pepe	¡Ah, sí! No olvido nunca aquel día de verano cuando hacía tanto calor y decidimos nadar en el río que había* detrás de la casa.
Juan	Sí, y sin traje de baño. Y vino mi madre con unas amigas a merendar y no pudimos salir del agua.
Pepe	Si, la vida era muy divertida en aquellos tiempos. Pero los tiempos cambian y cada época de la vida tiene sus ventajas.
Juan	A propósito, me sorprendió saber que te casaste. Cuando éramos jóvenes siempre decías que el matrimonio no era para ti. Es lástima que tu esposa y tus hijos no estén aquí. Tengo muchas ganas de conocerlos.
Pepe	Bueno, si tengo suerte y encuentro trabajo en el Ministerio, ellos van a venir la semana que viene. Primero voy a tener que encontrar un piso, y todo el mundo me dice que aquí en la ciudad cobran una fortuna.
Juan	Tienes razón, amigo. El nuestro es pequeño y muy viejo, pero pagamos casi la mitad de mi sueldo. Pero ya llegamos al Ministerio. Vamos a ver si tenemos suerte con el puesto y después nos preocupamos del piso.

Los dos entraron en el edificio y preguntaron por dónde se iba al despacho del amigo de Juan. Después, buscaron un ascensor y subieron al quinto piso donde los esperaba Felipe Guzmán.

Dialogue Practice

A. Prepare oral responses to the following questions.

1. ¿Para qué van los dos amigos al Ministerio?
2. ¿De qué hablan camino al Ministerio?
3. ¿Cuánto tiempo hace que no se ven los dos amigos?
4. ¿Cuándo fue la última vez que Pepe vio a Juan?
5. ¿Qué le pasó al cura el día de la boda?
6. ¿Qué pasó un día de verano cuando hacía mucho calor?
7. ¿Cuándo va a venir a la ciudad la familia de Pepe?
8. ¿Cómo es el piso de Juan?
9. Después de entrar en el Ministerio, ¿qué preguntaron?
10. Después de entrar, ¿qué buscaron, y a dónde subieron?

* **habia**   there was

124

LECCIÓN TRECE

Basic Words and Expressions

darse cuenta de to realize
por supuesto of course
tener confianza en to have confidence in
tener miedo de to be afraid of

acostarse (ue) to go to bed
cambiar to change
cerrar (ie) to close
contar (ue) to count, tell
dejar to leave behind
despedirse (de) (i, i) to say goodbye (to)
divertirse (ie, i) to have a good time
dudar to doubt
entender (ie) to understand
morirse (ue, u) to die
preocupar to worry
preocuparse (de) to worry about
recordar (ue) to remember
repetir (i, i) to repeat
vestirse (i, i) to get dressed

el alemán German

la cama bed
la confianza confidence
la costumbre custom
el empleo job, employment
el extranjero foreigner, abroad
la gente people
el miedo fear
el (la) recepcionista receptionist
el tema theme, topic
el tren train
la vida life

atrasado backward, late
cierto certain
claro clear, sure
dudoso doubtful
evidente evident
íntimo intimate
preciso necessary
raro strange

allá there

Basic Patterns

1. **Me di cuenta de que Pablo no estaba aquí.** I realized that Paul was not here.
2. **Juan se durmió en seguida.** John went to sleep immediately.
3. **La puerta se abre.** The door is opened.
4. **La puerta se abrió.** The door was opened.
5. **Las puertas se abrieron.** The doors were opened.
6. **Dudo que Pablo tenga miedo de esto.** I doubt that Paul is afraid of this.
7. **Es dudoso que él sepa escribir.** It's doubtful that he knows how to write.
8. **Es verdad que él sabe escribir.** It's true that he knows how to write.

Drills

Preterite Indicative of DAR

Repeat the model sentences and substitute the cues.

1. Se lo dimos a Pedro.
   (*él, tú, ellos, Ud., yo, nosotros*)
2. Me di cuenta de que Pablo no estaba aquí.
   (*él, Uds., tú, nosotros, yo, Ud.*)

Preterite Indicative of Stem-Changing Verbs

Substitute the subjects in parentheses.

1. Nos acostamos a las diez anoche.
   (*él, tú, ellos, yo, nosotros, el muchacho*)
2. Preferimos ir más tarde.
   (*tú, ellos, él, yo, nosotros, mi amigo*)
3. Me divertí mucho en la fiesta.
   (*nosotros, él, tú, Uds., yo, tu amigo*)
4. Me dormí en seguida.
   (*tú, él, nosotros, yo, ellos, Ud.*)
5. Mi hijo pidió demasiado.
   (*yo, él, tú, nosotros, ellos, Ud.*)
6. Los niños se vistieron fácilmente.
   (*él, yo, tú, ellos, nosotros, ella*)
7. Los novios se despidieron tristemente.
   (*nosotros, yo, él, tú, ellos, Ud.*)

Read the following sentences just as they are and then change the verbs to the preterite.

1. El se muere de hambre.
2. Ella se siente enferma.
3. Juan prefiere ir al cine.
4. Ellos se duermen aquí.
5. Lo siento mucho.
6. Uds. se despiden a las ocho.
7. José se viste solo.
8. El profesor repite la lección.
9. Vuelve a la ciudad.
10. ¿A qué hora te despiertas?
11. Te acuestas en la cama.
12. Pedro pierde su dinero.
13. Duermo en el coche.
14. Me visto todos los días.
15. Prefiere dormir aquí.
16. Me pide dos pesetas.
17. Pensamos ir al parque.
18. Ellos se divierten mucho.

Discussion

Preterite Indicative of DAR

The verb **dar** is conjugated in the preterite as follows.

dar	
di	dimos
diste	
dio	dieron

Preterite Indicative of Stem-Changing Verbs

Stem-changing verbs ending in **-ar** and **-er** are regular in the preterite tense.

sentarse (ie)		volver (ue)	
me senté	nos sentamos	volví	volvimos
te sentaste		volviste	
se sentó	se sentaron	volvió	volvieron

Verbs of this type which you have studied are **despertarse, entender, pensar, perder, sentarse, acostarse, contar, recordar.**

Stem-changing verbs ending in **-ir** change the stem vowel **e** to **i** and **o** to **u** in the third person singular and plural of the preterite tense.

preferir (ie, i)	dormir (ue, u)	pedir (i, i)
preferí	dormí	pedí
preferiste	dormiste	pediste
prefirió	durmió	pidió
preferimos	dormimos	pedimos
prefirieron	durmieron	pidieron

Verbs like **preferir** in this and previous lessons are **sentir, sentirse, divertirse.**
Verbs like **dormir** in this and previous lessons are **dormirse, morirse.**
Verbs like **pedir** in this and previous lessons are **despedirse, repetir, vestirse.**

You should now refer to the Appendix for a complete summary of the changes in stem-changing verbs in the present, present subjunctive, and preterite tenses.

Passive Voice: Reflexives

Change the following to the plural.

1. La puerta se abre.
2. Se vio la montaña.
3. Se vendió la cama.
4. Se paga la cuenta aquí.
5. Se oyó un ruido.
6. Se necesitaba una casa nueva.
7. La tienda se cierra.
8. El chico se perdió.

⊕ Write in Spanish and be able to do orally.

1. They say he is coming.
2. One says "Thanks."
3. You say "Of course."
4. People say he is returning.
5. One eats well here.
6. Tables are sold here.

⊕ Translate.

1. The store is closed at five.
2. The meal was eaten here.
3. This is done every day.
4. German is spoken here.
5. Many houses are sold.
6. Many jobs were lost.

Subjunctive with Verbs of Doubt and Necessity

Change the second verb according to the cue.

1. Dudo que Pablo tenga miedo de esto.
   (ellos, tú, él, nosotros, Uds., Ud.)
2. No creo que sean muy jóvenes.
   (tú, él, ellos, nosotros, Ud., Uds.)
3. Pablo necesita que le den un puesto.
   (tú, Ud., yo, ellos, nosotros, Uds.)

Begin with the cues and make all necessary changes.

1. Los muchachos se visten.
   (Creo que, Dudo que, Necesito que, No creo que)
2. El tren sale a las cinco.
   (Dudo que, Necesito que, Creo que, No creo que)
3. Tú te pones a trabajar.
   (Dudo que, Necesito que, No creo que, No dudo que)

⊕ Complete the sentences in Spanish.

1. Necesito que _____.
   (you to help me, them to help me, you (fam., sing.) to help me, you to do it)
2. Dudo que _____.
   (he'll leave at 8:00, he'll wake up, we will know it, they will get dressed, you (fam., sing.) will remember)

Passive Voice: Reflexives

When the subject acts, the verb is said to be active. When the subject is acted upon, the verb is passive.

Active   *Passive*
The boy opens the door.   The door is opened.

The passive voice is often expressed in Spanish by **se** and the third person of the verb. If the subject is singular, the verb is singular; if the subject is plural, the verb is plural.

Aquí se habla español.	Spanish is spoken here.
Se abren las puertas.	The doors are opened.
Se abre la puerta.	The door is opened.
Se vio el edificio.	The building was seen.
Las lecciones se aprendieron.	The lessons were learned.

If the subject is indefinite, several translations are possible.

se dice	it is said, they say, people say, one says.
Se come bien aquí.	One (You, People) eats well here.

Subjunctive with Verbs of Doubt and Necessity

The subjunctive mood is regularly used in Spanish to express four very concrete attitudes on the part of the speaker: command, emotion, doubt, and necessity. In previous lessons you have studied the subjunctive with verbs of command and emotion. Some verbs commonly used to express doubt or necessity are **dudar, necesitar, no creer, no pensar.**

Dudo que él sea mi amigo.	I doubt that he is my friend.
Necesito que me ayudes.	I need you to help me.
No creo que estudies mucho.	I don't believe you study much.
No creo que se vayan.	I don't think they are going.

When no doubt is inferred, the indicative is used.

Creo que estudias mucho.	I believe you study a lot.
No dudo que es mi amigo.	I don't doubt that he is my friend.
Creemos que se van.	We think that they are going.

Subjunctive after Impersonal Expressions

Repeat the model sentences and substitute the impersonal expressions.

1. El sabe escribir.
   (*Es dudoso, Es verdad, Es preciso, Es lástima*)
2. Vamos mañana por la mañana.
   (*Es posible, Es evidente, Es probable, Es importante*)

Change the second verb.

1. Es necesario que te despiertes temprano.
   (*él, ellos, tú, nosotros, yo, mi madre*)
2. Es posible que Juan recuerde la canción.
   (*tú, ellos, Ud., nosotros, yo, mi primo*)

⊕ Write in the proper forms of the verbs.

1. Es dudoso que ellos _____.
   (*escribir, acostarse, repetir, vestirse, contar*)
2. Es importante que nosotros _____.
   (*entender, cerrar la puerta, despedirse, contar*)

⊕ Complete the sentences according to the cues.

1. Es preciso . . .
   (*for them to study, for me to go, for them to remember, to go now, for you to go to bed*)
2. Es posible . . .
   (*to do it, for him to repeat it, for us to understand, to pay now, for me to come*)

Subjunctive after Impersonal Expressions

The subjunctive is used after many impersonal expressions when they indicate command, emotion, doubt, or necessity. Here are some which take the subjunctive.

Es dudoso.	It is doubtful.
Es importante.	It is important.
Es lástima.	It's a shame.
Es posible.	It's possible.
Es necesario.	It's necessary.
Es preciso.	It's necessary.
Es probable.	It's probable.

Es necesario que lo hagamos.	It's necessary for us to do it.
Es lástima que no se vayan ahora.	It's a shame they aren't going now.
Es posible que lo escriba.	It's possible that he'll write it.

Note that the subjunctive is not used unless the second verb has an expressed subject.

Es importante hacerlo.	It's important to do it.
Es importante que lo hagas.	It's important for you to do it.
Es preciso estudiar.	It's necessary to study.
Es preciso que estudiemos.	It's necessary that we study.

The subjunctive is not used after impersonal expressions which express truth or certainty, such as **es cierto, es evidente, es verdad, es claro.**

Es cierto que no se van.	It's certain that they aren't going.
Es verdad que habla español.	It's true that he speaks Spanish.

Combined Exercises

A. Express the Spanish sentences in English without referring to the Spanish. Then cover the Spanish and translate the English sentences. Repeat until you make no mistakes.

1.	Tengo confianza en él.	*I have confidence in him.*
2.	Tengo miedo del tren.	*I am afraid of the train.*
3.	Tenemos miedo de la gente.	*We are afraid of people.*
4.	Tengo miedo de acostarme.	*I am afraid of going to bed.*
5.	Tiene miedo de acostarse.	*He is afraid to go to bed.*
6.	Tienes miedo de acostarte.	*You are afraid of going to bed.*
7.	Tenemos miedo de acostarnos.	*We are afraid to go to bed.*
8.	Tienen miedo de acostarse,	*They are afraid of going to bed.*
9.	Me doy cuenta de que hace frío.	*I realize that it is cold.*
10.	Me di cuenta de que hacía frío.	*I realized that it was cold.*
11.	El se da cuenta de que es verdad.	*He realizes that it is true.*
12.	El se dio cuenta de que era verdad.	*He realized that it was true.*
13.	El se dio cuenta de que estaba atrasado.	*He realized that he was backward (behind the times).*
14.	Por supuesto el empleo es fácil.	*Of course the job is easy.*
15.	Naturalmente el alemán es fácil.	*Naturally German is easy.*
16.	A veces la vida es fácil.	*At times life is easy.*
17.	A propósito, las costumbres son alemanas.	*By the way, the customs are German.*
18.	Por supuesto la recepcionista es alemana.	*Of course the receptionist is German.*
19.	Las recepcionistas son alemanas.	*The receptionists are German.*
20.	Las costumbres son inglesas.	*The customs are English.*
21.	Las costumbres son raras.	*The customs are strange.*
22.	La gente me preocupa.	*People worry me.*
23.	La vida me preocupa.	*Life worries me.*
24.	Las costumbres me preocupan.	*The customs worry me.*
25.	Los extranjeros te preocupan.	*Foreigners worry you.*
26.	Los extranjeros le preocupan.	*Foreigners worry him.*
27.	Los extranjeros nos preocupan.	*Foreigners worry us.*
28.	Los extranjeros les preocupan.	*Foreigners worry them.*
29.	La vida les preocupaba.	*Life worried them.*

B. Prepare oral answers to the following questions.

1. ¿Cuántas horas durmió Ud. anoche?   2. ¿Crees que tienes demasiado dinero?   3. ¿Es posible estudiar en tu cuarto?   4. ¿Es posible que mucha gente estudie en tu cuarto?   5. ¿Te preocupan las notas?   6. ¿Tienen Uds. miedo de los exámenes?   7. ¿Se dio Ud. cuenta de que estamos en primavera?   8. ¿Se come bien en la cafetería?   9. ¿Te divertiste durante el fin de semana pasado?   10. ¿Piensas divertirte el fin de semana que viene?

C. Change the following sentences first to the preterite and then to the imperfect.

1. Lo hace Pedro.   2. Juan lo pone aquí.   3. Ellos duermen allí.   4. Prefiero acostarme.   5. Cierras la puerta.   6. Tengo confianza en Pedro.   7. Se paga bien allí.   8. Vamos a España.   9. Dejo mis libros en casa.   10. Entienden la lección.   11. Se repiten las lecciones.   12. Los niños cuentan hasta treinta. 13. Juan se despide de ellos.   14. Me levanto temprano y me visto. 15. Dejas tu ropa en la cama.   16. El camarero nos da la cuenta.

D. Substitute the cues.

1. La vida me preocupaba mucho.
    (*la gente, las costumbres, la verdad, las chicas, ellos*)
2. Me preocupo de todo.
    (*él, ellos, nosotros, yo, tú, la recepcionista*)
3. Tenía miedo de divertirme tanto.
    (*él, nosotros, tú, ellos, yo, el extranjero*)
4. Dudo que se muera.
    (*acostarse, salir, recordar, vestirse, saber, tener miedo, estar atrasado*)

⊕ E. Translate.

1. I don't believe he sleeps enough.
2. He had a good time, but he slept only four hours.
3. They got dressed and went downtown.
4. His daughter worried him because she refused to go.
5. He closed the door and went to sleep.
6. Of course he repeated the lesson, but they didn't learn it.
7. Give (*fam., sing.*) it to me; don't leave it there.
8. It's evident that you didn't put it there.
9. It's necessary to eat, but it's a shame that you eat so much.
10. The store was closed at five, but the doors weren't closed until five-thirty.

Reading and Conversation

Los Tiempos Cambian

Dos amigos, don Rafael Alvarez y don Jaime Mendoza se encontraron en la calle y se pusieron a* hablar.

Sr. Mendoza   Rafael, ¿qué tal? ¿Cómo te va? Hace mucho que no te veo por aquí.

Sr. Alvarez   Hola, amigo. Acabo de regresar del sur. Pasé varios días en el Parque Nacional.

Sr. Mendoza   De vacaciones, ¿eh? Fuiste con la familia, por supuesto.

Sr. Alvarez   No, fui solo. Fui a visitar a mi hija Margarita que trabaja allí en un hotel. Es un empleo muy bueno. Se paga bien y se puede conocer a muchas personas del extranjero. Ella habla inglés y alemán.

* **se pusieron a**   they began to

Sr. Mendoza	Pero, ¿vive allí sola entre extranjeros? ¿Cómo es que permites tal locura, hombre? No me digas que es por el dinero.
Sr. Alvarez	Hombre, se ve que estás muy atrasado ya. ¿No te das cuenta de que muchos jóvenes trabajan hoy día? Lo hacen por la experiencia, por el contacto íntimo con la vida. No hay nada malo en eso. Además tengo confianza en ella.
Sr. Mendoza	Sí, ¿pero no tienes miedo por tu hija? ¿Qué clase de empleo tiene? Tú sabes lo que* son estos extranjeros. Tienen unas costumbres tan raras.
Sr. Alvarez	¡Qué va! Son gente de confianza, como tú y yo. Además Margarita trabaja de recepcionista. Antes quería cuidar a los niños pero no se lo permití. Le conseguí el empleo de recepcionista. Tengo amigos allí.
Sr. Mendoza	En mis días esto no se permitía. ¡Cómo cambian los tiempos! ¿Y cuándo volviste?
Sr. Alvarez	Anoche en tren. No dormí en toda la noche por el ruido.
Sr. Mendoza	No dormiste, ¿eh? Por supuesto no te preocupaba nada dejar a la chica allá, ¿verdad?
Sr. Alvarez	Amigo, dejemos este tema. Ya te dije que los tiempos cambian y los jóvenes también. ¡Y hasta los viejos como nosotros podemos cambiar!

Dialogue Practice

A. Prepare oral responses to the following questions.

1. ¿Dónde se encontraron los dos amigos y qué se pusieron a hacer?
2. ¿De dónde acaba de regresar don Rafael?
3. ¿Por qué fue al Parque Nacional?
4. ¿Qué hace su hija allí?
5. ¿Por qué dice don Rafael que don Jaime está muy atrasado?
6. ¿Tenía miedo don Rafael por su hija?
7. ¿Por qué no pudo dormir don Rafael?
8. ¿Qué quería hacer Margarita en el Parque Nacional?
9. ¿Cómo consiguió el empleo de recepcionista?
10. ¿Por qué trabajan los jóvenes hoy día?

⊕ B. Using the dialogue as a model, translate the following into Spanish.

Mr. Alvarez went to visit his daughter who was working in a hotel in the National Park. They paid well there and she was working as a receptionist. Mr. Mendoza said that times were changing because in his day this wasn't permitted. Mr. Alvarez said that he had confidence in his daughter, but he didn't sleep much on the train.

* **lo que**   what

LECCIÓN CATORCE

Basic Words and Expressions

a menudo often
dar un paseo to take a walk

almorzar (ue) to eat lunch
beber to drink
caerse to fall down
coger to get, grasp, catch
empezar (ie) to begin
escoger to choose
faltar to need, lack
gustar to be pleasing to
ofrecer to offer
probar (ue) to prove, taste, try
quedar to remain, have left
seguir (i, i) to follow, continue
tardar to delay, be late

el almuerzo lunch
el arroz rice
el biftec steak
el café cafe, coffee
el cubierto table setting
la ensalada salad
el flan custard
la fruta fruit

el huevo (al plato) egg (fried)
la leche milk
la lechuga lettuce
la lista menu
el lugar place
la mantequilla butter
el minuto minute
el negocio business
la oficina office
el paseo walk, ride
la patata potato
el pescado fish
el plato plate
el pollo chicken
el postre dessert
la siesta afternoon nap
el tomate tomato
la tortilla omelette (*Spain*),
    cornmeal cake (*L. Am.*)
el vaso glass
la ventana window

fresco fresh, cool
frito fried
libre free

Basic Patterns

1. Busqué la lista.
2. Empecé a lavar los platos.
3. Le seguí hasta la esquina.
4. El leyó la lista.
5. Hace una hora que leo.
6. Hacía una hora que leía.
7. Lo leí hace una hora.
8. Me gusta el arroz con pollo.
9. A Pedro le falta dinero.
10. Me quedaba una semana.

I looked for the menu.
I began to wash the dishes.
I followed him to the corner.
He read the menu.
I have been reading for an hour.
I had been reading for an hour.
I read it an hour ago.
I like chicken with rice.
Pedro is lacking (needs) money.
I had a week left.

Drills

Verbs with Spelling Changes

Repeat the model sentences and then substitute the cues.

1. El camarero buscó la lista.
   (yo, él, nosotros, ellos, tú, mi hermano)
2. Elena empezó a lavar los platos.
   (ellos, tú, yo, él, nosotros, mis hermanas)
3. Almorcé aquí anteayer.
   (Ud., tú, ella, nosotros, Uds., mi padre)
4. Me acerqué a la ventana.
   (tú, ellos, yo, nosotros, él, nadie)
5. Le sigo hasta la esquina.
   (tú, él, nosotros, ellos, yo, el policía)
6. Le ofrezco pan y mantequilla.
   (nosotros, él, yo, Ud., ellos, la señora)
7. Juan escoge dos platos de la lista.
   (yo, Uds., ella, tú, nosotros, tu primo)

Read the following sentences just as they are and then change them to the preterite.

1. Empiezo a comer.
2. Coges el tren.
3. Sigues con tu empleo.
4. Te ofrezco un empleo.
5. Ellos almuerzan aquí.
6. Empiezan a estudiar.
7. Escojo arroz con pollo.
8. Llego a las cinco.
9. El lo niega siempre.
10. Pago la cuenta.
11. ¿Por qué ruegas?
12. ¿Cuándo comienzas?
13. Le conozco bien.
14. Juan parece americano.
15. Conduzco con cuidado.
16. Escogemos este café.

Substitute the cues.

1. Leí la lista con cuidado.
   (tú, él, nosotros, yo, ellos, Ud.)
2. Creímos que era verdad.
   (yo, él, tú, nosotros, Uds., Ud.)
3. Juan no oyó el ruido del coche.
   (yo, ellas, nosotros, Ud., tú, el muchacho)
4. Los niños se cayeron.
   (ella, yo, Ud., nosotros, tú, Uds.)

Discussion

Verbs with Spelling Changes*

For verbs ending in **-car, -gar, -zar,** like **buscar, acercarse, llegar, negar, pagar, rogar, comenzar, empezar, almorzar,** change the consonants **c, g, z** to **qu, gu, c** respectively, when these consonants would normally precede the letter **e.** This change occurs in the first person singular of the preterite and all forms of the present subjunctive.

Preterite

buscar (to look for)		**llegar** (to arrive)		**comenzar** (to begin)	
busqué	buscamos	llegué	llegamos	comencé	comenzamos
buscaste		llegaste		comenzaste	
buscó	buscaron	llegó	llegaron	comenzó	comenzaron

Present subjunctive

buscar		**llegar**		**comenzar**	
busque	busquemos	llegue	lleguemos	comience	comencemos
busques		llegues		comiences	
busque	busquen	llegue	lleguen	comience	comiencen

For verbs ending in **-ger** and **gir,** like **coger, escoger,** change **g** to **j** before **a** and **o.** Verbs ending in **-guir** do not retain the **u** when **g** precedes **o** or **a.**

escoger (to choose)

Present indicative	escojo	escoges	escoge	escogemos	escogen
Present subjunctive	escoja	escojas	escoja	escojamos	escojan

seguir (to follow)

Present indicative	sigo	sigues	sigue	seguimos	siguen
Present subjunctive	siga	sigas	siga	sigamos	sigan

For verbs ending in **-cer** and **-cir,** like **conocer, parecer, conducir, ofrecer,** change **c** to **zc** before **a** or **o.**

conocer (to know)

Present indicative	conozco	conoces	conoce	conocemos	conocen
Present subjunctive	conozca	conozcas	conozca	conozcamos	conozcan

conducir (to drive)

Present indicative	conduzco	conduces	conduce	conducimos	conducen
Present subjunctive	conduzca	conduzcas	conduzca	conduzcamos	conduzcan

Some verbs, like **leer, creer, oír, caer,** have a **y** in the third person singular and plural of the preterite.

leer (to read)		**oír** (to hear)		**creer** (to believe)		**caer (se)** (to fall down)	
leí	leímos	oí	oímos	creí	creímos	(me) caí	(nos) caímos
leíste		oíste		creíste		(te) caíste	
leyó	leyeron	oyó	oyeron	creyó	creyeron	(se) cayó	(se) cayeron

*See also Appendix.

Time Expressions with HACER (*past tenses*)

⊕ Translate the following.

1. I have been reading for an hour.
2. I had been reading for an hour.
3. I had been looking for an hour.
4. They had been talking for fifteen minutes.
5. It had been raining for a long time.
6. I went a week ago.
7. I saw it a month ago.
8. He returned two days ago.

Answer in Spanish.

1. ¿Cuánto tiempo hacía que leías?
2. ¿Cuánto tiempo hacía que hablabas?
3. ¿Cuánto tiempo hace que lo hiciste?

Uses of GUSTAR, FALTAR, PARECER, QUEDAR

Repeat the sentences and the words in parentheses.

1. Me gusta el arroz con pollo.
   (*la leche, los huevos, la ensalada, las frutas, el postre*)
2. A Pedro le falta dinero.
   (*a mí, a ti, a nosotros, a ellos, al camarero*)
3. Nos parecía buena la comida.
   (*a ellos, a ti, a nosotros, a mí, a Ricardo, a mis hijos*)
4. Les quedaba una semana más.
   (*dos pesetas, un minuto, una manzana, unas frutas, unos tomates, un año*)

⊕ Write in Spanish and then give orally.

1. He likes the apples. He likes the chicken. He liked the chicken. They liked the chicken. We liked the potatoes.
2. He needs the butter. I need the butter. I needed the butter. You needed the eggs. They needed the eggs.
3. They had a year left. You (*fam., sing.*) had a year left. He has a year left. We have a year left. They have a year left.
4. The fish seems fresh to him. The fish seemed fresh to him. The fish seemed good to me. The rice seemed good to her. The tables seemed large to them.

Time Expressions with HACER (*past tenses*)

Review the discussion of present tense time expressions with **hacer** in Lesson 11 (pp. 110, 111). With the imperfect tense the construction is: **Hacía + que + *imperfect tense.***

Hace dos meses que estudio.	I have been studying for two months.
Hacía dos meses que estudiaba.	I had been studying for two months.
Hacía un año que estábamos allí.	We had been there for a year.
Hacía mucho tiempo que leía.	He had been reading for a long time.

The English *ago* is expressed in Spanish by: *preterite* + **hace** + *time.*

Volví hace un año.	I returned a year ago.
Fuimos hace tres días.	We went three days ago.
Lo hice hace poco.	I did it a little while ago.

Uses of GUSTAR, FALTAR, PARECER, QUEDAR

Several of these verbs are used to express English words for which there is no direct equivalent in Spanish. For example, the English *I like that* must be translated as *That is pleasing to me.* **Eso me gusta.** When these verbs are used with indirect object pronouns, they have only two forms, the third person singular and plural.

Me gusta el libro.	The book pleases me. (I like the book.)
Me gustan los libros.	The books please me. (I like the books.)
Te falta dinero.	Money is lacking to you. (You need money.)
Te faltan libros.	Books are lacking to you. (You need books.)
Le parece fácil.	It seems easy to him.
Le parecen fáciles.	They seem easy to him.
Nos queda un año.	A year is remaining to us. (We have a year left.)
Nos quedan dos años.	Two years are remaining to us. (We have two years left.)
Les gustó la casa.	The house pleased them. (They liked the house.)
Les gustaron las casas.	The houses pleased them. (They liked the houses.)

Note that when the subject of the verb is plural, the plural verb form is used; when the subject is singular, the singular verb is used.

When the object is a proper name, it must be preceded by the personal **a;** when the object is a pronoun, the personal **a** followed by a prepositional pronoun may be used for clarification or emphasis.

A Juan le gustó mucho la película.	John liked the film very much.
A ellos les quedaban cinco pesetas.	They had five pesetas left.
A mí me faltaba tiempo.	I needed (lacked) time.

Cardinal Numbers 40–100

1. Write in Spanish and then give orally: 42 books, 67 pens, 83 men, 12 eggs, 50 windows, 33 minutes, 78 custards, 55 offices, 91 tables, 161 glasses, 100 men, 115 potatoes, 153 chickens, 1 table setting, 100 salads.
2. Count by tens from 10 to 100.
⊕ 3. Count by fives from 100 to 195.

EDITOR

—Lo siento, don Juan, pero ahora estas cosas se publican en las revistas ilustradas.

—He oído decir que sólo el 28 por 100 de la población mundial come lo suficiente. ¿Cómo es posible que tengamos suerte tan pocos?

Cardinal Numbers 40–100

40	cuarenta	31	treinta y uno
50	cincuenta	42	cuarenta y dos
60	sesenta	53	cincuenta y tres
70	setenta	64	sesenta y cuatro
80	ochenta	75	setenta y cinco
90	noventa	86	ochenta y seis
100	ciento (cien)	197	ciento noventa y siete

Tens and units are written separately beginning with 30.

dieciséis   **veintidós**   **cuarenta y cinco**   **ochenta y dos**

Ciento becomes **cien** when used immediately before a noun.

cien casas   **cien libros**   **ciento cincuenta libros**

Remember *one* is **una** before a feminine noun and becomes **un** before a masculine noun.

veintiún libros   **cuarenta y una casas**

OLIVOS
—Y si eres bueno, cuando seas mayor producirás spanish olive oil.

Combined Exercises

A. Translate first the Spanish and then the English without referring to the translations.

1.	Lo busqué ayer.	*I searched for it yesterday.*
2.	Lo empecé ayer.	*I began it yesterday.*
3.	Llegué la semana pasada.	*I arrived last week.*
4.	Lo pagué el año pasado.	*I paid it last year.*
5.	Lo negué anoche.	*I denied it last night.*
6.	Lo escojo a menudo.	*I choose it often.*
7.	Le sigo a menudo.	*I follow him often.*
8.	Me sigue a menudo.	*He follows me often.*
9.	Conduzco muy bien.	*I drive very well.*
10.	Conduje muy bien.	*I drove very well.*
11.	Le conozco muy bien.	*I know him very well.*
12.	Hace dos horas que estoy aquí.	*I have been here for two hours.*
13.	Hacía dos horas que estaba aquí.	*I had been here for two hours.*
14.	Hacía dos horas que leía.	*I had been reading for two hours.*
15.	Lo leí hace dos horas.	*I read it two hours ago.*
16.	Estuve aquí hace dos horas.	*I was here two hours ago.*
17.	Me gusta un poco de flan.	*I like a little custard.*
18.	Me queda un poco de flan.	*I have a little custard left.*
19.	Me falta un poco de flan.	*I need (am lacking) a little custard.*
20.	Te gustan las tortillas.	*You like tortillas.*
21.	Te quedan muchas tortillas.	*You have a lot of tortillas left.*
22.	Le faltan unas tortillas.	*You need (are lacking) some tortillas.*

B. Prepare oral answers to the following questions.

1. ¿Te gusta dormir una siesta a veces?   2. ¿Cuándo empezó Ud. a estudiar anoche?   3. ¿Buscaste tu libro de español en el parque?   4. Cuando estás en un café, ¿qué pides generalmente?   5. ¿Conoces al presidente de este país?   6. ¿Siempre conduces con cuidado?   7. ¿Llegaste a esta universidad hace diez años?   8. ¿Te falta una ventana en tu cuarto?   9. ¿Cuántos años de universidad te quedan?   10. ¿Tardaste mucho en leer esta lección?

C. Read aloud the following in Spanish.

1. John/begins, chooses, continues, falls down, drives, counts
2. I/choose, know, drive, eat lunch, begin, read, continue
3. I/chose, denied, arrived, drove, continued, looked for, tasted
4. They/read, continued, heard, believed, fell down, chose

D. Change the following to either the imperfect or the preterite according to the cues given below.

1.	Pago la cuenta.	*(ayer)*
2.	Busco la oficina.	*(todo el día)*
3.	Le conozco.	*(anoche)*
4.	Me falta un negocio.	*(siempre)*
5.	Me gusta ese lugar.	*(anteayer)*
6.	Juan cree en Dios.	*(siempre)*
7.	Dan un paseo.	*(todos los días)*
8.	Le parecen difíciles las lecciones.	*(muchas veces)*

9. Ellos se caen.   (*ayer*)
10. Tarda en venir.   (*de costumbre*)
11. Me ofrece un empleo.   (*hace dos días*)
12. Almuerzo allí.   (*a menudo*)
13. Pruebas un poco de todo.   (*ayer*)

E. Substitute the cues for the second verb.

1. Quiero que lo busques.
   (*él, Uds., ellos, nosotros, tú, mi amigo*)
2. Es preciso que lo comience Juan.
   (*tú, ellos, Ud., nosotros, el camarero*)

⊕ F. Translate.

1. I arrived at the office and began to work immediately.   2. I searched for the cafe, but I couldn't find it.   3. He believed the waiter and chose another cafe.   4. He tasted the steak, but he didn't like it.   5. We didn't like the place, and we didn't go back.   6. He wasn't feeling well and wanted to leave.   7. They had been eating in that restaurant for five years.   8. I ate there a week ago, but I didn't try the custard.   9. After the meal, they still had 155 desserts left.   10. I chose soup first and then fish.

Reading and Conversation

El Almuerzo

Felipe y Carlos trabajan en una oficina en Madrid. Son casi las dos y media de la tarde y entran en un café para almorzar.

Carlos Hay una mesa cerca de la ventana. Sentémonos allí.

Felipe Qué suerte encontrar una mesa libre a esta hora. Espero que venga pronto el camarero. Tengo mucha hambre.

Se sientan pero hay mucha gente y el camarero tarda unos minutos en venir. Por fin llega y les da la lista. Mientras leen, el camarero pone los cubiertos, pan y mantequilla.

Camarero ¿Qué les ofrezco, señores?

Carlos Primero voy a tomar una sopa de cebolla* y después una tortilla española.

Camarero ¿Nada más? Tenemos un biftec muy bueno con patatas fritas. El arroz con pollo también es bueno.

Carlos No, gracias. Me siento un poco mal hoy y no quiero comer mucho. Tráigame también un vaso de leche fría.

Felipe Pues yo me siento bien y tengo un hambre feroz.** Primero voy a tomar pescado y después huevos al plato. ¿Qué legumbres hay?

Camarero Espinacas†, ensalada de lechuga y tomate, alcachofas‡ . . .

* **cebolla** onion
** **feroz** ferocious
† **espinacas** spinach
‡ **alcachofas** artichokes

<table>
<tr><td>Felipe</td><td>Traiga una ensalada, por favor. No me gustan las alcachofas.</td></tr>
<tr><td>Camarero</td><td>Muy bien, ¿y para beber?</td></tr>
</table>

Los dos comen y hablan de cosas de la oficina. Cuando terminan, el camarero llega otra vez y pregunta si quieren postre.

<table>
<tr><td>Felipe</td><td>Sí, de postre flan y café solo.</td></tr>
<tr><td>Carlos</td><td>Para mí un poco de fruta fresca y café con leche. (A Felipe) Se come bien aquí. ¿Es muy caro este lugar?</td></tr>
<tr><td>Felipe</td><td>Es un restaurante muy bueno, pero no es caro. Vengo aquí a menudo. ¡Qué lástima que no te sientas bien! El pescado estuvo estupendo.</td></tr>
<tr><td>Carlos</td><td>Pues otro día lo pruebo. ¿Regresamos ahora?</td></tr>
<tr><td>Felipe</td><td>¿Para qué? Son las cuatro ahora y tú sabes que la oficina no se abre hasta las cinco. ¿Por qué no damos un paseo antes de volver?</td></tr>
<tr><td>Carlos</td><td>Muy bien, pero tengo sueño. Generalmente almuerzo en casa con la familia y después de comer, puedo dormir una siesta.</td></tr>
<tr><td>Felipe</td><td>¡Qué costumbre tan rara! Hoy día los hombres de negocios no tenemos tiempo para la siesta.</td></tr>
</table>

Dialogue Practice

A. Prepare oral responses to the following questions.

1. ¿Para qué entran Felipe y Carlos en un café?
2. ¿Dónde encuentran una mesa libre? ¿Por qué tarda unos minutos el camarero?
3. ¿Qué toma Carlos? ¿Por qué no quiere más?
4. ¿Qué toma Felipe? ¿Qué no le gusta a Felipe?
5. ¿Cuándo va a probar Carlos el pescado?
6. ¿Dónde come Carlos generalmente?
7. ¿Qué van a hacer después de comer?

⊕ B. Write the following passage in the correct past tense (preterite or imperfect).

Ayer Carlos y yo entramos en un restaurante. Encontramos una mesa libre y nos sentamos. Carlos dice que siempre pide biftec en este café y siempre le gusta. Mientras comemos, hablamos de nuestro trabajo. Al terminar, yo pago la cuenta y salimos.

LECCIÓN QUINCE

Basic Words and Expressions

al principio at first, at the beginning
¡De acuerdo! O.K.! Agreed!
en realidad as a matter of fact
hace fresco it's cool out
perder el tiempo to waste time

alojarse to stay (in a hotel)
anunciar to announce
asistir (a) to attend
contestar to answer
cubrir to cover
doblar to turn, to fold
importar to matter
romper to break
sonar (ue) to ring, to sound

el agua water
el baño bath
la calefacción heating

el curso course
la derecha right
el dólar dollar
el estudio study
la fuente fountain
la habitación room
el idioma language
la izquierda left
la lengua language
la manera way, manner
el pie foot
el propósito intention
el teléfono telephone

agradable pleasant
caliente hot
derecho straight
universitario university (*adj.*)

luego then

Basic Patterns

1.	**Mi hermano ha salido y mis padres no han vuelto todavía.**	My brother has left and my parents have not returned yet.
2.	**No me los ha dado.**	He has not given them to me.
3.	**Quería que yo comprara la casa.**	He wanted me to buy the house.
4.	**Esperaba que no saliéramos.**	He hoped that we would not leave.
5.	**Siento que no estuviera aquí.**	I am sorry that he was not here.
6.	**Vive en el tercer piso de la segunda casa.**	He lives on the third floor of the second house.
7.	**El hotel está en la Calle Treinta y cuatro.**	The hotel is on Thirty-fourth Street.
8.	**Lo importante es que el libro es bueno.**	The important thing is that the book is good.
9.	**Dígame lo que quiere.**	Tell me what you want.

Drills

Formation of Past Participle

⊕ Provide the past participle form for the following infinitives. Practice until you can give the correct form without referring to the list on the facing page.

hablar, comer, salir, trabajar, vivir, abrir, cantar, cubrir, decir, dormir, ir, volver, vender, ver, dar, escribir, pensar, poner, querer, romper, morir, contestar, hacer, ayudar

Present Perfect Indicative

Substitute the cues.

1. Mis padres han comido en casa.
   (*yo, nosotros, tú, ella, ellos, Ud.*)
2. He ido muchas veces a México.
   (*Ud., mis amigos, Roberto, tú, yo, nosotros*)
3. Han hecho muchas cosas interesantes.
   (*nosotros, yo, tú, ellos, María, Ud.*)

Change the following sentences to the present perfect.

Juan compró la casa. / *Juan ha comprado la casa.*
Los niños no me vieron. / *Los niños no me han visto.*

1. María me habló hoy.
2. Mis amigos salieron.
3. Luis no me los dio.
4. Juan me dijo la verdad.
5. Mi hermano fue a Barcelona.
6. Mis padres volvieron temprano.
7. No la vi hoy.
8. No le escribí una carta.
9. Pusimos los libros en la mesa.
10. Se murió el Sr. Mora.
11. Hicimos muchas cosas.

146

Discussion

Formation of Past Participle

The past participle of regular verbs is formed by adding **-ado** to the stem of **-ar** verbs and **-ido** to the stem of **-er** and **-ir** verbs.

hablar/habl *ado*	spoken
comer/com *ido*	eaten
vivir/viv *ido*	lived

Following are the most common irregular past participles.

abrir/abierto	opened
cubrir/cubierto	covered
decir/dicho	said
escribir/escrito	written
hacer/hecho	done
morir/muerto	died
poner/puesto	put
romper/roto	broken
ver/visto	seen
volver/vuelto	returned
ir/ido	gone

Present Perfect Indicative

The present perfect is formed with the present tense of **haber** and a past participle.

hablar

he hablado	I have spoken	**hemos hablado**	we have spoken
has hablado	you (*fam., sing.*) have spoken		
ha hablado	he, she, it has spoken, you (*formal, sing.*) have spoken	**han hablado**	you (*formal, pl.*), they have spoken

Contrary to English, nothing may come between the two parts of a perfect tense in Spanish.

¿Ha salido Juan?	Has John left?
No he hablado.	I have not spoken.

Object pronouns must precede the auxiliary verb.

Me han escrito.	They have written to me.
No la hemos visto.	We have not seen her.
No me lo han dado.	They have not given it to me.

Past Subjunctive

Substitute the cues for the second verb only.

1. Mi padre temía que yo no estudiara.
    (*ellos, tú, nosotros, Ud., yo, ella*)
2. Fue lástima que no viniera Juan.
    (*yo, ella, nosotros, Ud., ellos, tú*)

Repeat the sentence as it is written, then change the first verb to the imperfect and the second to the past subjunctive.

Insisto en que Juan conteste. / *Insistía en que Juan contestara.*

1. Quiero que Ud. hable español.
2. Insisto en que María salga.
3. Roberto pide que tú no bailes.
4. Prefiero que Uds. lo compren.
5. Mi padre no permite que yo trabaje.
6. Ruego que Alicia no cante en casa.
7. Aconsejan que Felipe viva con sus amigos.
8. Deseo que los niños no coman mucho.
9. Juan me dice que compre la casa.

⊕ In this drill, note that the first verb is in the present, but that the action which follows took place in the past. Answer the questions using the information in parentheses.

¿Qué teme Ud.? (*nosotros/no estudiar bastante ayer*) / *Temo que no estudiáramos bastante ayer.*

1.	¿Qué siente Ud.?	(*Juan/no venir ayer*)
2.	¿Qué espera Ud.?	(*tú/no comer demasiado ayer*)
3.	¿De qué se alegra Ud.?	(*los alumnos/estudiar ayer*)

Past Subjunctive

The past, or imperfect, subjunctive is formed by dropping **-ron** from the third person plural of the preterite and adding either of the following sets of endings.

hablar/habla *ron*

habla *ra* (*-se*)	hablá *ramos* (*-semos*)
habla *ras* (*-ses*)	
habla *ra* (*-se*)	habla *ran* (*-sen*)

dormir/durmie *ron*

durmie *ra* (*-se*)	durmié *ramos* (*-semos*)
durmie *ras* (*-ses*)	
durmie *ra* (*-se*)	durmie *ran* (*-sen*)

saber/supie *ron*

supie *ra* (*-se*)	supié *ramos* (*-semos*)
supie *ras* (*-ses*)	
supie *ra* (*-se*)	supie *ran* (*-sen*)

The **-ra** and **-se** forms are generally interchangeable, but since the **-ra** endings are somewhat more common they will be stressed here.

The past subjunctive follows a verb or expression in a past tense. Compare the following examples of present and past subjunctive.

Juan quiere que yo lo compre.	John wants me to buy it.
Juan quería que yo lo comprara.	John wanted me to buy it.
Temo que no vengan hoy.	I am afraid that they will not come today.
Temía que no vinieran.	I was afraid that they would not come.

The past subjunctive may follow a main verb or expression in the present tense, but the action referred to will clearly be past.

Siento que Juan esté enfermo hoy.	I am sorry that John is ill today.
Siento que Juan estuviera enfermo ayer.	I am sorry that John was ill yesterday.

Ordinal Numbers

Repeat the model sentences and substitute the cues.

1. María vive en la primera casa.
   (*segunda, tercera, cuarta, quinta, sexta, séptima, octava, novena, décima*)
2. El segundo coche es magnífico.
   (*primero, tercero, cuarto, quinto, sexto, séptimo, octavo, noveno, décimo*)
3. Estamos en la primera casa.
   (*piso, clase, coche*)
4. Es la primera casa a la derecha.
   (*cuarto, ventana, despacho*)

Use of Neuter LO

Substitute the cues for the italicized words.

1. Lo *interesante* de la casa es el interior.
   (*bonito, bueno, malo, feo*)
2. Lo *importante* es llegar temprano.
   (*difícil, necesario, divertido, preciso*)

Answer the questions as shown in the example.

¿Juan dijo eso? / *Sí, eso es lo que dijo.*

1. ¿María hizo eso?
2. ¿El periódico anunció eso?
3. ¿El médico aconsejó eso?
4. ¿El hombre gritó eso?

Answer the questions as shown in the example.

¿Qué hace Juan? / *Hace lo que quiere.*

1. ¿Qué dice María?
2. ¿Qué contesta el policía?
3. ¿Qué escribe el profesor?
4. ¿Qué pide la niña?
5. ¿Qué compran los jóvenes?
6. ¿Qué venden los alumnos?

Ordinal Numbers

primero (a)	first	**quinto (a)**	fifth	**octavo (a)**	eighth
segundo (a)	second	**sexto (a)**	sixth	**noveno (a)**	ninth
tercero (a)	third	**séptimo (a)**	seventh	**décimo (a)**	tenth
cuarto (a)	fourth				

They agree in number and gender with the nouns they modify.

Primero and **tercero** drop the final **o** before singular masculine nouns.

They are not normally used beyond the tenth; after the tenth they are replaced by cardinal numbers which follow the noun.

la primera casa, el primer hombre	the first house, the first man
el segundo hombre	the second man
Felipe Segundo	Phillip II
la Calle Doce	Twelfth Street

Use of Neuter LO

A neuter form of the definite article, **lo,** is often used with an adjective to refer to an idea or concept. We express this idea in English by words such as *thing* or *part* after the adjective.

Lo importante es estudiar mucho.	The important thing is to study a lot.
Todos dicen lo mismo.	Everybody says the same thing.
Lo interesante es que no sabe escribir.	The interesting part is that he doesn't know how to write.

Lo combined with **que** expresses the equivalent of *what* in the sense of *that which.*

Esto es lo que quiero.	This is what I want.
No vimos lo que hizo.	We did not see what he did.

Combined Exercises

A. Translate first the Spanish sentences and then the English.

1. Al principio no quería contestar.   *At first he didn't want to answer.*
2. Al principio perdía el tiempo.   *At first he wasted time.*
3. Al principio no asistía a clases.   *At first he didn't attend classes.*
4. Al principio no le importaba.   *At first it didn't matter to him.*
5. Al principio no quería alojarse en un hotel.   *At first he didn't want to stay in a hotel.*

6. En realidad hace fresco aquí.   *As a matter of fact, it's cool here.*
7. En realidad el hotel no tiene calefacción.   *As a matter of fact, the hotel does not have heating.*
8. En realidad no tiene agua caliente.   *As a matter of fact, it doesn't have hot water.*
9. En realidad no tiene cuarto de baño.   *As a matter of fact, it doesn't have a bathroom.*
10. En realidad la habitación no es muy buena.   *As a matter of fact, the room is not very good.*

11. Doble a la izquierda y luego vaya por la Calle Quinta.   *Turn left and then go along Fifth Street.*
12. Doble a la derecha y luego vaya por la Calle Doce.   *Turn right and then go along Twelfth Street.*
13. Doble a la izquierda y luego siga por la Calle de Bécquer.   *Turn left and then continue along Bécquer Street.*
14. Doble a la derecha y luego siga derecho.   *Turn right and then continue straight ahead.*

15. Suena el teléfono.   *The telephone is ringing.*
16. Ha sonado el teléfono.   *The telephone has rung.*
17. Han anunciado un nuevo curso de estudios.   *They have announced a new course of studies.*
18. Han anunciado una nueva escuela de lenguas.   *They have announced a new school of languages.*
19. Han anunciado una nueva escuela de idiomas.   *They have announced a new school of languages.*

B. Formulate answers to the following questions basing your answer on the information within parentheses.

¿Qué temía Ud.? *(Juan/no estudiar)* / *Temía que Juan no estudiara.*

1. ¿Qué esperaba Ud.?   *(María/ir a la fuente)*
2. ¿Qué mandaba Ud.?   *(el niño/no perder el dólar)*
3. ¿Qué sentía Ud.?   *(la habitación/no tener teléfono)*
4. ¿Qué prefería Ud.?   *(el hotel/tener calefacción)*
5. ¿Qué dudaba Ud.?   *(los alumnos/asistir a la clase)*
6. ¿De qué se alegraba Ud.?   *(nosotros/estar en Puebla)*

⊕ C. Translate.

1. It was doubtful that he had good intentions.   2. I was happy that it was cool out.   3. It was a shame that you left early.   4. He didn't believe that it was the best way to learn a language.   5. It is a shame that they did not answer.   6. It is doubtful that he bought the first car that he saw.   7. It is possible that he was a university student.

D. Prepare oral answers to the following questions.

1. ¿Cuánto tiempo hace que está aquí en la universidad?   2. ¿Ha estudiado
mucho este año?   3. ¿Qué es lo mejor de la vida universitaria?   4. ¿Ha
visto algo interesante hoy?   5. ¿Siempre dice Ud. lo que quiere decir?
6. ¿Siempre escribe Ud. lo que el profesor le pide?   7. ¿Temía Ud. no
recibir buenas notas el año pasado?   8. ¿Se alegraba Ud. de que tuviéramos
examen la semana pasada?   9. ¿Ha abierto su libro de español esta semana?
10. ¿Quiere Ud. que tengamos otro examen esta semana?

E. Review. Repeat the statement, then substitute the appropriate object pronouns for the italicized objects.

Juan vendió el libro a su amigo. / *Juan se lo vendió.*

1.   María quería dar *el dinero a su madre.*
2.   Los niños leyeron *la carta a sus amigos.*
3.   Roberto no pensaba mostrar *el coche a su padre.*
4.   Elena quería dar *libros a sus amigos.*
5.   Luis no quiere decir *la verdad a su madre.*

F. Review. Provide oral answers to the following questions.

1. ¿A qué hora se levantó Ud. hoy?   2. ¿Qué tiempo hacía cuando se
levantó?   3. ¿Ha llovido hoy?   4. ¿A qué hora se acostó Ud. anoche?
5. ¿Hacía frío cuando Ud. se levantó?   6. ¿A qué hora cena Ud.?   7. ¿Hace
mucho calor aquí en el verano?   8. ¿A qué hora termina esta clase?
9. ¿Hace mucho viento aquí en la primavera?   10. ¿Qué tiempo hace hoy?

Reading and Conversation

El Curso de Verano

Robert llama por teléfono a David. Suena el teléfono en casa de éste y contesta:

David   ¡Diga!*
Robert   Hola, David, soy yo, Robert. ¿Qué tal?
David   Pues, bien. ¿Qué hay de nuevo?
Robert   Oye, tengo una idea estupenda. He recibido carta de la Universidad
Panamericana donde asistí el verano pasado. Anuncian un curso de
estudios para el próximo verano que me parece excelente. Y lo in-
teresante es que me han dicho que este verano cuesta menos. ¿Por qué
no vamos?
David   Pero si tú ya has estado una vez, ¿por qué quieres volver?
Robert   Hombre, se sabe muy bien que la mejor manera de aprender una
lengua extranjera es vivir en el país donde se habla ese idioma. Además
la universidad está en Puebla, ciudad muy interesante y hermosa.
David   Ya lo sé. Como sabes, estuve en Puebla hace tres años y me gustó
mucho. ¿Pero tu padre permite que vuelvas?

* The standard way to answer the telephone in many Spanish-speaking countries; equivalent to
the English *hello.*

Robert	Creo que sí. El año pasado él temía al principio que yo no estudiara y que perdiera el tiempo, pero le convencí de mis buenos propósitos. En realidad, fue él quien insistió en que fuera.
David	¿Y en dónde te alojaste?
Robert	En un hotel cerca de la universidad. Tú sabes donde está la Calle Mayor, ¿verdad? Pues, se va por esta calle hasta llegar a una fuente. Luego se dobla a la izquierda y se va derecho por la Avenida Séptima hasta llegar a la Calle de Bécquer. El hotel está en la esquina de Bécquer y la Avenida Séptima.
David	¿Y es bueno el hotel?
Robert	Sí, muy bueno. Todas las habitaciones tienen cuarto de baño, agua caliente y calefacción. Pero lo que más me gustaba era que no cobraban mucho. Creo que pagaba unos tres dólares al día.
David	Pero, ¿dices que tiene calefacción? ¿Qué importa eso? Cuando yo estaba en Puebla hacía mucho calor.
Robert	Tienes razón. Durante los días de sol la temperatura es muy agradable, pero por la noche hace fresco.
David	Bueno, Robert, me gusta mucho tu idea de ir a estudiar a Puebla. Voy a hablar con mi padre a ver lo que a él le parece. Te llamo mañana, ¿bien?
Robert	De acuerdo, David. Hasta mañana.

Dialogue Practice

A. Prepare oral responses to the following questions.

1. ¿Qué ha recibido Robert?
2. ¿Qué dice la carta de la Universidad Panamericana?
3. ¿Por qué quiere volver Robert a la universidad?
4. ¿Cuándo estuvo David en Puebla? ¿Le gustó Puebla?
5. ¿Qué temía el padre de Robert?
6. ¿Quién insistió en que Robert fuera a Puebla?
7. ¿En dónde se alojó Robert? ¿Cuánto pagaba por el hotel?
8. ¿Le gusta a David la idea de ir a estudiar a Puebla?

REPASO (11-15)

⊕ A. Make complete sentences of the following using the tense indicated.

1. Yo/querer/que él/comprar/casa. *(past)*
2. Gustarme/los huevos/pero/faltarme/dinero. *(present)*
3. Ser preciso/Juan/saber escribir. *(past)*
4. María/llegar/martes/primero/agosto. *(past)*
5. Mi hermano/haber salido/y mis padres/no haber vuelto. *(present perfect)*

B. Answer in Spanish.

1. ¿Has conseguido trabajo para este verano?   2. ¿Estuviste en clase ayer o fuiste a otra ciudad?   3. ¿A qué hora viniste a la clase hoy y qué trajiste?   4. ¿Te diste cuenta de que hacía frío ayer?   5. ¿Esperaba que hiciera buen tiempo hoy?

C. Be able to give the past subjunctive forms of the following infinitives.

hablar, hacer, poner, caer, vender, poder, andar, saber, vivir, decir, leer, dar, oír, estar, ser, ir, querer, tener, venir, ver

D. Study the following responses thoroughly. After hearing the cue on the tape, choose the response which best completes the sentence.

1. agua caliente, una boda, sueldos, un pueblo
2. se conoce, te cases, tenemos suerte, buscas
3. a su dirección, a la ciudad, hace tres días, a tomar algo
4. la vida es cara, los trajeron, se levantan para salir, están allí
5. a tener suerte, a preocuparse, a encontrar un piso, a buscar trabajo
6. traje de baño, al despacho, merendar, al mundo
7. conocer a muchas personas, dormir temprano, dejar el tema, cambiar
8. piso, hija, sueño, tiempo
9. comer mucho, ir a casa, mucha hambre, correr a menudo
10. llegara pronto el camarero, fueran las dos y media, estuviera estupendo, para beber

E. This dictation is taken from the dialogue of Lesson Twelve. Write the Spanish without referring to your books and then check what you have written against the appropriate lines of the dialogue.

⊕ F. Translate.

1. My father didn't permit me to go.   2. It was a shame that he didn't come.   3. He had a week left, but he needed money.   4. The stores opened at 9:15 sharp.   5. These shirts are mine; those ties are yours.   6. He had been writing for 55 minutes.   7. I insisted on driving.   8. They got married last June.   9. We were eating when he came in.   10. They had a good time and then said good-bye.

Recommended Readings from Appendix

Las Culturas Antiguas and *Bosquejo de España.*

PERÚ AND GUATEMALA

GOLFO DE
MEXICO

OCEANO
ATLANTICO

MEXICO

GUATEMALA

Guatemala

MAR CARIBE

Golfo de
Panamá

VENEZUELA

CORDILLERA DE LOS ANDES

COLOMBIA

ECUADOR

PERU

BRASIL

OCEANO
PACIFICO

Lima

Lago
Titicaca

BOLIVIA

Machu Picchu in Perú. This is the "lost city" of the Incas, located in the midst of the Peruvian Andes.

Machu Picchu.

An Indian woman twists yarn
while watching her flock of sheep.

Woman gathering dried reeds in one of the villages along the shores of Lake Titicaca, on the border between Perú and Bolivia.

The llamas are the beasts of burden of the Peruvian farmers.

Outskirts of Lima.

Old main square with buildings and fountains dating back to the founding of the city of Lima in the sixteenth century.

Village scene in highland Guatemala.

Thatching a roof near Lake Atitlán, Guatemala.

Market scene,
Guatemala.

Making "tortillas."

Guatemalan textiles usually contain
colorful traditional Indian designs that
date back several centuries.

Indian fisherman in dugout canoe on Lake Atitlán, Guatemala.

Indian family weaving in small village in Guatemala. The childrens' faces are covered with cloth to ward off the "evil eye."

Guatemala City's Social Security Building—
one of the fine new buildings which
are found in the capital's Civic Center.

Cathedral and main plaza
in Guatemala City.

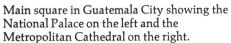

Main square in Guatemala City showing the
National Palace on the left and the
Metropolitan Cathedral on the right.

LECCIÓN DIECISÉIS

Basic Words and Expressions

al día siguiente on the following day
¡Ay de mí! Oh me!
estar aburrido to be bored
ser aburrido to be boring
dejar de + *inf.* to stop (doing something)
no dejar de + *inf.* not to fail (to do something)
ir de compras to go shopping
llover a cántaros to rain hard (bucketsful)
poder con to be able to deal with, cope with
¡Qué día! What a day!

apoderarse (de) to take over
formar to form
fumar to smoke
había there was, were
hubo there was, were
imaginarse to imagine
interesar to interest
interrumpir to interrupt

la alcoba bedroom
la cárcel jail

la cocina kitchen
el chocolate chocolate
el ejército army
la estabilidad stability
el gobierno government
el jefe leader, chief, boss
la junta legislative council
el loco madman
la lluvia rain
la sala living room
el vecino neighbor (*m.*)
la vecina neighbor (*f.*)

fuerte strong
serio serious
siguiente following

menos less, least
tan so
tanto so much

¿Cuál? Which? Which one?
esto this (*neut.*)

Basic Patterns

1. **Juanito está vistiéndose ahora.**
   Johnny is getting dressed now.
2. **El señor García está leyendo el periódico.**
   Mr. García is reading the newspaper.
3. **¿Qué quieres?**
   What do you want?
4. **¿Cuál quieres?**
   Which one do you want?
5. **Tengo tanto dinero como él.**
   I have as much money as he.
6. **María es más bonita que Juan.**
   Mary is prettier than John.
7. **María es tan alta como Juan.**
   Mary is as tall as John.
8. **La ventana fue cerrada por la criada.**
   The window was closed by the maid.
9. **La ventana estaba cerrada.**
   The window was closed.

Drills

Formation of Present Participle

Give the present participle for the following infinitives. Practice until you can give the correct forms without referring to the list on the facing page.

hablar, venir, estudiar, leer, comer, decir, vivir, pedir, contestar, seguir, traer, divertirse, oír, morirse, vestirse, hacer, repetir, creer, dormir, caerse

Progressive Tenses

Repeat the sentences and then substitute the cues.
1. Juanito está vistiéndose ahora.
   (*tú, ellos, nosotros, yo, ella, los niños*)
2. El Sr. García está leyendo el periódico.
   (*yo, ellos, Juan, nosotros, Ud., tú*)

Change the following sentences first to the present progressive and then to the past progressive.

1. Juan come mucho.
2. Digo la verdad.
3. El me lo pide.
4. Ellos se divierten.
5. Lo oigo.
6. Me muero de hambre.
7. Estudia en la cocina.
8. Duermes en la alcoba.
9. Se lo digo.
10. Trabaja en esa tienda.

⊕ Write the following in Spanish.

1. I am reading it (*letter*) to them.
2. He was bringing them (*books*) to me.
3. They were washing them (*dishes*).
4. He continues asking me for it (*tie*).
5. They kept on having a good time.

Discussion

Formation of Present Participle

The present participle of regular verbs is formed by adding **-ando** to the stem of **-ar** verbs and **-iendo** to the stem of **-er** and **-ir** verbs.

(hablar) habl *ando*   speaking
(comer) com *iendo*   eating
(vivir) viv *iendo*   living

The most common irregular forms are as follows. Note that the reflexive pronoun follows the present participle.

decir/diciendo	saying	**dormir/durmiendo**	sleeping
venir/viniendo	coming	**morirse/muriéndose**	dying
pedir/pidiendo	asking	**leer/leyendo**	reading
seguir/siguiendo	following	**caerse/cayéndose**	falling
divertirse/divirtiéndose	enjoying	**creer/creyendo**	believing
vestirse/vistiéndose	dressing	**oír/oyendo**	hearing
repetir/repitiendo	repeating	**traer/trayendo**	bringing

Progressive Tenses

The present participle is used with a form of **estar** or **seguir** and expresses a continuous action in the present or past tense. Object pronouns are attached to the participle.

Estoy comiendo.   I am eating.
Estaba comiéndola.   I was eating it (*the meal*).
Sigo leyéndoselo.   I keep on reading it (*the book*) to him.
Seguíamos durmiendo.   We continued sleeping.

The idea of continuous action is often expressed in Spanish by the present tense. Thus, the progressive tense is used only to stress the idea that the action is actually in progress.

Estudio español.   I am studying Spanish.   (*this year, but not at the moment*)
Estoy estudiando español.   I am studying Spanish.   (*actually, at this moment*)

Use of ¿QUÉ? and ¿CUÁL?

Write these questions in Spanish.

1. What is a woman?
2. What do you (*Ud.*) want?
3. Which one do you (*Ud.*) want?
4. What is the capital of Spain?
5. What are you (*Ud.*) reading?
6. What lesson are you (*Uds.*) studying?

Regular Comparisons of Adjectives and Adverbs

Substitute the cues.

1. Tengo tanto dinero como él.
   (*libros, camisas, zapatos, suerte, sombreros*)
⊕ 2. María es más bonita que Cecilia.
   (*fuerte, fea, divertida, aburrida, agradable*)

Be able to state the following with the variations given in parentheses.

1. I have more books than John.
   (*fewer, as many as*)
2. Mary is fatter than I.
   (*less fat, as fat as, the fattest in the class*)
3. My father is richer than yours.
   (*less rich, as rich as, the richest in town*)
4. There were more girls than boys.
   (*as many as, fewer*)
5. This lesson is more difficult than that one.
   (*as difficult as, the most difficult in the book*)

Use of ¿QUÉ? and ¿CUÁL?

The interrogative **qué** means *what* and usually calls for a definition. The interrogative **cuál** means *which* or *which one* and calls for a choice.

¿Qué es el hombre? What is man?
¿Cuál es el hombre? Which is the man?

Since **cuál** should not be used before a noun, **qué** or **cuál de** expresses *which* or *which one*.

¿Qué libro quieres? Which book do you want?
¿Cuál de los libros quieres? Which of the books do you want?

Regular Comparisons of Adjectives and Adverbs

The comparative of adjectives and adverbs is usually formed by using **más, menos,** or **tan** before the word.

Juan es más alto que María. John is taller than Mary.
Juan es menos alto que María. John is less tall than Mary.
Juan es tan alto como María. John is as tall as Mary.

Note that *than* is expressed by **que** and *as* is expressed by **como**.

The superlative degree is expressed with a definite article before the comparative form.

Juan es el alumno más inteligente de la clase. John is the most intelligent student in the class.
Juan es el más inteligente de la clase. John is the most intelligent in the class.
María es la menos inteligente de la clase. Mary is the least intelligent in the class.
Ellos son los más inteligentes de la clase. They are the most intelligent in the class.

Note that *in* is expressed by **de** in this type of sentence.

Before a noun, **tanto, (a, os, as),** *as much, as many,* is used instead of **tan,** *as.*

Tengo tanto dinero como tú. I have as much money as you.
Tienes tantas plumas como él. You have as many pens as he.

"True" Passive Voice

Substitute the cues.

La ventana fue cerrada por la sirvienta.
(*ventanas, puerta, libro, libros, tienda*)

Change the following sentences from active to "true" passive.

1. Mi hermano escribió la carta.
2. Los estudiantes terminaron la lección.
3. El profesor abrió las puertas.
4. Juan vendió el mercado.
5. María prepara la comida.

Change the following from "true" passive to reflexive.

1. La carta fue escrita por mi hermana.
2. Un gobierno nuevo fue formado por la junta.
3. El trabajo es empezado por Pedro.
4. Las puertas fueron abiertas por el profesor.

Change the following from reflexive to simple description with **estar.**

1. Se escribió la carta.
2. Las puertas se abrieron.
3. La lección se terminó.
4. Se arregló el coche.

Conjunctions E and U

⊕ Write in Spanish.

mother and daughter, summer and winter, children or men, Spanish and English, home or office, seven or eight

Diminutives and Augmentatives

⊕ Give the English equivalents.

1. casita, vasito, hermanito, cosita
2. mujerona, casona, hombrón, librón

"True" Passive Voice

The past participle is often used with **ser** to express the passive voice in Spanish.

La ventana fue cerrada por la sirvienta.	The window was closed by the maid.
Los libros fueron vendidos por el hombre.	The books were sold by the man.

Note that the word *by* is expressed by **por** and that the past participle agrees with the subject. Spanish does not use this construction as much as English, so if the agent (the one doing the action) is not expressed, Spanish often uses the reflexive substitute.

Se cerró la ventana.   The window was closed.

The past participle is sometimes used with **estar** to express a simple descriptive statement. It should not be confused with the passive voice.

La puerta está abierta.	The door is open.	(*descriptive*)
La ventana estaba cerrada.	The window was closed.	(*descriptive*)

Conjunctions E and U

When the conjunction **y** precedes **i** or **hi,** it changes to **e.** When **o** precedes another **o** or **ho,** it changes to **u.**

padre e hijo   father and son   **siete u ocho**   seven or eight

Diminutives and Augmentatives

The diminutive ending **-ito (-ita)** is often added to a word to denote smallness or affection. The augmentative ending **-on (-ona)** denotes largeness and sometimes ridicule.

casa/casita	small house
mujer/mujerona	large woman
Juan/Juanito	Johnny

Combined Exercises

A. Express first the Spanish in English and then the English in Spanish.

1.	tan fuerte como yo	*as strong as I*
2.	Es tan fuerte como yo.	*He is as strong as I.*
3.	Es tan fuerte como ella.	*He is as strong as she.*
4.	Es tan serio como ella.	*He is as serious as she.*
5.	Es más serio que ella.	*He is more serious than she.*
6.	Es menos agradable que ella.	*He is less pleasant than she.*
7.	Juan deja de estudiar tanto.	*John stops studying so much.*
8.	Juan dejó de comer tanto.	*John stopped eating so much.*
9.	Juan deja sus libros en casa.	*John leaves his books at home.*
10.	Juan dejó a sus amigos.	*John left his friends.*
11.	Juan salió de la casa.	*John left the house.*
12.	No dejes de estudiar, Juan.	*Don't stop studying, John.*
13.	Dejemos de interrumpir.	*Let's stop interrupting.*
14.	Me imagino que sí.	*I imagine so.*
15.	Me imagino que no.	*I imagine not.*
16.	Me imagino que se van.	*I imagine that they are going away.*
17.	Me imaginé que se fueron.	*I imagined that they went away.*
18.	¡Imagínate!	*Just imagine!*
19.	Había mucha gente en la cárcel.	*There were many people in the jail.*
20.	Hubo una revolución ayer.	*There was a revolution yesterday.*
21.	Había mucho que hacer.	*There was a lot to do.*
22.	De repente hubo un ruido.	*Suddenly there was a noise.*
23.	Me interesan las mujeres.	*Women interest me.*
24.	Me interesa la chica.	*The girl interests me.*
25.	Le interesaba el gobierno.	*Government interested him.*
26.	Nos interesaba ver esa película.	*We were interested in seeing that picture.*

B. Follow the Spanish command and form complete Spanish sentences.

Dígale a su amigo que no tiene tanto dinero como Ud. / *No tienes tanto dinero como yo.*

1. Dígale a su amigo que Ud. tiene tanto dinero como él.   2. Dígale a su amigo que Ud. es menos pobre que él.   3. Dígale que él es el alumno más alto de la clase.   4. Dígale que no es tan pobre como muchos.   5. Dígale que Ud. sigue estudiando tanto como él.   6. Dígale que Ud. todavía no ha dejado de fumar.   7. Dígale que a Ud. generalmente no le gusta la lluvia.   8. Dígale que no se vaya porque pronto va a llover a cántaros. 9. Dígale que no interrumpa tanto.   10. Pregúntele si le interesa un empleo en el ejército.   11. Pregúntele si se acuerda de Ud.   12. Pregúntele la dirección de su casa.

C. Answer in Spanish.

1. ¿Te gustan los días de lluvia?   2. ¿Generalmente te duermes en la cocina? 3. ¿Fuiste de compras ayer por la tarde?   4. Si estás cansado, ¿dejas de estudiar?   5. ¿Hay mujeres en el ejército de este país?   6. ¿Le gusta el chocolate a su hermanito?   7. ¿En qué cuarto se prepara la comida? 8. ¿Eres el estudiante más inteligente de la clase?   9. ¿Está abierta o cerrada la puerta de la clase?   10. ¿Cuál de sus clases le interesa más?

⊕ D. Write the following in three ways: the "true" passive, the reflexive construction, and description with **estar.**

Mi hermano abrió la puerta. $\begin{cases} \textit{La puerta fue abierta por mi hermano.} \\ \textit{Se abrió la puerta.} \\ \textit{La puerta estaba abierta.} \end{cases}$

1. La junta formó un nuevo gobierno.   2. María prepara la comida.   3. Mi hermanita lava los platos.   4. El jefe comenzó el trabajo.   5. Los estudiantes terminaron las lecciones.

⊕ E. Write the following in complete Spanish sentences. (Use past tenses.)

1.   Ellos/llevar/mucho/mis/vecinos/cárcel.
2.   Día siguiente/jefe/de la junta/formar/gobierno nuevo.
3.   Alcoba/ser/más grande/la sala.
4.   (Yo)/estar aburrido/porque/estar/llover/y querer/ir/compras.
5.   (Nosotros)/estar/morir/de hambre/y querer/chocolate.

⊕ F. Translate into Spanish.

1.   There were more men than women in the jail.
2.   This problem is very boring. I'll do it tomorrow.
3.   The window was opened by my neighbor, but it's closed now.
4.   The army took over the government, but they can't cope with those madmen.
5.   What a day! I had to buy seven or eight things and it was raining bucketsful.
6.   The children's names were (*They called themselves*) Johnny and Isabel.
7.   When I left the class, I left my books there.
8.   He kept on sleeping in the living room although his wife didn't like it.
9.   Don't fail (*fam., sing.; formal, sing.*) to read that book soon.
10.   She brought his meal to the jail, and he was eating there.

Reading and Conversation

Un Día de Lluvia*

El Sr. García y su esposa están sentados en la sala de su casa. Está lloviendo a cántaros. El Sr. García lee el periódico.

La Sra. García	¡Qué día más triste y aburrido! Quería ir de compras hoy con Carmen pero ahora está lloviendo tanto . . .
El Sr. García	Sí, y lo malo es que hace frío también.
La Sra.	Tal vez** podamos ir más tarde. Esta noche las tiendas están abiertas hasta las nueve. Vamos a ver si deja de llover pronto. ¿Quieres que Trini te traiga un chocolate o un café?
El Sr.	¡No, mujer! No tengo sed; tengo frío. Y además no me interrumpas. ¿No te das cuenta de que estoy leyendo el periódico?

---

* This dialogue reflects ideas, values and cultural norms which are not uncommon in a conservative upper-middle class setting in Latin America. No attempt has been made to reconcile values, pro or con, with those of the United States.
** **Tal vez** may or may not take the subjunctive, depending on the element of doubt in the speaker's mind.

La Sra.	Cálmate, Juan. Por Dios. No es para tanto. ¿Es que no se te puede hablar cuando estás leyendo? ¿Qué dice el periódico que te interesa tanto?
El Sr.	Imagínate. Hubo otra revolución en nuestro país vecino. ¿Es que esos locos no saben en qué puede acabar todo esto?
La Sra.	¿Otra vez? ¿Pero no me dijiste que el ejército se apoderó del gobierno hace una semana?
El Sr.	Sí, y formaron una junta con el general Ordóñez come jefe, pero ahora los otros de la junta le han llevado prisionero.
La Sra.	¿Cómo pudieron hacerle esto al jefe del país? ¿Cuál de los tres es el nuevo jefe?
El Sr.	No sé. Solo dice aquí que por la noche entraron en su alcoba y le sorprendieron en la cama. Al día siguiente, estaba en la cárcel.
La Sra.	Yo no creo que esto acabe nunca. Gracias a Dios tenemos un gobierno fuerte que puede con los radicales.
El Sr.	Sí, aquí hay estabilidad pero tenemos unos problemas muy serios. Puede ser que lo mismo pase aquí algún día. Pero Trini, ¿dónde estás? ¿No me traes el chocolate? Tengo sed.
La Sra.	¡Ay de mí! ¡Qué hombre! Trini está en la cocina. La llamo en seguida. Pero, mira Juan, ha dejado de llover y ha salido el sol. Voy a llamar a Carmen para que* vayamos ahora mismo de compras.

Dialogue Practice

A. Prepare oral responses to the following questions.

1. ¿Qué hacen los Sres. García?
2. ¿Qué tiempo hace?
3. ¿Qué quería hacer la Sra. García?
4. ¿Hasta qué hora están abiertas las tiendas?
5. ¿Qué le pasó al general Ordóñez?
6. ¿Dónde estaba al día siguiente?
7. ¿Qué cree la Sra. García de esta revolución?
8. ¿Qué quiere el Sr. García que le traigan?
9. ¿Por qué quiere la Sra. llamar a su vecina?

* **Para que**   always demands the subjunctive.

LECCIÓN DIECISIETE

Basic Words and Expressions

como de costumbre as usual
sin embargo nevertheless
tener lugar to take place

durar to last
equivocarse to be wrong
fijarse (en) to notice
gozar (de) to enjoy
jugar (ue) to play
practicar to play, to practice
quejarse (de) to complain (about)
viajar to travel

Alemania Germany
el apellido surname
el campeón champion
el campeonato championship
la carretera highway
el deporte sport
el equipaje baggage
el equipo team

el espectador spectator
el estadio stadium
el fútbol soccer
el helado ice cream
la ilusión illusion
el jugador player
la luna moon
el partido game, match
el perro dog
la popularidad popularity
el sóquer soccer
el tráfico traffic

alemán German
lleno full
mayor older, oldest
menor younger, youngest
mundial world (*adj.*)
peor worse, worst

dentro (de) within

Basic Patterns

1. **Me dijo que ya habían salido.**
   He told me that they had already left.

2. **Luis es mejor jugador que Tomás.**
   Luis is a better player than Thomas.

3. **Pelé es el mejor jugador del mundo.**
   Pele is the best player in the world.

4. **Juan canta mal y María canta peor, pero Roberto canta peor que todos.**
   John sings badly and Mary sings worse, but Robert sings the worst (of all).

5. **Tiene más de cincuenta mil dólares.**
   He has more than fifty thousand dollars.

6. **No tiene más que dos amigos.**
   He has only two friends.

7. **Juan tiene un perro grandísimo.**
   John has a huge dog.

Drills

Pluperfect Indicative

Substitute the cues for second verb only.

1. Dijo que habíamos salido.
   (*yo, ellos, tú, ella nosotros, Ud.*)
2. Dijo que habían hecho muchas cosas interesantes.
   (*tú, nosotros, ellos, yo, Juan*)

Change the following sentences to pluperfect.

Juan compró la casa. / *Juan había comprado la casa.*
Los niños no me vieron. / *Los niños no me habían visto.*

1. Mis amigos salieron.
2. Juan me dijo la verdad.
3. Mi hermano fue a Barcelona.
4. Mis padres volvieron temprano.
5. No la vi.
6. No le escribimos una carta.
7. Pusimos los libros en la mesa.
8. Hicieron muchas cosas.
9. Se murió el Sr. Mora.

Irregular Comparisons of Adjectives

Provide the opposite comparative or superlative adjectives.

Este equipo es mejor que aquél. / *Este equipo es peor que aquél.*
Juan es mi hermano mayor. / *Juan es mi hermano menor.*
Estos muchachos son los mejores alumnos de la clase. /
　　　　　　Estos muchachos son los peores alumnos de la clase.

1. Luis es el mejor jugador del equipo.
2. Este periódico es mejor que aquél.
3. María es mi hermana menor.
4. Juan y Luis son mis hermanos mayores.
5. Luis parece menor que Juan.
6. Estos libros son los mejores que tengo.
7. Estos libros son los peores de la biblioteca.

Discussion

Pluperfect Indicative

The pluperfect indicative is formed with the imperfect tense of **haber** and a past participle.

hablar

había hablado	I had spoken	**habíamos hablado**	we had spoken
habías hablado	you (*fam., sing.*) had spoken		
había hablado	he, she, it, you (*formal, sing.*) had spoken	**habían hablado**	they, you (*formal, pl.*) had spoken

Contrary to English, nothing may come between the two parts of the perfect tense in Spanish. Any object pronouns must precede the auxiliary verb.

¿Había salido Juan?	Had John left?
No había hablado.	I had not spoken.
No me lo habían dado.	They had not given it to me.

Irregular Comparisons of Adjectives

Irregular Adjectives

Adjective		Comparative		Superlative	
bueno	good	**mejor**	better	**el mejor**	best
malo	bad	**peor**	worse	**el peor**	worst
grande	large	**más grande**	larger	**el más grande**	largest
		mayor	older	**el mayor**	oldest
pequeño	small	**más pequeño**	smaller	**el más pequeño**	smallest
		menor	younger	**el menor**	youngest

Mayor and **menor** normally indicate age rather than size.
Bueno, malo, mejor, and **peor** precede the noun.

Juan es buen alumno.	John is a good student.
María es mejor alumna que Juan.	Mary is a better student than John.
María es la mejor alumna de la clase.	Mary is the best student in the class.
El Sr. Mora es mal profesor.	Mr. Mora is a bad professor.
El Sr. Díaz es peor.	Mr. Díaz is worse.
El Sr. Melón es el peor profesor de la universidad.	Mr. Melón is the worst professor in the university.
Roberto tiene diez años.	Robert is ten years old.
María es mayor.	Mary is older.
Teresa es la mayor de las tres.	Theresa is the oldest of the three.
Roberto es grande.	Robert is big.
Ricardo es más grande.	Richard is bigger.
Tomás es el más grande.	Thomas is the biggest.

Irregular Comparisons of Adverbs

Provide the comparative form of the adverbs.

María habla bien, ¿verdad? / *Sí, pero Luis habla mejor.*
Juan estudia mucho, ¿verdad? / *Sí, pero Luis estudia más.*

1. Juan trabaja poco, ¿verdad?
2. María canta mal, ¿verdad?
3. Pablo fuma mucho, ¿verdad?
4. Juan juega bien, ¿verdad?
5. Tomás escribe mal, ¿verdad?
6. María lee mucho, ¿verdad?

⊕ Provide the superlative form of the adverbs.

Juan habla bien, pero María habla mejor. / *Sí, pero Luis habla mejor que todos.*

(Use "Luis" in all of the following.)

1. Los muchachos trabajan poco, pero María trabaja menos.
2. Los alumnos cantan mal, pero Juan canta peor.
3. Juan y Pablo hablan mucho, pero María habla más.
4. Tomás y Juan juegan bien, pero Pablo juega mejor.
5. Las muchachas escriben mal, pero María escribe peor.
6. Pablo y María leen mucho, pero Roberto lee más.

DE and QUE before Numerals

Answer the questions by substituting the numbers in parentheses.

¿Tiene Ud. muchos libros?   (50+) / *Sí, tengo más de cincuenta.*

1. ¿Tiene Ud. muchos amigos?   *(80+)*
2. ¿Tiene Ud. muchas amigas?   *(4+)*
3. ¿Recibió Ud. muchas cartas hoy?   *(2+)*
4. ¿Compró Ud. muchas revistas?   *(1+)*
5. ¿Hay muchos parques en Madrid?   *(5+)*

Answer the following questions, substituting the numbers in parentheses.

¿Tiene Ud. muchos amigos?   (3) / *No, no tengo más que tres.*

1. ¿Tiene Ud. muchos libros?   *(2)*
2. ¿Tiene Ud. muchas amigas?   *(4)*
3. ¿Recibió Ud. muchas cartas hoy?   *(2)*
4. ¿Compró Ud. muchas revistas?   *(1)*
5. ¿Hay muchos parques en Madrid?   *(5)*

Use of -ÍSIMO

Provide a second sentence as shown in the example.

Esta casa es grande. / *Sí, pero ésa es grandísima.*

1. Este señor es alto.
2. Esta muchacha es hermosa.
3. Este examen es difícil.
4. Estos hombres son importantes.
5. Estas chicas estudian mucho.

Irregular Comparisons of Adverbs

Irregular Adverbs

Adverb		Comparative		Superlative	
bien	well	**mejor**	better	**mejor**	best
mal	badly	**peor**	worse	**peor**	worst
mucho	much	**más**	more	**más**	most
poco	little	**menos**	less	**menos**	least

Note there is no difference in Spanish between the comparative and superlative forms.

María y Luis hablan bien, pero Luis habla mejor.	Mary and Louis speak well, but Louis speaks better.
De los cuatro alumnos, Pablo habla mejor.	Of the four students, Paul speaks best.

DE and QUE before Numerals

Although **que** is normally used for *than* in comparisons, **de** is used before numerals in affirmative sentences.

Juan tiene más de cinco libros.   John has more than five books.

In negative sentences, **no más que** before a numeral is the equivalent of *no more than*, or *only*.

Juan no tiene más que dos dólares.   John has only two dollars.

Use of -ÍSIMO

The ending **-ísimo (-ísima, -ísimos, -ísimas)** can be added to an adjective to signify a high degree of the quality described. Only **-ísimo** may be added to an adverb. Adjectives and adverbs ending in a vowel drop the vowel before the ending is attached.

Es una casa grandísima.	It's an extremely large house.
Son hombres importantísimos.	They are very important men.
Las mujeres hablan muchísimo. *(adv.)*	The women talk very much.

Combined Exercises

A. Translate first the Spanish and then the English without referring to the translations.

1.	El partido tiene lugar hoy.	*The game takes place today.*
2.	El partido de fútbol tuvo lugar ayer.	*The soccer game took place yesterday.*
3.	El partido va a tener lugar en el estadio.	*The game is going to take place in the stadium.*
4.	Como de costumbre, no se fijó en los espectadores.	*As usual, he didn't notice the spectators.*
5.	Como de costumbre, ganaron el campeonato mundial.	*As usual, they won the world championship.*
6.	Como de costumbre, el estadio estaba lleno.	*As usual, the stadium was full.*
7.	Como de costumbre, el otro equipo jugó mejor.	*As usual, the other team played better.*
8.	Como de costumbre, se quejó de los jugadores.	*As usual, he complained about the players.*
9.	Como de costumbre, el partido duró tres horas.	*As usual, the game lasted three hours.*
10.	Si no me equivoco, su apellido es Mora.	*If I'm not mistaken, his surname is Mora.*
11.	Si no nos equivocamos, ha viajado mucho.	*If we are not mistaken, he has traveled a lot.*
12.	Si no me equivoco, son de Alemania.	*If I'm not mistaken, they are from Germany.*
13.	Si no me equivoco, son alemanes.	*If I'm not mistaken, they are Germans.*
14.	Si no me equivoco, no se practica ese deporte allá.	*If I'm not mistaken, that sport is not played there.*
15.	Si no me equivoco, fuma mucho.	*If I'm not mistaken, he smokes a lot.*
16.	Si no me equivoco, son los campeones.	*If I'm not mistaken, they are the champions.*
17.	Ese deporte goza de gran popularidad.	*That sport is very popular (enjoys great popularity).*
18.	El sóquer no goza de mucha popularidad aquí.	*Soccer does not enjoy much popularity here (is not very popular here).*
19.	Le gusta fumar.	*He likes to smoke.*
20.	Me gusta el helado.	*I like ice cream.*
21.	No le gustan los perros.	*He doesn't like dogs.*
22.	No nos gusta ese deporte.	*We don't like that sport.*
23.	Me gusta ver un buen partido de fútbol.	*I like to see a good soccer game.*
24.	No me gusta el tráfico.	*I don't like traffic.*

⊕ B. Translate.

1. He didn't tell us that the baggage had arrived.   2. We knew that they
had gone to the moon.   3. Within two years we had won the championship.
4. My older brother is a better player than Thomas.   5. My younger sister
is the best student in the class.   6. There are more than twenty teams, but
there is only one champion.   7. Your team played badly, but theirs played
worse. Yes, but ours played the worst (of all).   8. She is an extremely pretty
woman.   9. He is a very intelligent man.   10. He told me that the team
has only nine players. Ours has more than fifteen.   11. They found out we
had won the game.   12. He is the least intelligent of the family.

C. Prepare oral answers to the following questions.

1. ¿Le gusta el fútbol?   2. ¿Quién es más inteligente, Ud. o su padre?
3. ¿Quién es el más inteligente de la familia?   4. ¿Se queja Ud. de la
comida que se sirve aquí en la cafetería?   5. ¿Quiere Ud. viajar a la luna
algún día?   6. ¿Ha jugado en algún equipo? ¿Ganó un campeonato?
7. ¿Fue Ud. el mejor jugador del equipo?   8. ¿Tiene Ud. algún amigo
alemán?   9. ¿Le gusta el helado?   10. De todos sus amigos, ¿quién habla
mejor el español?

⊕ D. Review. Supply the proper forms of the possessive pronouns in parentheses.

1.   Su apellido es español; (hers) es inglés.
2.   Este perro es (ours); (theirs) está en casa.
3.   Este equipaje es (mine); (his) está en el avión.
4.   Esta casa es (his); (hers) está en la otra calle.

Reading and Conversation

El Fútbol

Juan le está hablando a David, amigo norteamericano, de un partido de fútbol
que tuvo lugar hace una semana entre la Argentina y México.

Juan   Lástima que no pudieras ir, David.
David   Sí. Hace casi un mes que estoy en la Argentina y todavía no he tenido
la oportunidad de ver lo que ustedes llaman fútbol.
Juan   ¿No has visto nunca este deporte?
David   Claro que sí. Lo que aquí llaman fútbol en mi país llamamos sóquer,
y aunque no goza de gran popularidad allá, es un deporte que se prac-
tica mucho. Pero dime algo del partido de la semana pasada.
Juan   Bueno. Como sabes, fui en coche con mi padre y había tanto tráfico
que llegamos tarde al estadio y el partido ya había empezado.
David   ¿Había muchos espectadores?
Juan   Más de cincuenta mil. El estadio estaba lleno.
David   El equipo argentino, ¿es muy bueno?

Juan	Bueno, el nuestro es un equipo muy joven. . . . de los cinco mejores jugadores el mayor tiene veintitrés años y el menor sólo diecinueve. En realidad este año es sólo regular, pero cuando mi padre era joven era el mejor del mundo. Ganó el campeonato mundial varias veces.
David	¿Quién es el mejor jugador?
Juan	Un muchacho que se llama Schultz. Es rapidísimo y juega muy bien.
David	¿Schultz dices? No es apellido muy argentino.
Juan	No, es alemán. Muchos de los jugadores vienen del extranjero. En este deporte parece que el país que paga más tiene el mejor equipo.
David	Pero hombre, dime, ¿quién ganó la semana pasada?
Juan	¿Tienes que preguntármelo? Pues, el otro equipo. Sin embargo, como ya te dije somos muy jóvenes y nos falta experiencia. Puede que me equivoque, pero estoy casi seguro de que dentro de dos años vamos a ser campeones del mundo otra vez.
David	Espero que no te equivoques.
Juan	¿Quién sabe? ¡A veces se vive de ilusiones . . . !

Dialogue Practice

A. Prepare oral responses to the following questions.

1. ¿A qué asistió Juan hace una semana?
2. ¿Cuánto tiempo hace que David está en la Argentina?
3. ¿Por qué llegaron tarde al estadio Juan y su padre?
4. ¿Cuántos espectadores había?
5. ¿Cómo es el equipo argentino?
6. ¿Cuántas veces había ganado el campeonato mundial?
7. ¿Quién es el mejor jugador del equipo?
8. ¿De dónde vienen muchos de los jugadores del equipo argentino?
9. En el fútbol, ¿qué país tiene el mejor equipo?

LECCIÓN DIECIOCHO

Basic Words and Expressions

¿**quién?** who?
de modo que so, so that
Hasta pronto. See you soon.
para que in order that, so that
sin más ni más without more ado, just like that

cenar to eat dinner
cortar to cut
deber ought, should, must
desayunarse to eat breakfast
doler (ue) to hurt
estropear to damage, ruin
gastar to spend (money)
habrá there will be
habría there would be
limpiar to clean
mostrar (ue) to show
ponerse to put on
quitar to take away from
quitarse to take off
recomendar (ie) to recommend

la abuela grandmother
el abuelo grandfather
el árbol tree

la boca mouth
la cabeza head
la cara face
la cena dinner
la cocinera cook
el desayuno breakfast
la escuela school
los Estados Unidos the United States
la lavandera washerwoman
la limpieza cleaning, cleanliness
la mano hand
la máquina lavadora washing machine
el pelo hair
el portero doorman
la ropa clothes
la tía aunt
el tío uncle

complicado complicated
limpio clean
seguro sure, certain
sucio dirty

incluso including, even

alguien someone

Basic Patterns

1.	**Hablarás con el portero esta mañana.**	You will speak with the doorman this morning.
2.	**Se lo mostraría a mi tía.**	I would show it to my aunt.
3.	**¿Cuántas casas tendrá?**	I wonder how many houses he has.
4.	**¿Cuántas casas tendría?**	I wonder how many houses he had.
5.	**Juan no debe gastar tanto dinero.**	John shouldn't waste so much money.
6.	**He de cenar con ellos.**	I am supposed to eat with them.
7.	**Me quité el abrigo.**	I took off my overcoat.
8.	**María me quitó el abrigo.**	Mary took off my coat.

Drills

Future and Conditional

Substitute the cues.

1. Hablarás con el portero esta mañana.
   (*yo, nosotros, él, ellos, tú, la chica*)
2. Se lo mostraría a mi tía.
   (*tú, yo, Uds., él, nosotros, mi abuelo*)
3. Podré hacerlo fácilmente.
   (*tú, él, nosotros, ellos, Ud., yo*)
4. Lo pondrían en la luna.
   (*tú, nosotros, Uds., él, yo, Ud.*)
5. Tu abuelo sabrá muchas cosas, ¿verdad?
   (*tener, querer, decir, hacer*)

Change the following sentences from present to future, then to conditional.

1. No puedo escribir.
2. Me visto temprano.
3. Dicen la verdad.
4. No hacemos muchas cosas.
5. Vienen a menudo.
6. Tengo cuidado.
7. No lo digo.
8. No lo haces.
9. Cuento hasta cien.
10. Hay mucha gente.
11. Subo en el ascensor.
12. Quieren salir.
13. No sabe nada.
14. Viene el martes.
15. Lo pongo en la mesa.
16. Te desayunas temprano.
17. Voy a México.
18. Te pido mucho dinero.
19. Mi tía limpia la casa.
20. Lo pruebo más tarde.
21. Ceno con mis tíos.
22. Ese árbol es mío.
23. Uds. están cansados.
24. Pepe me da la mano.
25. No puedo gastar tanto dinero.
26. Vamos a la escuela.

Future and Conditional of Probability

⊕ Write the following sentences in Spanish.

1. I wonder how many houses he has.
2. He probably has two houses.
3. I wonder how many houses he had.
4. He probably had two houses.
5. I wonder what the doorman wants.
6. He probably wants to ask us something.
7. What time do you suppose it is?
8. It must be one o'clock.
9. I wonder when they are coming.
10. They are probably coming tomorrow.

Discussion

Future and Conditional

The future tense of regular verbs is formed by adding the following endings to the whole infinitive. Note that the endings for **-ar, -er,** and **-ir** verbs are the same. The future tense is translated by *shall* or *will*.

hablar		comer		vivir	
hablar *é*	hablar *emos*	comer *é*	comer *emos*	vivir *é*	vivir *emos*
hablar *ás*		comer *ás*		vivir *ás*	
hablar *á*	hablar *án*	comer *á*	comer *án*	vivir *á*	vivir *án*

The conditional of regular verbs is formed by adding the following endings (the same for all verbs) to the whole infinitive. The conditional is translated by *would*.

hablar		comer		vivir	
hablar *ía*	hablar *íamos*	comer *ía*	comer *íamos*	vivir *ía*	vivir *íamos*
hablar *ías*		comer *ías*		vivir *ías*	
hablar *ía*	hablar *ían*	comer *ía*	comer *ían*	vivir *ía*	vivir *ían*

Several verbs have irregular stems in both the future and the conditional, but regular endings are used for both.

> **haber/habr-**
> **poder/podr-**
> **querer/querr-**
> **saber/sabr-**
> **poner/pondr-**
> **tener/tendr-**
> **venir/vendr-**
> **decir/dir-**
> **hacer/har-**

Juan vendrá mañana.	John will come tomorrow.
Juan vendría mañana.	John would come tomorrow.

Future and Conditional of Probability

The future is often used to express probability in the present. The conditional is used to express probability in the past. In a question they express the speaker's wonder or doubt.

¿Dónde estará?	I wonder where he is.
¿Dónde estaría?	I wonder where he was.
Estará en casa.	He is probably at home.
Estaría en casa.	He was probably at home.
¿Qué hora será (sería)?	I wonder what time it is (was).
Serán (Serían) las dos.	It is (was) probably two o'clock.

DEBER and HABER DE

Substitute the cues.

1. Juan no debe gastar tanto dinero.
   (*tú, ellos, nosotros, Ud., yo, la cocinera*)
2. He de cenar con ellos.
   (*él, nosotros, Uds., yo, tú, el alemán*)

⊕ Write in Spanish.

1. I must be there at six o'clock.
2. You should clean the house right now.
3. He is to eat breakfast with us.
4. You (*fam., sing.*) should not break things.
5. They were supposed to go to school.
6. I am supposed to wash the clothes.
7. We ought to ask the doorman.
8. I must write with a pencil.

Numbers from 100

⊕ Write the following and be prepared to give them orally.

156 houses, 372 faces, 510 machines, 801 schools, 215 pencils, 422 trees, 639 dogs, 740 teams, 991 stadiums, 1,550 champions, 1,500,000 spectators, 4,650,580 people

⊕ Write the following dates.

March 5, 1961; July 4, 1776; December 25, 1985; October 12, 1492; January 1, 1972; February 12, 1888

DEBER and HABER DE

Deber is used to express obligation.

> **Debo estar en casa.**   I must be (ought to be, should be) at home.
> **Debemos estudiar.**   We must (ought to, should) study.

The expression **haber de** also expresses obligation, but in a lighter sense.

> **He de estar allí a las dos.**   I am to be (am supposed to be) there at
> two o'clock.
> **Habíamos de estar allí.**   We were supposed to be there.

The above expressions tend to be confused with the future and conditional of probability in translation. Note, however, that neither of the following sentences expresses obligation, but only probability or conjecture.

> **¿Dónde estará?**   Where do you suppose he is?
> **Estará en casa.**   He must be (probably is) at home.

Numbers from 100

100	ciento (cien)	700	setecientos
200	doscientos	800	ochocientos
300	trescientos	900	novecientos
400	cuatrocientos	1.000	mil (dos mil, etc.)*
500	quinientos	1.000.000	millón
600	seiscientos		

Remember that **ciento** becomes **cien** when it immediately precedes a noun.

> **cien casas**   100 houses
> **ciento veinticinco casas**   125 houses

Millón and **millones** are followed by **de** when either immediately precedes a noun.

> **un millón de casas**   1,000,000 houses
> **dos millones quinientas casas**   2,000,500 houses

The hundreds always agree with the noun they modify.

> **doscientas casas, trescientos libros, cuatrocientas veinticinco casas**

Study the way the following numbers are formed.

> 1975   **mil novecientos setenta y cinco**
> 1555   **mil quinientos cincuenta y cinco**

---

* Note that a period is used instead of a comma.

Definite Article for the Possessive

Substitute the cues.

1. Me quité el abrigo.
   (*él, ellos, tú, nosotros, yo, Uds.*)
2. María le lavó la cara.
   (*yo, tú, nosotros, Ud., Uds., sus amigos*)
3. A Juan le dolía la cabeza.
   (*las manos, el pie, la boca, los pies*)

⊕ Give the English and then change to a past tense.

1. Tiene la cara limpia.
2. Me duelen los pies.
3. Juan se pone la camisa.
4. Se corta el pelo.
5. Le quito el lápiz.
6. Me duele la mano.
7. Ella les lava el pelo.
8. Me quitan la ropa.
9. Me corto la mano.
10. Te pones la ropa.

LOS RUIDOS
—Desde aquí no se ve Madrid. Pero se oye muy bien.

Definite Article for the Possessive

When the thing possessed is a part of the body or a personal item, the definite article is used instead of the possessive pronoun.

Tiene las manos muy sucias.	His hands are very dirty.
Se lavan la cara.	They wash their faces.
Me lavé las manos.	I washed my hands.
Me pongo el sombrero.	I put on my hat.

Note that when the action is performed on someone else, the indirect object pronoun is used.

Te lavo la cara.	I wash your face.
Le quité el lápiz.	I took away his pencil.

OTRA CONTAMINACION
DE LA ATMOSFERA

Combined Exercises

A. Express first the Spanish in English, then the English in Spanish, without referring to the translations.

1.	Juan se quitó el sombrero.	*John took off his hat.*
2.	Juan se quita el sombrero.	*John takes off his hat.*
3.	Juan le quita el sombrero (a Pepe).	*John takes his (Joe's) hat off.*
4.	Juan me quitó el sombrero.	*John took my hat off.*
5.	Nos lavamos la cara.	*We are washing our faces.*
6.	Les lavamos la cara.	*We are washing their faces.*
7.	Le lavamos la cara.	*We are washing your face.*
8.	Te lavaste la cara.	*You washed your face.*
9.	Se lavaron la cara.	*They washed their faces.*
10.	Me corté el pelo.	*I cut my hair.*
11.	María me cortó el pelo.	*Mary cut my hair.*
12.	¿Te cortaste el pelo?	*Did you cut your hair?*
13.	¿Por qué te cortas el pelo?	*Why do you cut your hair?*
14.	¿Por qué le cortaste el pelo?	*Why did you cut his hair?*
15.	Me duele la cabeza.	*My head hurts.*
16.	Le dolía la cabeza.	*His head hurt.*
17.	Me dolían los pies.	*My feet hurt.*
18.	¿Te duelen los pies?	*Do your feet hurt?*
19.	Hay muchos árboles en el parque.	*There are many trees in the park.*
20.	Había muchos árboles en el parque.	*There were many trees in the park.*
21.	Habrá muchos árboles en el parque.	*There will be many trees in the park.*
22.	Habría muchos árboles en el parque.	*There would be many trees in the park.*
23.	Hubo una revolución anteayer.	*There was a revolution the day before yesterday.*

B. Answer in Spanish.

1. ¿Has de cortarte el pelo mañana?   2. ¿Habrá una fiesta mañana?   3. ¿A qué hora cena su familia generalmente?   4. ¿A qué hora te desayunas generalmente?   5. ¿Comes mucho para el desayuno?   6. ¿Tienes las manos limpias o sucias?   7. ¿Te quitas la ropa antes de nadar?   8. ¿Crees que las máquinas son complicadas?   9. ¿Cuánto dinero gasta Ud. durante un mes? 10. ¿Tu familia tiene cocinera o lavandera?   11. ¿Cuántos años tendrá tu abuelo?   12. ¿Tu madre te pondrá la corbata mañana?   ¿Quién te la pondrá?

C. Read the following sentences in English. Then change them from the **deber** and **haber de** constructions to the future and then to the conditional.

1. Debo hablar con mis abuelos.   2. No debes estropear la máquina.   3. El portero debe recomendarme.   4. Mi tía debe limpiar el piso.   5. He de cortarme el pelo.   6. Debemos estar seguros.   7. Has de vivir en los Estados Unidos.   8. María debe lavarse la cara.   9. Deben mostrarnos esa máquina complicada.   10. La cocinera ha de prepararnos la cena.

⊕ D. Translate.

1. I wonder what time it is.
2. It must be ten o'clock, but I'm not sure.
3. I would clean my room, but my aunt has already done it.
4. In the United States we eat dinner about 6:00 p.m.
5. Someone cut his hair; it was probably his grandfather.
6. She didn't feel well because she had spent so much money.
7. Cleanliness is important; you (*fam., sing.*) should wash your hands often.
8. I'm supposed to eat dinner with Mary. I wonder where she lives.
9. There are 1,586 students in the school, but 358 are sick today.
10. I took the pencil away from her, but she didn't like it.

Reading and Conversation

Buscando Trabajo

María es una chica de veintidós años que acaba de llegar a Madrid de su pueblo en el sur del país. Está hablando con su amiga, Rosa.

Rosa ¿Viste el anuncio en el periódico de esta mañana? Los Sres. Alonso buscan una chica. Es una familia muy buena y estarás muy contenta con ellos.

María ¿Sí? ¿Tú los conoces? ¿Viven cerca de aquí?

Rosa En esta misma calle, número sesenta y seis, de modo que si trabajas allí, nos veremos todos los días. Irás esta mañana a hablar con la señora, ¿verdad?

María Pero no me conoce la señora. Yo no puedo presentarme y pedirle trabajo sin más ni más.

Rosa No te preocupes. Hablaré con el portero esta mañana para que te recomiende a la señora. Debes ir a verla sobre las doce y media.

María Muy bien. ¿Qué querrá esa señora? ¿Alguien para la limpieza, una lavandera o una cocinera?

Rosa Tendrás que hablar con ella, pero sé que ya tienen cocinera. Es una amiga mía que se llama Pilar. Creo que tendrás que lavar la ropa, limpiar y cuidar a los niños durante la tarde. Imagínate, incluso tienen máquina lavadora.

María ¡Ay de mí! Yo tendría miedo de estropearla. Son muy complicadas estas máquinas.

Rosa ¡Qué va! Aprenderás en seguida. ¡Ay, Dios mío! Será tarde, ¿verdad? Tengo que irme corriendo. Mi señora quiere que vaya de compras esta mañana temprano.

María	Rosa, dime algo más. ¿Cuántos niños tiene la familia?
Rosa	No estoy segura, pero tendrán dos, Roberto e Isabel, si no me equivoco. El hijo es mayor; tendrá unos siete u ocho años ya. La niña tiene menos.
María	Bueno, estaré allí a las doce en punto. Gracias, Rosa. Y, a propósito, ¿pagan bien?
Rosa	Pues no sé, pero a Pilar le dan cuatro mil quinientas al mes y además almuerzo y cena. Buen sueldo, ¿no te parece? ¿Qué harás con tanto dinero?
María	No sé, pero siempre es más fácil gastar el dinero que ganarlo. Adiós. Hasta pronto.
Rosa	Bien. Esta tarde me dirás si has tenido suerte.

Dialogue Practice

A. Prepare oral responses to the following questions.
1. ¿De qué región del país es María?
2. ¿Qué vio Rosa en el periódico esta mañana?
3. ¿Por qué María no quiere pedirle trabajo a la señora?
4. ¿Quién va a recomendarla?
5. ¿Qué tendrá que hacer María en la casa de los Sres. Alonso?
6. ¿Quién es la cocinera?
7. ¿Por qué tuvo Rosa que irse corriendo?
8. ¿Cómo se llaman los niños y cuántos años tienen?
9. ¿Cuánto le pagan a Pilar?

⊕ B. Using the dialogue as a model, write the following paragraph in Spanish.

Mary, I saw an advertisement in this morning's paper. Mr. and Mrs. Alonso are looking for a girl (maid), and they live on this same street so that we can see each other every day. You'll talk to Mr. and Mrs. Alonso tomorrow, won't you? The cook is a friend of mine, and they pay her well. You'll have to care for the two children, Robert and Isabel, during the afternoon.

LECCIÓN DIECINUEVE

Basic Words and Expressions

cuenta corriente charge account
¿En qué puedo servirle? What can I do for you? May I help you?
pagar al contado to pay cash
quedarle bien to fit one well
venir bien con to look well with

anunciar to announce
probarse (ue) to try on
regalar to give (as a gift)
regatear to bargain, dicker

el abrigo de piel fur coat
el almacén department store
la blusa blouse
el bolso purse
el calcetín sock
el collar necklace
la dependienta clerk (*f.*)
el dependiente clerk (*m.*)

el escaparate display window
la falda skirt
la ganga bargain
el guante glove
la joya jewel
la joyería jewelry store
la liquidación sale
las mangas cortas short sleeves
las mangas largas long sleeves
la media stocking, hose
el nilón nylon
los pantalones trousers
el par pair
el suéter sweater
la zapatería shoe store

parecido similar, alike
precioso pretty

ninguno (a) not any, none
sino but (on the contrary)

Basic Patterns

1. **¿Dónde está el coche en que vamos?**
   Where's the car we're going in?
2. **La ventana por la cual entró está rota.**
   The window through which he entered is broken.
3. **El amigo de mi hermano, el cual es mexicano, vive con nosotros.**
   My brother's friend, who is a Mexican, lives with us.
4. **El que está hablando es mi padre.**
   The one who is talking is my father.
5. **Quiero comprar un coche que no sea caro.**
   I want to buy a car that is not expensive.
6. **No hay ningún coche aquí que quiera comprar.**
   There is no car here that I want to buy.
7. **Habré salido antes de las dos.**
   I will have left before two.
8. **Juan dijo que habría comprado el libro.**
   John said that he would have bought the book.
9. **Mi amigo no es español, sino alemán.**
   My friend is not Spanish, but German.
10. **Siento que haya salido.**
    I am sorry that he has left.
11. **Sentía que hubieran venido.**
    I was sorry that they had come.

Drills

Relative Pronouns

⊕ Fill the blanks with the proper relative pronoun. Note that only the prepositions **a, de, en, con** are used in this drill.

1. ¿Dónde está el coche en _____ vamos?
2. La casa en _____ vivo es muy grande.
3. La chica a _____ hablo es de Alemania.
4. ¿Ha visto Ud. a los muchachos con _____ fuimos al cine?
5. Allí está la chica de _____ yo le hablaba.
6. ¿Dónde está la pluma con _____ escribía?

⊕ Fill the blanks with the proper relative pronoun. Prepositions other than the ones listed above are used in this drill.

1. Allí está la puerta por _____ entró el jefe.
2. El almacén detrás de _____ vive es muy grande.
3. La muchacha al lado de _____ está sentado es muy bonita.
4. Aquélla es la ventana desde _____ se ve mejor.
5. ¿Es grande la zapatería cerca de _____ vive Ud.?
6. No tiene joyas, sin _____ no puede asistir a la fiesta.

⊕ In this drill give the proper relative pronoun for the first of the two antecedents provided.

1. La corbata de mi padre, _____ compró ayer, es muy fea.
2. El hijo del Sr. Mora, _____ llegó ayer, es médico.
3. Las hijas de nuestro amigo, _____ viven en Madrid, han ido de compras.
4. Los amigos de Juan, _____ vienen a vernos hoy, quieren conocer a María.

⊕ Complete the following sentences in Spanish as indicated.

1. (*He who*) estudia mucho aprendo mucho.
2. (*The ones who*) vienen esta noche son de México.
3. (*Those who*) trabajan mucho ganan mucho.
4. (*The one which*) compré tiene mangas largas.

Discussion

Relative Pronouns

When using relative pronouns in Spanish, prepositions must precede verbs. So to express the equivalent of *Here's the house I live in,* or *There's the girl I wrote to last week,* you must change to the more formal construction of *Here is the house in which I live,* or *There is the girl to whom I wrote last week.*

After the prepositions **a, de, en, con,** the relative **que** is used to refer to things, while **quien(es)** refers to persons.

Aquí está la casa en que vivo.	Here's the house I live in.
¿Dónde está la pluma con que escribía?	Where's the pen I was writing with?
Allí está la chica a quien escribí la semana pasada.	There's the girl I wrote to last week.

After other prepositions, the relative **el cual, la cual, los cuales,** or **las cuales** is used.

La ventana por la cual entró está rota.	The window through which he entered is broken.
Allí está el hotel cerca del cual vive.	There's the hotel he lives near.
Son los dos jugadores sin los cuales no podemos ganar.	They are the two players without whom we cannot win.

To refer back to the first of two antecedents, **el cual, la cual, los cuales,** or **las cuales** is used.

La amiga de mi hermana, la cual vive en México, está enferma. (*refers to* **amiga,** *not* **hermana**)	My sister's friend, who lives in Mexico, is ill.
Los padres de Juan, los cuales están aquí esta noche, son médicos.	John's parents, who are here tonight, are doctors.

El que, la que, los que, las que, are equivalent to *he (she) who, the ones who, the one which,* etc.

El que habla mucho es Juan.	The one who talks a lot is John.
Los que estudian más aprenden más.	The ones (those) who study most learn most.
La que no dice nada es María.	The one who is not saying anything is Mary.

Subjunctive in Adjective Clauses

⊕ Provide the proper form of the infinitives in parentheses. Not all the following sentences will require the subjunctive.

1. Buscamos una chica que (*ser*) tan bonita como María.
2. Buscamos a la chica que (*estar*) aquí ayer.
3. Quiero comprar un collar que no (*ser*) muy caro.
4. No hay ningunas joyas aquí que (*ser*) caras.
5. Quería encontrar un traje que me (*gustar*).
6. Conozco a un señor que (*hablar*) alemán.
7. ¿Hay alguién que (*tener*) una cuenta corriente?
8. ¿Dónde están los zapatos que yo (*comprar*) ayer?
9. No hay nadie que (*pagar*) al contado.

Future Perfect and Conditional Perfect Indicative

In the following sentences, change **hoy** to **mañana** and present perfect to future perfect.

Hoy he terminado mi trabajo. / *Mañana habré terminado mi trabajo.*

1. Hoy Juan ha comprado un piso.
2. Hoy tú has escrito muchas cartas.
3. Hoy me han hablado mucho.
4. Hoy hemos dicho muchas cosas
5. Hoy he aprendido mucho.
6. Hoy han comprado un suéter.

Change the following sentences to the conditional perfect.

Juan compró la casa. / *Juan habría comprado la casa.*
Los niños no me vieron. / *Los niños no me habrían visto.*

1. Mis amigos salieron.
2. Juan me dijo la verdad.
3. Mis padres volvieron temprano.
4. Mi hermano fue a Barcelona.
5. No la vi.
6. No le escribimos una carta.
7. Tú compraste un par de calcetines.

Subjunctive in Adjective Clauses

In this type of sentence, a statement is made about a person or object which is determined in a following clause. If the antecedent, that is, the person or object being described, is indefinite or negative, the subjunctive is used. In the following examples, the antecedents are italicized.

Busco *una sirvienta* que hable inglés. I am looking for *a maid* (any maid) who speaks English.

No hay *nadie* aquí que hable alemán. There is *no one* here who speaks German. (*negative antecedent*)

Busco a *la sirvienta* que estuvo aquí ayer. I am looking for *the maid* who was here yesterday. (*a definite antecedent, therefore no subjunctive*).

Future Perfect and Conditional Perfect Indicative

The future perfect is formed with the future of **haber** and a past participle; the conditional perfect is formed with the conditional of **haber** and a past participle.

Future perfect
hablar

habré hablado	**habremos hablado**
habrás hablado	
habrá hablado	**habrán hablado**

Conditional perfect
hablar

habría hablado	**habríamos hablado**
habrías hablado	
habría hablado	**habrían hablado**

The future perfect is translated *shall have* or *will have spoken*. The conditional perfect is translated *would have spoken*.

Habrán llegado antes de las seis. They will have arrived before six.
Mis amigos dijeron que habrían venido. My friends said that they would have come.

PERO, SINO, and SINO QUE

Form one sentence from the two given by using **sino.**

No va al cine. Va al teatro. / *No va al cine, sino al teatro.*
No viene Luis. Viene Carlos. / *No viene Luis, sino Carlos.*

1. No compró medias. Compró calcetines.
2. No está triste. Está contento.
3. No tenemos hambre. Tenemos sed.
4. No tienen frío. Tienen calor.

Form one sentence from the two given by using **sino que.**

No estudiaban. Leían una revista. / *No estudiaban, sino que leían una revista.*

1. No perdió el libro. Lo vendió.
2. No dijeron nada. Escuchaban.
3. No dormía. Leía el periódico.
4. No fuimos al centro. Nos quedamos en casa.

Perfect Tenses of Subjunctive

Begin each of the following with **Temo que,** changing present perfect to present perfect subjunctive.

Juan ha salido. / *Temo que Juan haya salido.*

1. Juan ha comprado unas camisas.
2. No han estado aquí.
3. María no ha venido.
4. Hemos llegado tarde.
5. Tú has estudiado demasiado.

Begin each of the following sentences with **Sentía que,** changing pluperfect to pluperfect subjunctive.

Juan había comprado el libro. / *Sentía que Juan hubiera comprado el libro.*

1. No habían aprendido nada.
2. Habías escrito tantas cartas.
3. No habían estado aquí.
4. No había venido hoy.
5. Habíamos llegado tarde.
6. Juan lo había vendido.

PERO, SINO, and SINO QUE

These words express the equivalent of the English *but;* however, **pero** implies the idea of *but nevertheless,* while **sino** implies *but on the contrary.* To use **sino,** there must be a contradiction of a previous negative statement.

Juan es español, pero habla muy bien el inglés.	John is Spanish, but (nevertheless) he speaks English very well.
Juan no es español, sino alemán.	John is not Spanish, but (on the contrary) German.

Sino que is used under the same conditions as **sino,** but only when a conjugated verb follows.

No me escribió, sino que vino a verme.	He didn't write to me, but (on the contrary) came to see me.

Perfect Tenses of Subjunctive

The present perfect of the subjunctive is formed with the present subjunctive of **haber** and a past participle. It may be translated *have spoken* or *will have spoken* in situations where a preceding word or expression demands use of the subjunctive.

hablar

haya hablado	hayamos hablado
hayas hablado	
haya hablado	hayan hablado

Siento que hayan venido.	I am sorry that they have come.
Espero que lo haya comprado.	I hope that he has bought it.

The pluperfect of the subjunctive is formed with the past subjunctive of **haber** and a past participle. It may be translated *had spoken* or *would have spoken* in situations where a preceding word or expression demands use of the subjunctive.

hablar

hubiera (-se) hablado	hubiéramos (-semos) hablado
hubieras (-ses) hablado	
hubiera (-se) hablado	hubieran (-sen) hablado

Sentía que hubieran venido.	I was sorry that they had come.
Esperaba que lo hubiera comprado.	I hoped that he had (would have) bought it.

Combined Exercises

A. Express first the Spanish in English and then the English in Spanish, without referring to the translations.

1.	una gran liquidación	*a big sale*
2.	Hay una gran liquidación en el almacén.	*There is a big sale at the department store.*
3.	Hay una gran liquidación en la zapatería.	*There is a big sale at the shoe store.*
4.	Hay una gran liquidación en la joyería.	*There's a big sale at the jewelry store.*
5.	Hay una gran liquidación de abrigos de piel.	*There's a big sale of fur coats.*
6.	habría comprado	*he would have bought*
7.	Habría comprado un par de zapatos.	*He would have bought a pair of shoes.*
8.	Habrían comprado zapatos y sombreros.	*They would have bought shoes and hats.*
9.	Habríamos comprado calcetines y medias.	*We would have bought socks and stockings.*
10.	Habrías comprado una blusa de mangas cortas.	*You would have bought a short-sleeved blouse.*
11.	venir bien con	*to look well with (go well with)*
12.	El suéter viene bien con los pantalones.	*The sweater goes well with the trousers.*
13.	La corbata viene bien con el traje.	*The tie goes well with the suit.*
14.	El collar viene bien con el vestido.	*The necklace goes well with the dress.*
15.	Las medias vienen bien con la falda.	*The stockings go well with the skirt.*
16.	Los zapatos vienen bien con el bolso que me regaló.	*The shoes go well with the purse he gave me.*
17.	le queda bien	*it fits you well*
18.	El vestido le queda bien.	*The dress fits you well.*
19.	Los zapatos no me quedan bien.	*The shoes don't fit me well.*
20.	La ropa no les queda muy bien.	*The clothing doesn't fit them very well.*
21.	cuenta corriente	*charge account*
22.	Tengo cuenta corriente en el almacén.	*I have a charge account at the department store.*
23.	Tienen cuenta corriente en la joyería y en la zapatería.	*They have a charge account at the jewelry store and at the shoe store.*
24.	pagar al contado	*to pay cash*
25.	Siempre pago al contado.	*I always pay cash.*
26.	¿Hay que pagar al contado?	*Do you have to pay cash?*
27.	No hay que pagar al contado aquí.	*It's not necessary to pay cash here.*

B. Answer in Spanish.

1. ¿Qué se vende en un almacén?   2. ¿Dónde se compran zapatos?
3. ¿Dónde se compran joyas?   4. ¿Le quedan bien los zapatos?   5. ¿Tiene
Ud. cuenta corriente en algún almacén?   6. ¿Siempre paga Ud. al contado?
7. ¿Le gustan las camisas de mangas cortas?   8. ¿Dónde se anuncian las
grandes liquidaciones?   9. ¿Le gusta regatear?   10. ¿Siempre son
simpáticos y amables los dependientes?

⊕ C. Translate.

1. Where is the car that you are going in?   2. He will have bought the
jewels.   3. I am afraid that he has bought (will have bought) the jewels.
4. He would have bought the suit.   5. I was afraid that he had bought
(would have bought) the suit.   6. He is looking for a suit that doesn't cost
much.   7. He was looking for a suit that wouldn't cost much.   8. There
is no purse in this store that I want to buy.   9. There was no purse in that
store that I wanted to buy.   10. The store he lives near (near which he lives)
has many bargains.

Reading and Conversation

De Compras

Los periódicos han anunciado una gran liquidación de ropa para hombres
y mujeres en los grandes almacenes del centro. Dos jóvenes españolas, María
y Juana, van de compras.

María	Juana, mira ese vestido de nilón que hay en el escaparate. ¡Qué bonito es!, ¿verdad?
Juana	¿Cuál? ¿El que está detrás de la blusa de mangas cortas?
María	Sí, es ése. Vendrá muy bien con el suéter que me regaló mi madre, ¿no te parece? ¿Por qué no entramos para probármelo?
Juana	Bien, pero me parece que va a ser muy caro. ¿Cuánto costará?
María	No sé, no tiene precio. Pero la dependienta nos lo dirá.

(Las dos jóvenes entran en el almacén.)

Dependienta	Buenas tardes, señoritas. ¿En qué puedo servirlas?
María	Ese vestido que está en el escaparate, ¿cuánto cuesta, por favor?
Dependienta	Mil cuatrocientas pesetas. Es un precio especial de liquidación.
María	Me parece muy caro. ¿No me lo vendería por novecientas?
Dependienta	Temo que se haya equivocado, señorita. Ud. debe saber que en esta tienda y en todos los grandes almacenes no se regatea.

María	Pero, ¿no tiene otro parecido que sea menos caro?
Dependienta	No, lo siento. Lo que sí hay es liquidación de guantes, bolsos y medias.
María	No, lo que necesito es un vestido, pero no quiero pagar más de novecientas.
Juana	Pero por lo menos pruébatelo. Es precioso. Me parece que te va a quedar muy bien.
María	No voy a probarme ningún vestido que cueste tanto. Además, una amiga de mi madre, la cual trabaja en una tienda de ropa para mujeres, me dijo que allí tienen verdaderas gangas.
Juana	Entonces, ¿por qué no vamos allá? Siento que no hayas pensado en eso antes. Hemos perdido mucho tiempo aquí.
María	Tiempo sí, pero por lo menos no hemos gastado nada.

Dialogue Practice

A. Prepare oral responses to the following questions.

1. ¿Qué han anunciado los periódicos?
2. ¿A dónde van las dos jóvenes españolas?
3. ¿En qué parte del escaparate está el vestido de nilón?
4. ¿Con qué vendrá bien el vestido?
5. ¿Cuánto cuesta el vestido?
6. ¿Por qué no lo compró María?
7. ¿Cuánto quería pagar María por el vestido?
8. ¿En dónde dice la dependienta que no se regatea?
9. ¿Por qué dijo María que no quería probarse el vestido?
10. ¿Dónde trabaja la amiga de la madre de María?

⊕ B. Using the dialogue as a model, write the following paragraph in Spanish.

Juana, look at that nylon blouse in the window, the one that is in front of the short-sleeved dress. It will go very well with the skirt that my father gave me. I wonder how much it costs. I wonder if they have another one like it (similar) that is less expensive. Let's not buy anything here. A friend of my father, who works in a jewelry store, told me that they have some real bargains there. Let's go there. I am afraid that we have lost a lot of time here.

LECCIÓN VEINTE

Basic Words and Expressions

a pesar de in spite of
¡Cuánto (-a, -os, -as) . . . ! What a lot of . . . !
¡Ojo! Take care! Watch out!
por ejemplo for example
venga lo que venga come what may, no matter what happens

descansar to rest
detenerse to stop
encantar to fascinate
molestar to bother
organizar to organize
quedarse to stay, remain

el ambiente atmosphere
el ángel angel
el caballero gentleman
la cantidad quantity
el clima climate
el dólar dollar
la geografía geography
el guardia guard
la historia history
el indio Indian
la maravilla marvel

el mestizo mestizo, mixed blood
la molestia bother
la morena brunette
la nación nation
la plaza plaza, central square
la política politics
el presidente president
el rato while
la rubia blonde
la tierra land
la variación variation
la variedad variety

corto short
diferente different
igual equal

a menos que unless
con tal que provided that
en caso de que in case that
en cuanto as soon as
entre between, among
hasta que until
luego que as soon as
sin que without

Basic Patterns

1. **Paco vendrá cuando yo le llame.**   Paco will come when I call him.
2. **Paco vino cuando yo le llamé.**   Paco came when I called him.
3. **Si yo tuviera dinero, iría a España.**   If I had money, I would go to Spain.
4. **Si yo tengo el dinero, voy a España.**   If I have the money, I am going to Spain.
5. **Le hablé como si fuera niño.**   I talked to him as if he were a child.
6. **Salen para Madrid.**   They are leaving for Madrid.
7. **Anduvieron por la calle.**   They walked down the street.
8. **Quisiera comprar un sombrero.**   I would like to buy a hat.

Drills

Subjunctive after Certain Conjunctions

Substitute the cues for the second verb only.

1. Paco vendrá en cuanto yo le diga.
   (*tú, Ud., nosotros, ellos, yo, el guardia*)
2. Salieron antes de que Juan llegara.
   (*yo, Uds., tú, Ud., nosotros, el presidente*)

⊕ Repeat the following, supplying the proper form of the infinitives in parentheses.

1. Voy a Madrid en cuanto (*tener*) dinero.
2. Estudio antes de (*dormir*).
3. Le di el libro para que (*leerlo*).
4. Leía el periódico cuando él (*entrar*).
5. Vinieron sin que yo se lo (*decir*).
6. Me quedo aquí a menos que (*molestarte*).
7. Se detuvieron para (*descansar*).
8. Iremos al parque con tal que no (*llover*).
9. María esperaba hasta que (*llegar*) sus amigos.
10. Juan salió antes de que nosotros (*entrar*).
11. Llevo mi abrigo en caso de que (*llover*).
12. Voy luego que me lo (*decir*).

⊕ Write in Spanish.

1. I'll eat before he arrives.
2. I ate before he arrived.
3. They ate as soon as he arrived.
4. They will go provided it doesn't snow.

Subjunctive in *If* Clauses

Substitute the cues, changing both verbs.

Si yo tuviera dinero iría a España.
(*él, tú, nosotros, Uds., yo, el caballero*)

Change the following to indicate that the *if* clause is contrary to fact.

1. Si tengo dinero, voy a España.
2. Si Pedro está aquí, le hablaré.
3. Si la casa está sucia, la limpio.
4. Si tenemos tiempo, lavamos la ropa.
5. Si voy a España, puedo aprender español.

⊕ Write the following sentences in Spanish.

1. If I were president, I would help the foreigners.
2. I would write to him if I had a pencil.
3. If he isn't sick, he'll go to school.
4. I wouldn't have gone if I had known that.

202

Discussion

Subjunctive after Certain Conjunctions

The subjunctive is used after the following conjunctions if the action referred to by the main verb has not yet taken place. Thus, the conjunctions in the left column will always be followed by the subjunctive.

antes de que	before	**luego que**	as soon as
a menos que	unless	**en cuanto**	as soon as
para que	in order that, so that	**cuando**	when
con tal que	provided that	**hasta que**	until
en caso de que	in case (that)		
sin que	without		

Vamos a salir antes de que lleguen.	Let's leave before they arrive.
Salieron antes de que Juan llegara.	They left before John arrived.
Le llamo para que salgamos ahora.	I'll call him so that we may leave now.
Se lo diré en cuanto vuelva.	I'll tell him as soon as he returns.

If the action has already taken place, the indicative is used.

Lo compré en cuanto llegué.	I bought it as soon as I arrived.
Juan lo hizo cuando volví.	John did it when I returned.

The subjunctive is not used with **para que** and **antes de que** if the subject of both clauses is the same; the infinitive is used and **que** is omitted.

Juan lo hace antes de estudiar.	John does it before he studies.
Salió para buscarlo.	She left in order to look for it.

Subjunctive in *If* Clauses

The imperfect subjunctive is used in *if* clauses that are contrary to fact; the other clause will be in the conditional.

Si yo tuviera el dinero, iría a España.	If I had the money, I would go to Spain.
Si Juan fuera presidente, haría más por los indios.	If John were president, he would do more for the Indians.
Yo habría hablado con él si hubiera tenido tiempo.	I would have talked to him if I had had time.

The present indicative is used in *if* clauses that are not contrary to fact; the other clause will be in the future or present tense.

Si tengo dinero, voy a España.	If I have the money, I am going to Spain.
Si Pedro está aquí, le hablaré.	If Peter is here, I'll talk to him.
Si no llueve, iremos al campo.	If it doesn't rain, we'll go to the country.

Subjunctive after COMO SI

⊕ Write in Spanish.

1. I talked to him as if he were a child.
2. They talked as if they had known him.
3. She looks at me as if I were a gentleman.
4. He eats as if he were dying of hunger.
5. He left as if he were afraid.

POR and PARA

Read the following, filling in the blanks with **por** or **para**. Then translate.

1. Vivió en España _____ un año.
2. Juan estudia _____ la mañana.
3. ¿Hay una carta _____ mí?
4. Deben terminarlo _____ el lunes.
5. Le doy dos mil pesetas _____ el coche.
6. Dan un paseo _____ el parque.
7. Salí esta mañana _____ Valencia.
8. Trabajé _____ Juan. (*he paid me*)
9. Trabajé _____ Juan. (*in his place*)
10. Se fue _____ el café.

⊕ Write in Spanish.

1. They walked toward the plaza.
2. They walked through the plaza.
3. The letter was written by an Indian.
4. He gave me 10,000 pesetas for the land.
5. I study in order to learn.
6. We went by train.
7. Mary studied for two hours.
8. These chairs are for the class.
9. The house is for my family.
10. Thanks for everything.

QUISIERA and DEBIERA

⊕ Write in Spanish.

1. You shouldn't read so much.
2. I would like to see that movie.
3. Would you give me your book?
4. He should visit his friends often.

Subjunctive after COMO SI

The imperfect or pluperfect subjunctive must be used after **como si.** The present subjunctive is never used after this expression.

Me mira como si estuviera loco.	He looks at me as if I were crazy.
Me habla como si no me conociera.	He talks to me as if he didn't know me.
Me mira como si me hubiera olvidado.	He looks at me as if he had forgotten me.

POR and PARA

Para is more limited in its meaning than **por.** It stresses the goal or destination of an action.

Salió para Madrid.	He left for Madrid.
La lección es para el lunes.	The lesson is for Monday.
El regalo es para ti.	The gift is for you.
Comemos para vivir.	We eat in order to live.
Trabaja para la fábrica.	He works for the factory.

Por is involved with explaining or amplifying the action itself. Some possible meanings are (1) through or during time,

Estuvo en Madrid por un año.	He was in Madrid for a year.
Andaba por el parque.	I was walking through the park.
Lo haré por la tarde.	I'll do it in the afternoon.

(2) cause or means of action,

Vamos por avión.	We are going by plane.
Fue visto por todos.	It was seen by all.
No fueron por la lluvia.	They didn't go because of the rain.

and (3) for the sake of, on behalf of, in exchange for.

Lo hice por mis niños.	I did it for my children.
Gracias por su ayuda.	Thanks for your help.
Pagué cinco pesetas por el libro.	I paid five pesetas for the book.
Trabajé por Diego.	I worked for Diego. (took his place)

QUISIERA and DEBIERA

These two words are often used as a substitute for the simple present tense. They are used to soften requests and orders which might otherwise seem too blunt.

Quisiera sopa de cebolla.	I would like onion soup.
Ud. debiera estudiar más.	You ought to study more.

Combined Exercises

A. Express the Spanish sentences in English and the English sentences in Spanish, without referring to the translations.

1. Venga lo que venga, voy a España.   *Come what may, I am going to Spain.*
2. Venga lo que venga, organizamos un partido.   *Come what may, we are organizing a game.*
3. Venga lo que venga, la fiesta tendrá lugar.   *Come what may, the fiesta will take place.*

4. Me encanta México.   *Mexico fascinates me.*
5. Me encantan los niños.   *The children fascinate me.*
6. Le encantó la historia.   *History fascinated him.*
7. Me molestaron los niños.   *The children bothered me.*
8. Nos molestó el clima.   *The climate bothered us.*
9. Les molestaron las fiestas.   *The fiestas bothered them.*

10. Me fijé en las chicas.   *I noticed the girls.*
11. ¿No se fijó en el guardia?   *Didn't you notice the guard?*
12. ¿No te fijaste en la fiesta?   *Didn't you notice the fiesta?*
13. ¡Ojo! Fíjate bien en lo que haces.   *Take care! Watch what you're doing.*
14. ¡Ojo! Fíjese bien en lo que hace.   *Take care! Watch what you're doing.*

15. Se detienen un rato.   *They stop a while.*
16. Me detengo un rato.   *I stop a while.*
17. Te detienes en el mercado.   *You stop in the market.*
18. Me detuve a pesar de tener prisa.   *I stopped in spite of being in a hurry.*
19. Nos detuvimos un rato.   *We stopped a while.*
20. Se detuvieron a charlar.   *They stopped to chat.*

21. ¡Cuánta variedad hay!   *What a lot of variety there is!*
22. ¡Cuántas naciones hay!   *What a lot of nations there are!*
23. ¡Cuántos ángeles hay!   *What a lot of angels there are!*

B. Answer the questions in Spanish.

1. Si ves a un amigo, ¿te detienes a hablar con él? 2. ¿Te has fijado en la cantidad de chicas bonitas que hay en esta clase? 3. ¿Te encantan las morenas? ¿Y las rubias? 4. ¿Te molestó tener que estudiar anoche? 5. ¿Vas a descansar después de clase o tienes otra? 6. ¿Son iguales, parecidos o còmpletamente diferentes los países de Latinoamérica? 7. En cuanto termine esta clase, ¿qué vas a hacer? 8. ¿Había algún presidente bueno o no había ninguno? 9. ¿Cuántos dólares daría Ud. por un buen coche? 10. Si tuvieras mucho dinero, ¿qué país visitarías? 11. ¿Quisiera Ud. ir por avión o por tren? 12. ¿Qué debieran Uds. hacer para aprender más?

C. Read the following and then change to the past tense, using the cues provided.

1. Voy a casa antes de que llueva.   *(Fui a casa)*
2. Espero allí hasta que lleguen.   *(Esperaba allí)*
3. Se lo diré luego que venga.   *(Se lo dije)*
4. Se lo doy con tal que me pague cinco dólares.   *(Se lo daba)*
5. Estudiaré cuando Uds. se vayan.   *(Estudiaba)*
6. Nado en el río sin que nadie me vea.   *(Nadaba)*

7. En caso de que vuelva, le espero. *(le esperaba)*
8. Lo haré hasta que me digan que no. *(Lo hacía)*
9. Grito para que me oigan. *(Grité)*
10. Entra en la sala sin que nadie lo sepa. *(Entré)*
11. Le contestaré cuando me escriba. *(Le contesté)*
12. Estudiaré geografía en cuanto el Sr. García la enseñe. *(Estudiaba)*
13. Si estoy allí, se lo diré. *(se lo diría)*
14. Si ellos me lo dan, te doy una parte. *(te daría una parte)*
15. Si es una molestia, te quejas. *(te quejarías)*

⊕ D. Translate.

1. We stopped until it stopped raining.   2. Have you noticed the variations in the politics of certain countries?   3. It bothered him to have to work too much.   4. This country is wonderful (a marvel), but I'd like to visit others.   5. Every country has its own atmosphere. For example, Mexico is a land of many mestizos and Indians.   6. It's no bother. Besides, it fascinates me to see so many blondes and brunettes.   7. I'll go to the movies with you provided you pay.   8. I worked for him until he left for the United States. 9. I did the work as soon as he asked for it.   10. If he had studied, he would have known the lesson.

Reading and Conversation

Sábado en Chapultepec

John es un estudiante de los Estados Unidos. Este verano vive en México con una familia mexicana. Los dos hijos de esta familia, Carlos y Miguel, están con él en el parque de Chapultepec. Los tres se detienen a charlar un rato.

John ¡Cuánta gente hay en el parque hoy! ¡Todo el mundo viene los sábados!

Carlos Sí, es verdad, y la cantidad de chicas que hay es una maravilla. Por ejemplo, esas dos morenas que compran helados, son bonitas, ¿no te parece?

John Como dos angelitos. ¡Ojo! ¿No te has fijado en los chicos que hablan con el guardia? Van con ellas.

Carlos ¡Ay! Es cierto; no me di cuenta. ¿Por qué no nos sentamos aquí a descansar? ¿Qué te pasa, Juan? Pareces triste.

John Estaba pensando en que tengo que volver a los Estados Unidos la semana que viene. Ha sido un verano muy corto.

Miguel Tal vez puedas regresar a México otro año, ¿no? ¿Te ha gustado México?

John Claro. Me encanta y también he aprendido mucho, pero me gustaría visitar otros países. En los Estados Unidos mucha gente cree que toda Latinoamérica es igual, y no lo es.

Carlos ¡Qué tontería! ¿De veras creen eso? ¿No se dan cuenta de que todos estos países son muy diferentes en geografía, clima, costumbres, política y otros aspectos?

Miguel	Incluso dentro de las varias regiones mexicanas hay gran variedad.
Carlos	Y mucho más entre las naciones. Hay veinte y cada una tiene su propio ambiente. Por ejemplo, México es un país de mestizos e indios y el Perú lo es también. Sin embargo las diferencias entre los dos países son grandes.
Miguel	En la Argentina y Chile casi no hay indios y a pesar de esto no son iguales. Y aunque todos hablamos la misma lengua, menos el Brasil y Haití, cada país presenta ciertas variaciones en su manera de hablar.
Carlos	También la historia de estas naciones, por ejemplo Bolivia y Cuba, ha sido muy diferente. Y a propósito de la historia, Juan, siento mucho que no hayas podido visitar San Juan Teotihuacán. Es una parte muy interesante de nuestra historia.
John	Sí, pero he tenido tanto que hacer, tantos viajes y otras cosas, que no he podido.
Carlos	Todavía te quedan unos días. Venga lo que venga, te llevo allí antes de que salgas de México. Si yo tuviera coche, iríamos mañana.
Miguel	Mañana es domingo. Tal vez papá nos lleve. No está lejos.
John	Sería estupendo, pero, ¿él no lo habrá visto ya muchas veces? No quisiera molestar.
Carlos	Hombre, no es ninguna molestia. Además . . .
Miguel	Miren allí. Parece que se está organizando un partido de fútbol. Vamos.

Dialogue Practice

A. Prepare oral responses to the following questions.

1. ¿Por qué se detienen los tres chicos?   2. ¿Qué hacen las dos morenas?
3. ¿En qué no se ha fijado Carlos?   4. ¿Por qué parece triste John?   5. ¿Qué cree mucha gente en los Estados Unidos?   6. ¿Hablan la misma lengua en todos los países de Latinoamérica?   7. ¿Qué tiene que hacer Carlos antes de que John salga?   8. ¿Qué harían los tres si Carlos tuviera coche?   9. ¿Qué se organiza cerca de allí?

⊕ B. Using the dialogue as a model, make complete sentences of the following.

1. Si (yo)/tener coche/(nosotros)/ir/mañana. (*past subjunctive and conditional*)
2. (Yo)/llevarte/antes de que/(tú)/salir. (*present*)
3. Cada país/presentar/cierto/variación/manera/hablar. (*present*)
4. (Tú)/no haberse fijado en/chicos/que hablar/con/guardia. (*present perfect and present*)
5. (Yo)/sentir/(tú)/no haber podido visitar/San Juan. (*present and present perfect subjunctive*)

C. Follow the directions in Spanish and form complete Spanish sentences. Use the dialogue as a model.

1. Dígale a su amigo que Ud. está triste porque tiene que volver a los Estados Unidos.
2. Dígale que le encanta México pero que le gustaría ver otros países.
3. Pregúntele si se ha fijado en las dos morenas que compran helado.
4. Pregúntele si su padre ya habrá estado en San Juan.
5. Dígale que Ud. tiene que hablarle antes de que salga de México.

REPASO (16-20)

⊕ A. Using the dialogue of Lesson Sixteen, write a short narration describing a revolution in a neighboring country. Include, but do not limit your narration to, the following.

1. A week ago the army took over the government and formed a junta.
2. Last night the other generals of the junta put the leader in jail. 3. Now there is no stability in the country. They still have some serious problems.

B. Answer the questions in Spanish.

1. Si tuvieras coche, ¿a dónde irías? 2. ¿Le gustan las camisas de mangas largas? 3. ¿Habrá fiesta en clase mañana? 4. ¿Se quitaría Ud. el sombrero antes de entrar en la clase? 5. ¿En qué cuarto se prepara la comida?
6. ¿Cuál es la capital de España? 7. ¿Te has quejado mucho de tus notas este año?

C. Study the following responses thoroughly. After hearing the cue on the tape, choose the response which best completes the sentence.

1. llover, llueve, llueva, vaya
2. tanto dinero como yo, tan dinero como yo, más dinero como yo, tanto dinero
3. para el profesor, por el profesor, del profesor, se cerró
4. lleno, salida, salido, salió
5. hablarás, hablé, hablaré, vengo
6. el tío, limpio, la mano, el pelo
7. compro un coche, compraría un coche, compraré un coche, sin embargo
8. será la una, serán la una, está la una, será las una
9. lavar sus manos, lavarse las manos, cortarse el pelo, lavarme las manos
10. me quedé bien, te quedas bien, te quejas bien, te queda bien

D. This dictation is taken from the dialogue of Lesson Seventeen. Write the Spanish without referring to your books, and then check what you have written against the dialogue.

E. Read the sentence just as it is written; then change it to each of the following tenses: imperfect, preterite, future, conditional, present perfect, and past perfect.

1. Vengo a clase a las ocho de la mañana. 2. Es un hombre muy simpático.
3. Me lavo la cara todos los días. 4. Ellos se quejan de todo. 5. Lo hacemos para que vean la verdad.

⊕ F. Translate.

1. Paco is taller than John, but he is not the tallest in the family.
2. I put on my hat and left, but I left my overcoat.
3. They told him that we had not studied.
4. I am supposed to be there at 8:00, but I must clean my room first.
5. I wonder who that girl is. It's probably Mary.
6. There were 550 trees in the park on June 1, 1934.
7. John's head hurt; he was bored.
8. When she comes, I'll tell her.
9. She waited until her friends arrived.
10. They said that they would try the soup.
11. The door is open; it was opened by the teacher.
12. The stores open at 8:00 and close at 5:30.

Recommended Readings from Appendix

Del Loor de España and *Poesías.*

COLOMBIA AND ARGENTINA

Private home in Guatavita,
a new planned town in Colombia.

San Agustín Park,
in the Huila Province of Colombia.

Plaza de Bolívar in Bogotá.

In many dry areas, deep-water wells are the only means of irrigation.

Hotel El Monasterio in Popayán.

View of Cartagena.

View of Buenos Aires. More than eight million people live in Argentina's capital.

One of the main squares in Buenos Aires.

Livestock on the Argentine pampa near Buenos Aires.

Artisan hand-tooling leather.

View of Mt. Acongagua, highest mountain in the Argentine Andes.

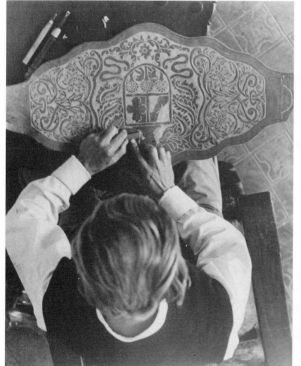

APPENDIXES:
Reading
Selections

The eight reading selections that follow are keyed to the text and graded for grammatical difficulty. They may be introduced according to the following schedule:

La Ciudad de México Se Hunde

Mexico City Is Sinking

La **ciudad** de México es una de las metrópolis más **altas** del mundo, y con una **población** de casi siete millones de habitantes, es también una de las ciudades de más rápido **crecimiento.** Pero la gran metrópoli tiene un problema **único entre** las ciudades de este hemisferio y del **mundo,** el problema de su progresivo **hundimiento.** Son muy **conocidos** los hundimientos del **suelo causados** por la extracción de **carbón** o de **petróleo,** pero la capital de México es el único **ejemplo** de hundimiento **producido** por extracción de **agua.** La explicación del fenómeno es que la ciudad está **situada** sobre un **lago** subterráneo, y con su crecimiento rápido es necesario **extraer** más agua para la industria y para los **habitantes** nuevos. **Como** consecuencia de la extracción continua de agua, la ciudad se hunde más **cada** año, y ahora muchos de los **edificios** y monumentos de importancia histórica están **hundidos hasta** tres **metros** o más.

Para resolver **este** problema de gran importancia para los mexicanos, hay planes muy ambiciosos, pero la solución va a ser muy difícil y también muy **costosa.**

city
high • population

growth
unique • among
world
sinking • known
earth • caused • coal
oil • example
produced • water
located
lake
to extract
inhabitants • as

each • buildings
sunken • up to
meters (39.3 *inches*)

this

expensive

Stalin y el Oro de España

Stalin and the Gold of Spain

(*El relato de uno de los mayores atracos de la historia*.) — story • biggest • robberies

En 1936 España pasa **por** la terrible crisis de una **guerra** civil **entre** los **partidarios** de la República (los republicanos) y los nacionalistas de Franco. No es una guerra en que una región geográfica de la nación **lucha contra otra, sino** una guerra ideológica en que a veces los hijos de la misma familia luchan en diferentes facciones, una guerra con la mala reputación de ser el combate **más** brutal de la historia moderna. En este momento trágico para España, la Unión Soviética **ayuda** a los republicanos mientras **Alemania** ayuda a los nacionalistas. Los republicanos, que **creen** que las reservas de oro del país van a caer en **manos** de Franco y los nacionalistas, deciden **confiar** el **tesoro** "para su **mayor seguridad**" a José Stalin, y tres meses después del **comienzo** de la guerra uno de los **altos** funcionarios soviéticos en España recibe un telegrama de Stalin que lee **así:** "Prepare con el **jefe** del **gobierno** republicano el **envío** de las reservas de oro de España a la Unión Soviética."

(glosses: through • war • between • followers • fights • against • another • but • most • helps • Germany • believe • hands • entrust • treasure • greater • safety • beginning • high, senior • as follows • chief • government • shipment)

Durante tres noches **desde** las siete de la tarde a las diez de la mañana, una caravana de **camiones** transporta 7800 **cajas** de oro español con un **valor** de 600 millones de dólares a unos **barcos** soviéticos que esperan en el **sur** del país, y los barcos **llevan** el fabuloso tesoro a la Unión Soviética para su "custodia" en Moscú.

(glosses: during • from • trucks • boxes • value • ships • south • carry, take)

Pasan los años y Rusia **todavía guarda** el oro español. Insiste que el oro es una garantía por el **pago** de las **armas** y otro material **enviados** a la República española durante la guerra civil. Insiste también que además del valor del oro que guarda la Unión Soviética, que los españoles **deben** otros 50 millones de dólares.

(glosses: still • keeps, holds • payment • arms • shipped • owe)

Este atraco representa un **desastre** para España y los comienzos de un **largo** período de **pobreza** y **sufrimiento.**

(glosses: disaster • long • poverty • suffering)

Bosquejo de México

Sketch of Mexico

México es uno de los países más grandes y más progresivos de Latinoamérica, pero es también un país de muchos contrastes raciales y geográficos. Tiene **más de cuarenta y cinco** millones de **habitantes** y su territorio **equivale** a **la cuarta parte** del territorio de los Estados Unidos. En el norte hay un gran **semidesierto** y no hay mucha **gente** en esa parte del país. En las montañas del centro el **clima depende de** la elevación, pero en muchos **lugares** hace frío, **sobre todo** por la

(glosses: more than forty-five • inhabitants • is equal • one fourth • semidesert • people • climate • depends on • places • especially)

noche. En las **costas** y en Yucatán el **clima** es tropical y hay muchas **selvas.**

coasts • climate
jungles

La capital, la ciudad de México, es una ciudad grande y moderna con más de siete millones de habitantes. Hay **avenidas,** parques hermosos, y muchos **edificios** altos y modernos que dan a la ciudad un **ambiente agradable** y cosmopolitano. La ciudad de México se llama el París del Nuevo Mundo y es verdad que es una de las ciudades más hermosas del mundo. **Los domingos** muchas familias traen su comida al famoso parque de Chapultepec para pasar el día **al aire libre, jugar** al fútbol, y visitar al **zoológico.** Cerca del parque está el nuevo **Museo** de Antropología donde **se ve** toda la historia de los **indios** de México, sus **costumbres,** su religión y otros aspectos de su civilización. Los mexicanos de hoy no olvidan su historia y tienen mucho **interés** y **orgullo** en las grandes civilizaciones **indígenas** del país. También en la ciudad está la Universidad Nacional de México que es de una arquitectura muy moderna y en muchos de los edificios hay **pinturas murales** de famosos artistas mexicanos. El **edificio** más **impresionante** es la biblioteca donde se ve toda la historia del país.

avenues • buildings
atmosphere
pleasant

On Sundays

in the open air • to play • zoo
museum
one sees • Indians
customs

interest • pride
native

mural paintings
building • impressive

Otras ciudades importantes de México son Guadalajara, Monterrey, y Acapulco. Guadalajara es la **segunda** ciudad del país y está al norte de la capital. Monterrey, la **tercera** ciudad en **población,** está en el norte y es una ciudad industrial. Acapulco es famoso por sus **playas** y hoteles que **atraen** muchos turistas de los **Estados Unidos** y de otros países del mundo.

second

third • population

beaches • attract
United States

La **mayoría** de la población de Mexico son **indios** y **mestizos.** Más del treinta **por ciento** son indios puros que **generalmente** son **pobres** y viven en el campo. Algunos todavía hablan las **lenguas antiguas en vez del** español, pero **hoy día** muchos vienen a las ciudades grandes para buscar trabajo, **causando** grandes problemas para la economía.

majority • Indians • of mixed
Indian and European blood • percent
generally • poor
languages • ancient • instead
of • today
causing

En México hay muchas **ruinas** de antiguas civilizaciones y muchos turistas las visitan **cada** año. La antigua capital de los **aztecas,** Tenochtitlán, es ahora la ciudad de Mexico y cada día **se encuentran** más ruinas de la civilización azteca. **Por ejemplo,** cuando **construyeron** el **Metro** para la ciudad, encontraron una gran **cantidad** de artefactos de la antigua capital. Al norte de la capital están las ruinas de Teotihuacán con sus **pirámides** del sol y de la **luna** que son más grandes que las pirámides de **Egipto.** En el sur hay ruinas y antiguas ciudades de los **mayas,** otro grupo de indios con una civilización muy **avanzada.**

ruins
each
Aztecs
are found
for example
they built • subway
quantity

pyramids • moon
Egypt
Mayans
advanced

En la historia moderna de México, el país **sufrió** dos **guerras** muy importantes que **debemos** mencionar. La **primera** fue la guerra **contra** los Estados Unidos

suffered
wars • we ought
first • against

cuando México perdió casi **la mitad** de su territorio nacional. **Antes de** 1848 (mil ochocientos cuarenta y ocho), **fecha** del **Tratado** de Guadalupe Hidalgo **entre** México y los Estados Unidos, los estados de California, Tejas, Arizona, Nuevo México y partes de Colorado, Utah, y Nevada **formaron** parte de la república de México, pero en esta **época había** muchos problemas económicos y políticos en México, el **resultado** de una **serie** de malos **gobiernos** y mucha corrupción. Además, en los años antes de la guerra muchos **norteamericanos vinieron** a estos territorios, **sobre todo** a Tejas y California y **querían** ser independientes de los problemas de México. **Los de** Tejas comenzaron la guerra y **ganaron** su independencia en 1845 (mil ochocientos cuarenta y cinco). Después, los Estados Unidos, **bajo** la influencia de la doctrina de "Manifest Destiny" **decidieron** hacer la guerra contra México para **obtener** el resto del territorio. **A pesar de** esta guerra, México y los Estados Unidos **hoy día** tienen buenas relaciones políticas y económicas.

half
before
date • treaty • between

formed
period • there were
result
series • governments
citizens of the U.S.A.
came • especially
wanted
the people from
won
under

decided • to obtain
in spite of
today

Le segunda guerra de gran importancia para México fue su revolución que **ocurrió** entre los años de 1910–1917 (mil novecientos diez hasta mil novecientos diecisiete). **Murieron** muchos mexicanos en esta guerra contra la **dictadura** de Porfirio Díaz, uno de los más famosos dictadores de Latinoamérica. Los revolucionarios ganaron la guerra y **como resultado,** el gobierno del país **cambió** radicalmente. Si México es un país moderno y progresivo hoy es **a causa de** la revolución de 1910 (mil novecientos diez). Pancho Villa del norte del país y Emiliano Zapata del sur son dos de los héroes más importantes de esta guerra.

occurred

died
dictatorship

as a result
changed
because of

México hoy día es una nación que **conserva** su **pasado** en las tradiciones indias y españolas, pero también entra en la **edad** moderna. Hay industrias **de toda clase** y el **nivel** de vida en las ciudades es muy alto. El país tiene muchos problemas que no encontramos aquí en los Estados Unidos pero cada día el progreso es más evidente.

conserves • past

age • of all kinds
standard

Observaciones sobre Latinoamérica

Muchas personas, al pensar en Latinoamérica, creen que hay **poca** diferencia **entre** los muchos países de esta parte del mundo. Creen que estos países son **más o menos parecidos,** y que tienen las mismas aspiraciones y los mismos problemas políticos y económicos. Pero como vamos a ver, hay grandes diferencias **dentro de** esta región y es difícil hablar de esta parte del mundo con **generalidades.**

little • among

more or less similar

within
generalities

La composición racial de Latinoamérica es un buen ejemplo de la **variedad** que hay en esta región. Hay partes de Latinoamérica como México, Centroamérica y las regiones **montañosas** de Sudamérica donde el **indio** es el elemento racial predominante. En estos países casi el **noventa por ciento** de la **población** son indios puros o mestizos, es decir, de **sangre** india y europea. En otras partes de Sudamérica, **como** la Argentina, el Uruguay, y Chile, donde **no había** concentraciones de indios al llegar los españoles al Nuevo Mundo, la población es casi toda de origen **europeo.** Entre los europeos, no todos son de España y Portugal. Hay muchos italianos en la Argentina **por ejemplo,** y hay **ingleses,** irlandeses, y **alemanes** en muchos países. En partes de Centroamérica, Venezuela, Colombia, Cuba, y las **Antillas Menores** viven un gran número de negros y mulatos. **Así,** ¿qué es un latinoamericano, **por lo menos** del **punto de vista étnico? Claro** es que **depende de** qué parte del continente **se habla.**

variety

mountainous
Indian
ninety percent • population
blood

like
there weren't

European

for example
Englishmen • Germans

Lesser Antilles*
thus
at least • point of view • ethnic •
of course • it depends • one speaks

En el **clima** y la geografía de estos países también encontramos muchas diferencias. En las regiones bajas, las **islas** del **Caribe** y la costa de muchos países, el clima es tropical y esto **influye** mucho en la economía y la agricultura. Hay grandes **desiertos** en el norte de Chile pero en el sur de este país llueve casi todos los días. En las regiones montañosas, El Perú, Eucador, Colombia, México, y otros, el clima **depende de** la elevación. Las montañas hacen muy difíciles la comunicación y la construcción de **carreteras.** La agricultura en las montañas también es muy variada **a causa de** la elevación. El centro de Chile y la Argentina están **dentro de** una región **templada** y la **tierra** es muy fértil. A causa del clima y la geografía, los productos de estos países son muy diferentes; por ejemplo, la Argentina es un país famoso por su **ganado** y **trigo,** Chile y Bolivia por sus minerales, Venezuela por su petróleo, Colombia por su café, etcétera.

climate

islands • Caribbean
influences
deserts

depends on

highways
because of

within • temperate • land

cattle • wheat

Hasta en la comida hay gran variedad en Latinoamérica. La base de la comida en México es el **maíz.** **Les gusta a los mexicanos** comer **tortillas, enchiladas,** y **frijoles,** pero en el Perú no tienen esta clase de comida. Allí la base es la patata. En la Argentina comen mucha carne porque tienen mucho ganado.

corn
Mexicans like • *thin, flat corn cakes • tortilla with meat filling and chili • beans*

La religión de **la mayor parte** de los latinoamericanos es el Catolicismo, pero **aun** en la religión hay diferencias importantes. **En los últimos años** el protestantismo es muy evidente en varios países, por ejemplo, México. Muchos indios todavía **conservan** elementos de sus **antiguas** religiones o los **mezclan** con el catolicismo. En la vida política hay **gobiernos** democráticos (de muchas formas diferentes de **la nuestra**), **dictaduras,**

the majority
even
in recent years

conserve
ancient • mix
governments
ours • dictatorships

---

* Chain of islands in the eastern part of the Caribbean Sea.

gobiernos militares, y comunismo. No hay dos países **iguales respecto a** su forma de gobierno. — equal, alike • with respect to

El español **se habla** en gran parte de Latinoamérica pero hay otras **lenguas** muy importantes. Por ejemplo, el inglés se habla en las Bahamas, Jamaica, Trinidad, **Guayana*** y Belize; el portugués en el Brazil; el **holandés** en Curacao y Guayana holandesa; el **frances** en Haití y Guayana francesa. En el Perú y Bolivia muchos indios todavía hablan quechua, la lengua antigua de los Incas. Paraguay tiene dos lenguas oficiales, el español y el guaraní, y en México todavía hay personas que hablan nahuatl, la lengua antigua de los aztecas. — is spoken / languages / Dutch / French

En cuanto a los problemas económicos, los países latinoamericanos **sí tienen** algo en común. La economía de estos países no es tan variada como la nuestra y depende demasiado de uno o dos productos. En el caso de Bolivia, por ejemplo, donde la riqueza principal es el **estaño,** cuando el **precio** de este mineral baja en el mercado **mundial,** muchas veces hay una crisis económica que **conduce** a grandes problemas políticos en el gobierno del país. Y podemos hacer la misma observación de Venezuela y el petróleo, de Chile y el **cobre,** etcétera. — do have / tin • price / world (*adj.*) / leads / copper

Otro problema en Latinoamérica es que en muchos países una pequeña parte de la población (más o menos el 5%) tiene la **mayor** parte de la tierra. Las **riquezas** de algunos países están en **manos** de unas pocas familias importantes, **mientras** la mayor parte de los **habitantes** de estos países viven con muy poco dinero. Algunas naciones, como México y Costa Rica, **ya no sufren** de este problema **tanto como** en el **pasado,** pero en muchos países es todavía uno de los grandes problemas de hoy. — greatest / wealth • hands / while / inhabitants / no longer suffer • as much as / past

Así vemos que Latinoamérica es una región de una **enorme** riqueza cultural. Al visitar esta parte del mundo, vemos que **cada** país nos **presenta** algo diferente, algo nuevo, algo **sorprendente.** Es un mundo de una **variedad** casi infinita. — enormous / each • presents / surprising / variety

* Independent country, formerly British Guiana.

Las Culturas Antiguas

The Ancient Cultures

Muchas veces pensamos que la historia del Nuevo Mundo comienza con la **llegada** de **Cristóbal Colón** en mil cuatrocientos noventa y dos (1492), pero **nos equivocamos** sin **duda pensando** solamente en la cultura **occidental.** La historia del Nuevo Mundo comienza más de veinte **mil** años **antes de** la llegada de los conquistadores cuando los primeros hom- — arrival • Christopher Columbus / we are / mistaken • doubt • thinking / western / thousand • before

222

bres llegaron de Asia **pasando sobre lo que** hoy es el **estrecho** de Bering, y durante miles de años de migración **poblaban poco a poco** al Nuevo Mundo desde Alaska a la **Tierra del Fuego.*** **Claro es** que estos primeros habitantes no eran civilizados, **sino** que eran tribus **nómadas** que siempre **vagaban** de un **lugar** a otro **en busca de** comida. La civilización vino mucho más tarde con el **descubrimiento** del **maíz.** Con este descubrimiento las **tribus** podían **dejar de viajar** continuamente y concentrarse en pueblos, **dedicándose** a la **agricultura.** La importancia de la agricultura hizo necesaria la construcción de ciudades y mercados, el estudio de la **naturaleza** y de las estaciones del año, una religión para **explicar** el **orden** de las cosas, y una **arquitectura** para la construcción de **edificios.** El descubrimiento del maíz era la base y la civilización **floreció** en muchas partes.

> passing • over • what
> strait
> populated • little by little
> it is clear
> but
> nomadic • wandered • place
> in search of
> discovery • corn
> tribes • stop traveling
> dedicating themselves •
> agriculture
>
> nature
>
> explain • order
> architecture • buildings
>
> flourished

No **sería** posible **describir** todas las civilizaciones del Nuevo Mundo porque hay muchas y todavía hay mucho que no sabemos de ellas, pero **entre** todas estas civilizaciones hay tres que **se destacan** por su importancia **tanto** hoy día **como** en la historia. Son la civilización de los **aztecas,** los **mayas,** y los **incas.**

> would be • to describe
>
> among
> stand out
> as much • as
> Aztecs • Mayans • Incas

El centro de la cultura azteca estaba **situado** donde hoy día se encuentra la ciudad de México. Hernán Cortés, un conquistador español, **conquistó** a los aztecas en mil quinientos veintiuno, (1521), y él y sus capitanes nos han dado una descripción de su cultura. Tenían una gran ciudad en **medio** de un lago y **habían** conquistado a casi todas las tribus del centro de México. Los aztecas eran muy **avanzados** en la agricultura, las **ciencias,** la arquitectura, y el arte. **Observando** las **estrellas, habían elaborado** un calendario muy exacto, y **construyeron edificios** y templos que **decoraron** con **pinturas** y **esculturas** muy complicadas. Tenían un alfabeto **jeroglífico** y un buen sistema de **números.** Pero **a pesar de** su cultura avanzada, parece que los aztecas **no inventaron** estas cosas **sino que** adaptaron los **conocimientos** de otras civilizaciones a sus necesidades. **Hasta** su religión era una **mezcla** de las religiones de otras civilizaciones. Cuando los aztecas vinieron al **valle** de México, ya **había** otras tribus más avanzadas allí y tuvieron que pedirles **permiso** a estas tribus para quedarse allí. Pero eran una gente **guerrera** y poco a poco conquistaban a las otras tribus, **utilizando** sus **conocimientos** y cultura. **Desafortunadamente, la mayor parte** de su capital fue **destruída** por los españoles, pero ya queda bastante de su civilización para **recrearla** en **detalle.** Su símbolo era una **águila encima de** un **nogal devorando** una **serpiente** y este símbolo forma parte de la **bandera** de México hoy día.

> situated, located
>
> conquered
>
> middle
> had
> advanced
> sciences
> observing • stars • they had
> constructed • buildings
> they decorated • paintings •
> sculptures • hieroglyphic
> numbers • in spite of
> did not invent • but
> knowledge
> even • mixture
>
> valley • there were
>
> permission
> warlike˙
> using • knowledge
> unfortunately • the majority
> destroyed
> recreate it • detail
> eagle • on top of • *type of cactus* •
> devouring • serpent • flag

* Island at southern tip of South America.

La **segunda** cultura de que vamos a hablar es la de los mayas. Su civilización empezó en lo que hoy es Guatemala y más tarde **se trasladó** a Yucatán. Hay ruinas de muchas de sus ciudades en todo este territorio, por ejemplo, Bonampak, Palenque, Uxmal, Chichén-Itzá; y muchas de estas ruinas no fueron **descubiertas** hasta este **siglo.** No se sabe mucho del origen de los mayas **ni** por qué dejaron sus ciudades en ruinas porque al llegar los españoles, la civilización estaba en decadencia y las ciudades abandonadas. Lo que sí sabemos es que eran magníficos arquitectos, **ingenieros,** artistas, **escultores, matemáticos, y astrónomos.**

second

moved

discovered • century
nor

engineers • sculptors •
mathematicians • astronomers

La civilización de los incas en el Perú no comenzó hasta cerca de 1000 AD, pero **llegó a ser** el **imperio** más grande y mejor organizado del Nuevo Mundo. Su imperio **incluía** los países del Perú, Ecuador, Bolivia, y partes de la Argentina y Chile. Generalmente **nos referimos a** estos indios como los incas, pero este **nombre** no es correcto en realidad. Los indios de esta región se llamaban quechuas y todavía hablan la lengua quechua. **Sin embargo** la historia de esta gente cuenta que Dios, el sol, vio la miseria y la **pobreza** del hombre y **decidió mandar** a sus hijos al mundo.

it became • empire

included

we refer to
name

nevertheless
poverty
decided • to send

Se llamaban Manco Capac y su hermana Mama Ocllo, los primeros Incas. Ellos fundaron su capital en la ciudad de Cuzco y la **palabra** "Inca" **se refería** solamente al **rey** y su familia. El Inca era todo **poderoso** porque era hijo del Sol, el dios de los incas, y la mejor manera de **describir** su **gobierno** es decir que era una **teocracia** comunista. Todo **pertenecía** al Inca y las **cosechas se dividían según** las necesidades de los pueblos del imperio. Los incas construyeron edificios monumentales, tenían un magnífico sistema de **carreteras** y comunicaciones y un gobierno **estable** y organizado. Cuando Francisco Pizarro llegó al Perú, los incas **acababan de pasar por** una **guerra** civil entre dos hijos del Inca que **se disputaban** el **poder.** Esta guerra y la **suerte** de Pizarro en hacer prisionero al rey hizo más fácil la **conquista** de los incas. Hoy las ruinas mejor preservadas son las de Macchu Picchu, una **fortaleza** en los Andes que fue abandonada por los incas y no fue descubierta hasta este **siglo.**

word • referred to
king • powerful

describe • government
theocracy • belonged
crops were divided
according to
highways
stable

had just gone through • war
fought over • power
luck
conquest

fortress
century

Bosquejo de España

Outline of Spain

En una **conferencia** sobre España un hombre **distinguido** de ese país **se refirió** accidentalmente a "Las Españas". En cierta manera tenía razón porque lo que llamamos España **se compone de** regiones muy **dis-**

lecture • distinguished
referred

is composed of • different

tintas en cuanto a la historia, costumbres, dialectos, y maneras de vivir. Para tener **por lo menos** una idea de lo que es España vamos a examinar las varias regiones y los elementos modernos que mejor **caracterizan** al país.

> as far as
> at least
> characterize

Empecemos nuestro viaje por España en el norte, en los **Pirineos** donde vemos montañas muy altas, **valles** fértiles y en los valles, pueblos pequeños, **limpios,** y **pintorescos.** Muchos turistas vienen a esta región para practicar el **esquí, sobre todo** cerca de ciudades como Huesca. Al este encontramos el Mediterráneo y la Costa Brava que es hoy una nueva Riviera española. La ciudad de Barcelona está cerca y es la primera ciudad industrial de España. **Situada** en la provincia de Cataluña, todavía conserva su propia lengua, el catalán, **junto con** el español.

> Pyrenees • valleys
> clean
> picturesque
> skiing • above all
>
> located
>
> together with

Al oeste de los Pirineos, en la costa del Atlántico y en la **frontera** entre España y Francia, están las Provincias **Vascongadas.** Aquí la gente tiene fama de ser muy **trabajadora** y **ha contribuído** mucho a la cultura y economía del país. Aquí se hablan español y **vascüence,** una lengua muy antigua de la que no se sabe mucho. Los orígenes de esta gente se han perdido en la historia pero hay una **leyenda** que dice que el **diablo** fue a las Provincias Vascongadas y quería aprender la lengua para poder **tentar** a la gente. La lengua era tan difícil que después de siete años no lo **había aprendido** y tuvo que salir. ¡**Por eso** dicen que los **vascos** son tan buenos! Siempre han tenido un **fuerte sentido** de independencia y varias veces **han tratado de separarse** de España para formar su propio país.

> boundary
> Basque (*adj.*)
> hard working • have contributed
> *Basque language*
>
> legend • devil
>
> tempt
> had learned
> therefore • Basques
> strong sense
> have tried to separate

Más al oeste encontramos la región **montañosa** de Asturias y Galicia. Aquí llueve mucho y hay muchos **bosques** y valles fértiles. La gente es de origen céltico y conserva **bailes e** instrumentos **parecidos** a los de **Escocia.** El centro del país, Castilla, es una **meseta** alta donde llueve poco. Es el **corazón** de España con la capital, Madrid, y otras ciudades importantes como Toledo y Burgos. Aquí hay mucho **trigo** y otros cereales y parece que cada pueblo tiene su **castillo.** Muchos de estos están en ruinas hoy día, pero el **gobierno** está haciendo **esfuerzos** para **preservarlos** y **ha convertido** varios de los castillos **antiguos** en hoteles modernos, siempre **conservando** el **ambiente** medieval. En toda esta región del norte vemos personas de **ojos azules** y **pelo rubio;** es decir, de origen europeo.

> mountainous
>
> forests
> dances and • similar
> Scotland • high plain
> heart
>
> wheat
> castle
> government
> efforts • preserve them • has
> converted • ancient
> conserving • atmosphere
> blue eyes
> blond hair

Viajando de Madrid al sureste llegamos a Valencia que se llama "la **huerta** de España" porque es una región muy rica en productos **agrícolas** como **naranjas, arroz,** y legumbres de toda clase. La gente tiene sus propias costumbres, una comida típica, y un dialecto diferente aunque todos hablan español. En el sur del

> traveling
> orchard
> agricultural • oranges
> rice

país, en Andalucía, encontramos una de las regiones más interesantes de España. Cuando pensamos en un español "típico", generalmente pensamos en el español de Andalucía porque es **moreno**, de ojos **negros**, y su dialecto es parecido al que se habla en Latinoamérica. También aquí es donde tiene sus orígines el **flamenco**, el **baile** típico de los **gitanos**. En las regiones **costeras** de Andalucía el **clima** es muy **agradable** y muchos turistas de otras partes de Europa pasan el invierno aquí. Las ciudades mas importantes son Sevilla, Córdoba, Granada, y Cádiz. Extremadura, al norte y **junto a** Portugal, es la región más **pobre** de España porque es muy árido. **Sin embargo,** muchos de los primeros conquistadores y exploradores del Nuevo Mundo vinieron de esta región.

brunette, dark • black

gypsy dance • dance • gypsies
coastal • climate • pleasant

next to • poor
nevertheless

Así vemos que en **realidad** parece que hay varias "Españas," cosa que **añade** mucho al interés y la atracción de vivir o **viajar** en España.

reality
adds
travel

La historia moderna de España empezó con la **guerra** civil en mil novecientos treinta y seis (1936). El **ejército** del general Francisco Franco, ayudado por los **alemanes,** **luchó contra** el ejército de los llamados "republicanos," ayudados por los **rusos.** La guerra **duró** tres años y Francisco Franco **llegó por fin a ser** el dictador de un país **débil** y casi **destruido.** Sin embargo, en los años después de la guerra, España **ha progresado** mucho hasta que hoy día, **disfruta de** un **nivel** de vida bastante alto, y la economía se hace más **estable** cada año. Franco **ha prometido convertir** el país en una monarquía constitucional y **ha nombrado** al **príncipe** Juan Carlos como el **próximo rey** de España.

war
army
Germans
fought against
Russians • lasted
finally became
weak • destroyed
has progressed
enjoys • standard
stable
has promised to convert
has named • prince
next king

No se puede terminar una descripción de España sin mencionar Madrid, que además de ser la capital política del país, es también la capital cultural. Es una ciudad de unos tres **millones** de habitantes que en cierto modo conserva el ambiente de un pueblo por sus muchos **barrios** diferentes. En el centro hay muchos teatros y el museo de arte, el Prado, que es uno de los más grandes y famosos de Europa. Situada en las **afueras** de Madrid, la ciudad universitaria es **grandísima** y moderna. **En cuanto a** las diversiones, parece que lo que les gusta más a los **madrileños** es sentirse **libres** para caminar, sentarse **al aire libre** en un café, o charlar con amigos. La vida de la ciudad es **acelerada** pero siempre hay tiempo para **descansar** con amigos.

millions

districts, neighborhoods

outskirts
extremely large• as for
person from Madrid
free • in the open air

fast • rest

Así, ¿cuál es correcto, España o las Españas? De todas maneras, como dicen **los mismos españoles,** "España es diferente."

thus
the Spanish themselves

Del Loor de España

La *primera crónica general de España** es una historia escrita en el **siglo** trece. Se escribió **bajo** la dirección de Alfonso X, el **Sabio,** un **rey** de España que había **contribuido** mucho al **desarrollo** de la cultura y la **sabiduría** del país. Antes de leer la selección, sería interesante saber algo del **fondo** histórico.

> century • under
> wise • king
> contributed • development
> knowledge, wisdom
> background

Después de la caída del Imperio Romano**, España, como todas las provincias romanas, fue **invadida** por varias **tribus visigóticas** que **reinaban** en el país durante varios siglos. En el año de setecientos once, los **moros** del norte de Africa **invadieron** España y en muy pocos años **se apoderaron de** casi todo el país. Esta presencia de los moros duró casi ochocientos años, y durante estos años los cristianos de España participaban en una **lucha** épica para **expulsar** a los moros del país. La lucha era larga y difícil pero en el año de mil cuatrocientos noventa y dos los ejércitos combinados de Fernando e Isabel por fin **vencieron** la última de las **fortalezas** de los moros en España. El **autor** de esta selección escribe de la primera invasión de los moros y cómo vencieron a los **poderosos** reyes **góticos.** En este momento decide hacer una descripción de cómo era su país en aquel tiempo. Es una descripción llena de emoción, patriotismo, y **tristeza. Debe recordarse** que la selección fue escrita durante la **época** de las **guerras contra** los moros, y aunque los españoles habían ganado muchas **batallas,** todavía no habían **vencido** a los moros. La selección es una adaptación del original.

> invaded
> Visigothic tribes • ruled
> Moors • invaded
> took over
> struggle • to expel, drive out
> conquered
> fortresses
> author
> powerful
> Gothic
> sadness
> It should be remembered
> epoch • wars against
> battles
> conquered

Después que el rey Rodrigo† y los cristianos fueron vencidos, todos los **godos,** una gente muy noble, que había ganado muchas batallas en todas partes, fueron vencidos también.

> Goths

Todos deben por eso aprender que no es bueno **alabarse;** ni el rico por su **riqueza,** ni el poderoso por su **poder,** ni el fuerte por su fortaleza, ni el sabio por su sabiduría. Pero si alguién quiere alabarse, que se alabe en su servicio a Dios porque Dios puede **herir** y puede **curar;** puede **destruir** y puede **crear.** Todos los pueblos, la gente, las lenguas, y los países cambian, pero Dios siempre queda igual.

> to praise oneself • wealth
> power
> wound
> cure • destroy • create

Dios ha dado honores y riquezas a todos los países del mundo en varias formas; pero de todos los países, dio más a España que a los otros porque dio a este

---

* La primera crónica general de España   The first general chronicle of Spain, the name Alfonso gave to his history of Spain.
** La caída del Imperio Romano   the fall of the Roman Empire (about 400 AD).
† Rodrigo   the greatest of the Gothic kings.

país en abundancia todo lo que puede querer un hombre. Los godos habían viajado por todas partes de Europa y de Asia y habían vivido en muchos países, pero después de mirar bien a todas estas tierras encontraron que España era el mejor de todos. Ellos querían más a España porque entre todos los otros países, España tenía más riquezas, **fertilidad,** y abundancia.

fertility

Esta España de que hablamos es como el **paraíso** de Dios porque tiene cinco ríos grandes que son el Ebro, el Duero, el Tajo, el Guadalquivir, y el Guadiana. Entre los ríos hay montañas y **valles,** y los **llanos** son grandes y **anchos.** Por la fertilidad de la tierra y la abundancia de agua, el país tiene muchas frutas y otras cosas buenas. Hay de todo, frutas de toda clase, pescado del **mar,** mucha leche y todas las cosas que se hacen de ella. Está lleno de **venados** y **caza,** cubierta de **ganados, caballos,** y **mulas.** Es **seguro** por sus castillos, **alegre** por sus buenos **vinos, satisfecho** por su pan, rica de metales de todas clases, **estaño, hierro, plata, oro, piedras preciosas, sales** de mar y muchos minerales más. También hay **seda, miel, azúcar,** y todas las cosas finas que necesita el hombre para vivir contento.

paradise

valleys • plains
broad

sea
deer • game • cattle
horses • mules • safe • happy
wines • satisfied
tin • iron • silver • gold
precious stones • salts
silk • honey • sugar

Además este país, España, es muy bravo en la batalla, con **soldados** muy buenos. Es **leal** a sus señores, dedicado al estudio, **cortés** en palabra, y correcto en todo **bien.** No hay tierra en todo el mundo que sea su igual en abundancia, **ni** en la **cantidad** de fortalezas; y hay pocos en el mundo tan grandes como ella. ¡Ay, España! ¡No hay lengua en el mundo ni persona sabia que pueda contar su bien!

soldiers • loyal
courteous
good things
nor • quantity

Pues, este país tan noble, tan rico, tan poderoso, tan honrado, fue invadido y vencido. Por la **cobardía** de unos pocos, todos perdieron porque todas la ciudades de España fueron vencidas por los moros y **destruídas** por las manos de sus **enemigos.**

cowardice

destroyed
enemies

Después de la batalla todos estaban **muertos** y toda la tierra quedaba **vacía** de gente, llena de **sangre, bañada de lágrimas.** ¡Pobre España! Tanta fue la **muerte** que **sufrió,** y no había nadie que **llorara** su suerte porque los que antes estaban libres ya eran **esclavos,** los que antes eran señores ya tenían que trabajar para ganarse la vida, los que antes tenían ropa fina ya no tenían con que vestirse, y los bravos soldados todos murieron en la batalla. Y con esto murió también la **enseñanza** de la **ley** y de la **santa fe** cristiana.

dead
empty • blood
bathed in tears
death • suffered • cried

slaves

teaching • law • holy
faith

Anonymous *España*

Romance del Prisionero

Ballad of the Prisoner

Que por mayo era, por mayo,	For it was in the month of May
cuando hace la calor,	
cuando los **trigos encañan**	wheat forms stalks
y están los **campos** en **flor,**	fields • flower
cuando canta la **calandria**	lark
y responde el **ruiseñor,**	nightingale
cuando los **enamorados**	lovers
van a servir al **amor;**	love
sino yo, triste, **cuitado,**	except • wretched, afflicted
que vivo en esta prisión,	
que ni sé cuándo es de día	
ni cuándo las noches son,	
sino por una **avecilla**	little bird
que me cantaba al **albor.**	dawn
Matómela un **ballestero;**	*me la mató (archaic)* • crossbowman
déle Dios mal **galardón.**	reward

Luis de Góngora y Argote
(1561–1627) *España*

Romancillo

a popular type of verse

La más **bella** niña	beautiful
de nuestro **lugar,**	village
hoy **viuda** y sola	widowed
y ayer **por casar,**	not yet married
viendo que **sus ojos**	"her eyes," *i.e., her loved one*
a la **guerra** van,	war
a su madre dice	
que escucha su **mal:**	complaint, sorrow
dejadme llorar	let me cry
orillas del mar.	at the shore of the sea
Pues **me distes,** madre,	you gave me *(in marriage)*
en tan **tierna edad,**	tender age
tan corto el **placer,**	pleasure
tan **largo** el **penar,**	long • suffering
y **me cautivastes:**	you made me the captive
de **quien** hoy se va	him who
y lleva las **llaves**	keys
de mi libertad,	
dejadme llorar	
orillas del mar.	

En llorar conviertan
mis ojos, de hoy más,
el sabroso oficio
del dulce mirar,
pues que no se pueden
mejor ocupar,
yéndose a la guerra
quien era mi **paz.**
   Dejadme llorar
   orillas del mar.

May my eyes henceforth
convert the pleasant task
of sweet glances into tears

having gone
peace

No me pongáis freno
ni queráis culpar;
que lo uno es justo,
lo otro por demás.
Si me **queréis** bien,
no me hagáis mal,
harto peor **fue**
morir y **callar.**
   Dejadme llorar
   orillas del mar.

Don't stop me (from crying)
nor try to blame
for one (crying) is just
the other (blaming me) not wanted, too much
love, wish
don't do me wrong
much • *fue = sería*
keep silent

Dulce madre mía,
quién no llorará,
aunque tenga el **pecho**
como un **pedernal,**
y **no dará voces**
viendo **marchitar**
los más **verdes** años
de mi **mocedad?**
   Dejadme llorar
   orillas del mar.

sweet

breast
flint
would not cry out
wither
green
youth

Váyanse las noches,
pues ido se han
los **ojos que hacían**
los míos velar;
váyanse, y no vean
tanta **soledad**
después que en mi **lecho**
sobra la mitad.
   Dejadme llorar
   orillas del mar.

Let the nights pass on

eyes that would not let
mine close

loneliness
since • bed
half is wasted, half is unused

Gustavo Adolfo Bécquer (1836–1870) *España*

Rima

Los **suspiros** son **aire** y van al aire.
Las **lágrimas** son agua y van al **mar.**
Dime, mujer: cuando el **amor** se olvida,
¿sabes tú adónde va?

Rhyme

sighs • air
tears • sea, ocean
love

Antonio Machado (1875–1939) *España*

Cantar

¡**Ojos** que a la luz se abrieron
un día para, despés
ciegos tornar a la tierra,
hartos de mirar sin ver!

Song, poem

eyes

blind • to turn
fed up, disgusted

José Martí (1853–1895) *Cuba*

Versos Sencillos

Yo soy un hombre sincero
de donde **crece** la **palma;**
y antes de morirme, quiero
echar mis versos del **alma.**

Yo vengo de todas partes,
y **hacia** todas partes voy:
arte soy entre las artes;
en los **montes,** monte soy.

Temblé una vez—en la **reja,**
a la **entrada** de la **viña—,**
cuando la **bárbara abeja**
picó en la **frente** a mi niña.

Gocé una vez, **de tal suerte**
que gocé cual nunca: cuando
la sentencia de mi **muerte**
leyó el **alcalde** llorando.

Simple Verses

grows • palm tree

pour out • soul

toward

mountains

I trembled • *iron bars which cover a
window or form a door* • entrance •
vineyard • savage • bee
stung • forehead

I was happy • in such a way
that I have never been since
death
warden

Federico García Lorca (1898–1936) *España*

Canción de Jinete

Rider's Song

Córdoba.*
Lejana y sola.

distant

Jaca negra, luna grande,
y **aceitunas** en mi **alforja.**
Aunque sepa los **caminos**
yo nunca llegaré a Córdoba.

small black horse
olives • saddlebag
roads

Por el **llano,** por el viento,
jaca negra, luna **roja,**
la **muerte** me está mirando
desde las **torres** de Córdoba.

plain
red
death
towers

¡Ay qué camino tan largo!
¡Ay mi jaca **valerosa!**
¡Ay que la muerte me espera,
antes de llegar a Córdoba!

brave

Córdoba.
Lejana y sola.

* city in Southern Spain

Verbs

Regular Verbs (-AR)

Infinitive	Present participle	Past participle
hablar (to speak)	**hablando** (speaking)	**hablado** (spoken)

Present	*Imperfect*	*Preterite*
(I speak, do speak, am speaking)	(I was speaking, used to speak)	(I spoke)

yo **hablo**	**hablaba**	**hablé**
tú **hablas**	**hablabas**	**hablaste**
él ella } **habla** Ud.	**hablaba**	**habló**
nosotros **hablamos**	**hablábamos**	**hablamos**
vosotros **habláis**	**hablabais**	**hablasteis**
ellos } Uds. } **hablan**	**hablaban**	**hablaron**

Future	*Conditional*	*Present subjunctive*
(I shall speak)	(I would speak)	
yo **hablaré**	**hablaría**	**hable**
tú **hablarás**	**hablarías**	**hables**
él ella } **hablará** Ud.	**hablaría**	**hable**
nosotros **hablaremos**	**hablaríamos**	**hablemos**
vosotros **hablaréis**	**hablaríais**	**habléis**
ellos } Uds. } **hablarán**	**hablarían**	**hablen**

Imperfect subjunctive (**-ra**)	*Imperfect subjunctive* (**-se**)	*Affirmative imperatives*
yo **hablara**	**hablase**	*sing.* **habla**
tú **hablaras**	**hablases**	*pl.* **hablad**
él ella } **hablara** Ud.	**hablase**	
nosotros **habláramos**	**hablásemos**	*Negative imperatives*
vosotros **hablarais**	**hablaseis**	*sing.* **no hables**
ellos } Uds. } **hablaran**	**hablasen**	*pl.* **no habléis**

Regular Verbs (-ER)

Infinitive	Present participle	Past participle
comer (to eat)	comiendo (eating)	comido (ate)

Present (I eat, do eat, am eating)		Imperfect (I was eating, used to eat)	Preterite (I ate)
yo	como	comía	comí
tú	comes	comías	comiste
él ella Ud.	come	comía	comió
nosotros	comemos	comíamos	comimos
vosotros	coméis	comíais	comisteis
ellos Uds.	comen	comían	comieron

Future (I shall eat)		Conditional (I would eat)	Present subjunctive
yo	comeré	comería	coma
tú	comerás	comerías	comas
él ella Ud.	comerá	comería	coma
nosotros	comeremos	comeríamos	comamos
vosotros	comeréis	comeríais	comáis
ellos Uds.	comerán	comerían	coman

Imperfect subjunctive (-ra)		Imperfect subjunctive (-se)	Affirmative imperatives
yo	comiera	comiese	*sing.* come
tú	comieras	comieses	*pl.* comed
él ella Ud.	comiera	comiese	
nosotros	comiéramos	comiésemos	Negative imperatives
vosotros	comierais	comieseis	*sing.* no comas
ellos Uds.	comieran	comiesen	*pl.* no comáis

Regular Verbs (-IR)

Infinitive	Present participle	Past participle
vivir (to live)	viviendo (living)	vivido (lived)

Present (I live, do live, am living)		Imperfect (I was living, used to live)	Preterite (I lived)
yo	vivo	vivía	viví
tú	vives	vivías	viviste
él ella Ud.	vive	vivía	vivió
nosotros	vivimos	vivíamos	vivimos
vosotros	vivís	vivíais	vivisteis
ellos Uds.	viven	vivían	vivieron

Future		Conditional	Present subjunctive
(I shall live)		(I would live)	
yo	viviré	viviría	viva
tú	vivirás	vivirías	vivas
él ella Ud.	vivirá	viviría	viva
nosotros	viviremos	viviríamos	vivamos
vosotros	viviréis	viviríais	viváis
ellos Uds.	vivirán	vivirían	vivan

Imperfect subjunctive (-ra)		Imperfect subjunctive (-se)	Affirmative imperatives
yo	viviera	viviese	sing. vive
tú	vivieras	vivieses	pl. vivid
él ella Ud.	viviera	viviese	
nosotros	viviéramos	viviésemos	Negative imperatives
vosotros	vivierais	vivieseis	sing. no vivas
ellos Uds.	vivieran	viviesen	pl. no viváis

Compound Tenses

Present perfect
(I have spoken, eaten, lived)
he hablado, comido, vivido
has hablado
ha hablado
hemos hablado
habéis hablado
han hablado

Past perfect (*pluperfect*)
(I had spoken, eaten, lived)
había hablado, comido, vivido
habías hablado
había hablado
habíamos hablado
habíais hablado
habían hablado

Future perfect
(I shall have spoken, eaten, lived)
habré hablado, comido, vivido
habrás hablado
habrá hablado
habremos hablado
habréis hablado
habrán hablado

Conditional perfect
(I would have spoken, eaten, lived)
habría hablado, comido, vivido
habrías hablado
habría hablado
habríamos hablado
habríais hablado
habrían hablado

Present perfect subjunctive
haya hablado, comido, vivido
hayas hablado
haya hablado
hayamos hablado
hayáis hablado
hayan hablado

Past perfect subjunctive (*pluperfect subjunctive*)
hubiera (hubiese) hablado, comido, vivido
hubieras hablado
hubiera hablado
hubiéramos hablado
hubierais hablado
hubieran hablado

Stem-Changing Verbs

Some verbs ending in **-ar** and **-er** have changes in the stem vowel in the present indicative and the present subjunctive.

cerrar **(ie)** *(to close)*
Pres. ind. **cierro, cierras, cierra,** cerramos, cerráis, **cierran**
Pres. subj. **cierre, cierres, cierre,** cerremos, cerréis, **cierren**

volver **(ue)** *(to return)*
Pres. ind. **vuelvo, vuelves, vuelve,** volvemos, volvéis, **vuelven**
Pres. subj. **vuelva, vuelvas, vuelva,** volvamos, volváis, **vuelvan**

Other verbs of this type are **acordarse, acostarse, almorzar, comenzar, contar, costar, despertarse, empezar, encontrar, llover, mostrar, negar, nevar, pensar, perder, probar, recordar, rogar, sentarse.**

Some **-ir** verbs change the stem vowel in the present indicative, present subjunctive and preterite tenses.

sentir **(ie, i)** *(to feel)*
Pres. ind. **siento, sientes, siente,** sentimos, sentís, **sienten**
Pres. subj. **sienta, sientas, sienta, sintamos, sintáis, sientan**
Preterite sentí, sentiste, **sintió,** sentimos, sentisteis, **sintieron**
Pres. part. **sintiendo**

dormir **(ue, u)** *(to sleep)*
Pres. ind. **duermo, duermes, duerme,** dormimos, dormís, **duermen**
Pres. subj. **duerma, duermas, duerma, durmamos, durmáis, duerman**
Preterite dormí, dormiste, **durmió,** dormimos, dormisteis, **durmieron**
Pres. part. **durmiendo**

pedir **(i, i)** *(to ask for)*
Pres. ind. **pido, pides, pide,** pedimos, pedís, **piden**
Pres. subj. **pida, pidas, pida, pidamos, pidáis, pidan**
Preterite pedí, pediste, **pidió,** pedimos, pedisteis, **pidieron**
Pres. part. **pidiendo**

Other verbs like **sentir** and **dormir** are **divertirse, morir, preferir.**
Other verbs like **pedir** are **conseguir, despedirse, repetir, seguir,** and **vestirse.**

Spelling Changes

1. Verbs ending in **-car, -gar,** and **-zar** change *c* to **qu,** *g* to **gu,** *z* to **c** before the letter *e*.

   buscar (to look for)
   Preterite   **busqué,** buscaste, buscó, buscamos, **buscasteis,** buscaron
   Pres. subj.   **busque, busques, busque, busquemos, busquéis, busquen**

   llegar (to arive)
   Preterite   **llegué,** llegaste, llegó, llegamos, llegasteis, llegaron
   Pres. subj.   **llegue, llegues, llegue, lleguemos, lleguéis, lleguen**

   comenzar (to begin)
   Preterite   **comencé,** comenzaste, comenzó, comenzamos, comenzasteis,
                 comenzaron
   Pres. subj.   **comience, comiences, comience, comencemos, comencéis, comiencen**

Other verbs of this type are **acercarse, almorzar, empezar, equivocarse, negar, pagar, rogar, sacar, tocar.**

2. Verbs ending in **-ger, -gir, -guir** change *g* to **j,** *gu* to **g** before *o* or *a*.

   escoger (to choose)
   Pres. ind.   **escojo,** escoges, escoge, escogemos, escogéis, escogen
   Pres. subj.   **escoja, escojas, escoja, escojamos, escojáis, escojan**

   *seguir (**i, i**) (to follow)*
   Pres. ind.   **sigo,** sigues, sigue, seguimos, seguís, siguen
   Pres. subj.   **siga, sigas, siga, sigamos, sigáis, sigan**

Other verbs of this type are **coger** and **conseguir.**

3. Verbs ending in **-cer** and **-cir** change *c* to **zc** before *o* and *a*.

   conducir (to drive)
   Pres. ind.   **conduzco,** conduces, conduce, conducimos, conducís, conducen
   Pres. subj.   **conduzca, conduzcas, conduzca, conduzcamos, conduzcáis,
                 conduzcan**

Other verbs of this type are **conocer, ofrecer,** and **parecer.**

Irregular Verbs

andar (*to walk*)
Preterite   anduve, anduviste, anduvo, anduvimos, anduvisteis, anduvieron

caer (*to fall*)
Pres. ind.   caigo, caes, cae, caemos, caéis, caen
Preterite   caí, caíste, cayó, caímos, caísteis, cayeron
Pres. part.   cayendo
Past part.   caído

conducir (*to drive*)
Pres. ind.   conduzco, conduces, conduce, conducimos, conducís, conducen
Preterite   conduje, condujiste, condujo, condujimos, condujisteis, condujeron

conocer (*to know, be acquainted with*)
Pres. ind.   conozco, conoces, conoce, conocemos, conocéis, conocen

creer (*to believe*)
Preterite   creí, creíste, creyó, creímos, creísteis, creyeron
Pres. part.   creyendo
Past part.   creído

dar (*to give*)
Pres. ind.   doy, das, da, damos, dais, dan
Pres. subj.   dé, des, dé, demos, deis, den
Preterite   di, diste, dio, dimos, disteis, dieron

decir (*to say, tell*)
Pres. ind.   digo, dices, dice, decimos, decís, dicen
Preterite   dije, dijiste, dijo, dijimos, dijisteis, dijeron
Future   diré, dirás, dirá, diremos, diréis, dirán
Conditional   diría, dirías, diría, diríamos, diríais, dirían
Imperative   (fam., sing.) di
Pres. part.   diciendo
Past part.   dicho

estar (*to be*)
Pres. ind.   estoy, estás, está, estamos, estáis, están
Pres. subj.   esté, estés, esté, estemos, estéis, estén
Preterite   estuve, estuviste, estuvo, estuvimos, estuvisteis, estuvieron

hacer (*to do, make*)
Pres. ind.   hago, haces, hace, hacemos, hacéis, hacen
Preterite   hice, hiciste, hizo, hicimos, hicisteis, hicieron
Future   haré, harás, hará, haremos, haréis, harán
Conditional   haría, harías, haría, haríamos, haríais, harían
Imperative   (fam., sing.) haz
Past part.   hecho

ir (*to go*)
Pres. ind.   voy, vas, va, vamos, vais, van
Pres. subj.   vaya, vayas, vaya, vayamos, vayáis, vayan
Imperfect   iba, ibas, iba, íbamos, ibais, iban
Preterite   fui, fuiste, fue, fuimos, fuisteis, fueron
Imperative   (fam., sing.) ve
Pres. part.   yendo

leer (*to read*)
Preterite   leí, leíste, *leyó*, leímos, leísteis, *leyeron*
Pres. part.   *leyendo*
Past part.   leído

oír (*to hear*)
Pres. ind.   oigo, oyes, oye, oímos, oís, *oyen*
Preterite   oí, oíste, *oyó*, oímos, oísteis, *oyeron*
Pres. part.   *oyendo*
Past. part.   oído

poder (*to be able*)
Pres. ind.   *puedo, puedes, puede,* podemos, podéis, *pueden*
Preterite   *pude, pudiste, pudo, pudimos, pudisteis, pudieron*
Future   *podré, podrás, podrá, podremos, podréis, podrán*
Conditional *podría, podrías, podría, podríamos, podríais, podrían*
Pres. part.   *pudiendo*

poner (*to put, place*)
Pres. ind.   *pongo,* **pones, pone,** ponemos, ponéis, ponen
Preterite   *puse, pusiste, puso, pusimos, pusisteis, pusieron*
Future   *pondré, pondrás, pondrá, pondremos, pondréis, pondrán*
Conditional *pondría, pondrías, pondría, pondríamos, pondríais, pondrían*
Imperative   (*fam., sing.*) **pon**
Past part.   *puesto*

querer (*to wish, want*)
Pres. ind.   *quiero, quieres, quiere,* queremos, queréis, *quieren*
Preterite   *quise, quisiste, quiso, quisimos, quisisteis, quisieron*
Future   *querré, querrás, querrá, querremos, querréis, querrán*
Conditional *querría, querrías, querría, querríamos, querríais, querrían*

saber (*to know*)
Pres. ind.   sé, **sabes, sabe, sabemos, sabéis,** saben
Pres. subj.   *sepa, sepas, sepa, sepamos, sepáis, sepan*
Preterite   *supe, supiste, supo, supimos, supisteis, supieron*
Future   *sabré, sabrás, sabrá, sabremos, sabréis, sabrán*
Conditional *sabría, sabrías, sabría, sabríamos, sabríais, sabrían*

salir (*to leave*)
Pres. ind.   *salgo,* **sales, sale,** salimos, salís, salen
Future   *saldré, saldrás, saldrá, saldremos, saldréis, saldrán*
Conditional *saldría, saldrías, saldría, saldríamos, saldríais, saldrían*
Imperative   (*fam., sing.*) *sal*

ser (*to be*)
Pres. ind.   *soy, eres, es, somos, sois, son*
Pres. subj.   *sea, seas, sea, seamos, seáis, sean*
Imperfect   *era, eras, era, éramos, erais, eran*
Preterite   *fui, fuiste, fue, fuimos, fuisteis, fueron*
Imperative   (*fam., sing.*) *sé*

tener (*to have*)
Pres. ind.   *tengo, tienes, tiene,* **tenemos, tenéis,** *tienen*
Preterite   *tuve, tuviste, tuvo, tuvimos, tuvisteis, tuvieron*
Future   *tendré, tendrás, tendrá, tendremos, tendréis, tendrán*
Conditional *tendría, tendrías, tendría, tendríamos, tendríais, tendrían*
Imperative   (*fam., sing.*) **ten**

traer (to bring)

Pres. ind.	*traigo,* **traes, trae, traemos, traéis, traen**
Preterite	*traje, trajiste, trajo, trajimos, trajisteis, trajeron*
Pres. part.	*trayendo*
Past part.	**traído**

venir (to come)

Pres. ind.	*vengo, vienes, viene,* **venimos, venís,** *vienen*
Preterite	*vine, viniste, vino, vinimos, vinisteis, vinieron*
Future	*vendré, vendrás, vendrá, vendremos, vendréis, vendrán*
Conditional	*vendría, vendrías, vendría, vendríamos, vendríais, vendrían*
Imperative	*(fam., sing.)* *ven*
Pres. part.	*viniendo*

ver (to see)

Pres. ind.	*veo,* **ves, ve, vemos, veis, ven**
Pres. subj.	*vea, veas, vea, veamos, veáis, vean*
Imperfect	*veía, veías, veía, veíamos, veíais, veían*
Past part.	*visto*

Exercises from Drills

These exercises are taken from the Drills section of each lesson and are identified by the title under which they appear in the lesson. These answers are not included in the tape program. In sentences where the **tú** form or the **Ud., Uds.** forms are not specifically called for in the English, the authors have used them arbitrarily.

Lesson 2

Number and Gender of Adjectives

nueva, nuevos, nuevas; vieja, viejos, viejas; interesante, interesantes, interesantes; hermosa, hermosos, hermosas; buena, buenos, buenas; pequeña, pequeños, pequeñas; grande, grandes, grandes

Lesson 3

Uses of Ser and Estar

1. Somos amigos.
2. Está aquí.
3. Está contenta.   (Es feliz.)
4. Es un médico bueno.
5. Estamos cansados.
6. Mi hermano es de Nueva York.
7. ¿Dónde está la televisión?
8. Las sillas son bonitas.
9. Estamos contentos   (Somos felices.)
10. María es joven y bonita.

Present Tense with Future Meaning

1. Leo el libro mañana.
2. Estudio la lección mañana.
3. Compramos la tienda mañana.
4. Escriben la carta mañana.
5. Entras en la clase mañana.

Lesson 4

Possessive Adjectives

mis amigos, su médico, nuestra universidad, sus exámenes, sus cartas, mi medicina, su pluma, sus padres, su silla, nuestros alumnos, su mesa, tu tienda, su hermano, nuestro libro, su novio

Tener Que + Infinitive

1. Tengo que estudiar.
2. Tiene que ir.
3. Tenemos que correr.
4. Tengo que vivir.
5. Tienen que venir.
6. Tienes que abrir la puerta.
7. Ud. tiene que preparar la comida.
8. Tiene que tener la medicina.

Lesson 5

Cardinal Numbers (11–30)

3. once, catorce, quince, dieciséis, veinte, veintiocho, treinta
4. Necesitamos veintiún libros más. Necesitamos veintiuna casas más.

Lesson 6

Shortening of Adjectives **Bueno** and **Malo**

1. Es un buen hombre.
2. Son buenas muchachas.
3. Es una mala cosa.
4. Es un mal día.
5. Son buenos amigos.

Lesson 7

Present Indicative of Stem-Changing Verbs

cuesta, digo, perdemos, comienzan, llueve, Ud. come, podemos, cuestan, queremos, pide, volvemos, pierden, decimos, buscas, llevan, presento, vuelve, puedo, nieva, comenzamos

1. Queremos tomar el autobús aquí, pero no sabemos el número.
2. Ellos no dicen nada porque no pueden.
3. Tenemos que volver ahora, pero no queremos.

Double Negative

1. No compra nada.
2. No puede hacer nada.
3. No dicen nada.
4. No estudia nada.
5. No olvida a nadie.   (Note use of personal "a.")

Direct Object Pronouns

1. Lo sé.
4. Me cree.
7. No me comprenden.
10. La traigo.
13. No le oímos.

2. Le conozco.
5. Nos visitan.
8. Los venden.
11. La miran.
14. Me conoce.

3. Lo (la) tenemos.
6. Me conoces.
9. No nos ven.
12. No los ve.
15. La comienzo.

Lesson 9

Demonstrative Adjectives

esta ciudad, esa ciudad, aquella ciudad; este avión, ese avión, aquel avión; estos hombres, esos hombres, aquellos hombres; estas lecciones, esas lecciones, aquellas lecciones; esta luz, esa luz, aquella luz; este coche, ese coche, aquel coche; esta carta, esa carta, aquella carta; estos anuncios, esos anuncios, aquellos anuncios; este chico, ese chico, aquel chico; esta tienda, esa tienda, aquella tienda

Demonstrative Pronouns

1. Prefiero ésta.
2. Quiero ver aquéllos.
3. Esa es buena.
4. Ese es grande.
5. Voy a leer éstos, ésas, y aquéllos.

Reflexive Pronouns

1. Quiero lavarme.
2. Tiene que levantarse.
3. Tenemos que despertarnos.
4. Levántese Ud.   (Levántate tú.)
5. Van a sentarse.
6. Prefieres irte.
7. Quiere dormirse.
8. No se siente Ud. allí.

Lesson 10

Present Subjunctive of Regular Verbs

1. (yo) abra, admita, ande, aprenda, arregle, camine
2. (tú) cenes, comas, compres, comprendas, corras, escribas
3. (Juan) espere, estudie, hable, lea, llame, mire
4. (nosotros) olvidemos, pasemos, presentemos, recibamos, regresemos
5. (ellos) respondan, terminen, tomen, trabajen, vivan

Present Subjunctive of Stem-Changing Verbs

1. (yo) pierda, pueda, quiera, vuelva, pida
2. (tú) duermas, encuentres, muestres, pienses, prefieras
3. (él) sienta, se despierte, se siente, duerma
4. (nosotros) perdamos, podamos, sintamos, durmamos, pidamos
5. (ellos) vuelvan, pidan, muestren, se sienten, pierdan

1. Prefiero que Ud. no duerma aquí.
2. No quiero que María pierda el dinero.
3. El profesor nos aconseja que pensemos.
4. Prefiero volver ahora.
5. El señor no quiere que nosotros pidamos más sueldo.
6. El profesor insiste en que nosotros no durmamos en la clase.
7. No quieren que los huéspedes se sienten en esta silla.
8. Nos aconseja que no volvamos a este barrio.
9. Mi madre prefiere que nosotros no pidamos nada.
10. Quiere que Uds. se despierten temprano.

Subjunctive for Let's

6. Levantémonos.
7. Sentémonos.
8. Trabajemos.
9. Hagámoslo.
10. Salgamos.
11. Traigámoslo.

6. No, no lo vendamos ahora.
7. No, no nos lavemos ahora.
8. No, no trabajemos ahora.
9. No, no salgamos ahora.
10. No, no lo hagamos ahora.
11. No, no lo traigamos ahora.

Familiar Commands: Negative

1. Juan, estudia.
2. Roberto, no hables.
3. Sr. Mora, no trabaje Ud.
4. Sr. Mora, no salga Ud.
5. María, sal.
6. Pepe, ven aquí.
7. Niños, coman.
8. Sr. López, no lea Ud.

Lesson 11

Formation of Adverbs

1. Lo hizo rápidamente. (con cuidado, perfectamente)
2. Condujo perfectamente. (fácilmente, rápidamente, difícilmente)
3. Escribieron claramente. (naturalmente, perfectamente, con cuidado)
4. Le hablé con respeto. (amablemente, claramente)
5. Anduvo rápidamente. (naturalmente, con cuidado, difícilmente)

Days of the Week

1. Llega el lunes.
2. Estudiamos los domingos.
3. El sábado es fiesta.
4. No hay clases el martes.
5. Mañana es jueves.
6. Tuvimos clase el miércoles.

Months of the Year

1. Viernes, primero de junio.
2. Lunes, cuatro de julio.
3. Sábado, diez de agosto.
4. Martes, veintiséis de mayo.
5. Miércoles, primero de enero.
6. Jueves, trece de febrero.
7. Domingo, doce de noviembre.
8. Miércoles, once de septiembre.
9. Vayamos el veintiuno de diciembre.
10. ¿Cuál es la fecha? Es el diez de junio.

Lesson 12

Possessive Pronouns

1. Mi abrigo no es tan bonito como el de ella.
2. Este ascensor no sube tan rápidamente como el de Ud.
3. Nuestra casa está al lado de la de Ud.
4. Estos zapatos son más bonitos que los de ellos.
5. Nuestra casa está detrás de la de ellos.

Distinctions Between Preterite and Imperfect Usage

1. Juan comía cuando yo entré.
2. María era muy joven cuando se casó con Roberto.
3. Mi padre nació en México.
4. Mi esposo pagó la última cuenta esta tarde.
5. La casa era muy grande.
6. Cuando yo era joven, vivía al lado de la biblioteca.

Lesson 13

Passive Voice: Reflexives

1. Se dice que viene.
2. Se dice "gracias."
3. Se dice "por supuesto."
4. Se dice que vuelve.
5. Se come bien aquí.
6. Aquí se venden mesas.

1. La tienda se cierra a las cinco.
2. Aquí se comió la comida.
3. Esto se hace todos los días.
4. Aquí se habla alemán.
5. Se venden muchas casas.
6. Se perdieron muchos empleos.

Subjunctive with Verbs of Doubt and Necessity

1. Necesito que Ud. me ayude.
   (*ellos me ayuden, tú me ayudes, Ud. lo haga*)
2. Dudo que él salga a las ocho.
   (*él se despierte, lo sepamos, ellos se vistan, tú recuerdes*)

Subjunctive after Impersonal Expressions

1. Es dudoso que ellos escriban.
   (*se acuesten, repitan, se vistan, cuenten*)
2. Es importante que nosotros entendamos.
   (*cerremos la puerta, nos despidamos, contemos*)

1. Es preciso que ellos estudien.
   (*que yo vaya, que ellos recuerden, ir ahora, que Ud. se acueste*)
2. Es posible hacerlo.
   (*que él lo repita, que comprendamos, pagar ahora, que yo venga*)

Lesson 14

Time Expressions with **Hacer** (*past tenses*)

1. Hace una hora que leo.
2. Hacía una hora que leía.
3. Hacía una hora que miraba.
4. Hacía quince minutos que hablaban.
5. Hacía mucho tiempo que llovía.
6. Fui hace una semana.
7. Lo vi hace un mes.
8. Volvió hace dos días.

Uses of **Gustar, Faltar, Parecer, Quedar**

1. Le gustan las manzanas. Le gusta el pollo. Le gustó el pollo. Les gustó el pollo. Nos gustaron las patatas.
2. Le falta la mantequilla. Me falta la mantequilla. Me faltaba la mantequilla. Le faltaban los huevos. Les faltaban los huevos.
3. Les quedaba un año. Te quedaba un año. Le queda un año. Nos queda un año. Les queda un año.
4. El pescado le parece fresco. El pescado le parecía fresco. El pescado me parecía bueno. El arroz le parecía bueno. Las mesas les parecían grandes.

Cardinal Numbers 40–100

ciento cinco, ciento diez, ciento quince, ciento veinte, ciento veinticinco, ciento treinta, ciento treinta y cinco, ciento cuarenta, ciento cuarenta y cinco, ciento cincuenta, ciento cincuenta y cinco, ciento sesenta, ciento sesenta y cinco, ciento setenta, ciento setenta y cinco, ciento ochenta, ciento ochenta y cinco, ciento noventa, ciento noventa y cinco

Lesson 15

Formation of Past Participle

hablado, comido, salido, trabajado, vivido, abierto, cantado, cubierto, dicho, dormido, ido, vuelto, vendido, visto, dado, escrito, pensado, puesto, querido, roto, muerto, contestado, hecho, ayudado

Past Subjunctive

1. Siento que Juan no viniera ayer.
2. Espero que tú no comieras demasiado ayer.
3. Me alegro de que los alumnos estudiaran ayer.

Lesson 16

Progressive Tenses

1. Estoy leyéndosela.
2. Estaba trayéndomelos.
3. Estaban lavándolos.
4. Sigue pidiéndomela.
5. Seguían divirtiéndose.

Regular Comparisons of Adjectives and Adverbs

2. María es más fuerte que Cecilia.
   María es más fea que Cecilia.
   María es más divertida que Cecilia.
   María es más aburrida que Cecilia.
   María es más agradable que Cecilia.

Conjunctions e and u

madre e hija, verano e invierno, niños u hombres, español e inglés, casa u oficina, siete u ocho

Diminutives and Augmentatives

1. small house, small glass, little brother, small thing
2. big woman, large house, big man, big book

Lesson 17

Irregular Comparisons of Adjectives and Adverbs

1. Sí, pero Luis trabaja menos que todos.
2. Sí, pero Luis canta peor que todos.
3. Sí, pero Luis habla más que todos.
4. Sí, pero Luis juega mejor que todos.
5. Sí, pero Luis escribe peor que todas.
6. Sí, pero Luis lee más que todos.

Lesson 18

Future and Conditional of Probability

1. ¿Cuántas casas tendrá?
2. Tendrá dos casas.
3. ¿Cuántas casas tendría?
4. Tendría dos casas.
5. ¿Qué querrá el portero?
6. Querrá preguntarnos algo.
7. ¿Qué hora será?
8. Será la una.
9. ¿Cuándo vendrán?
10. Vendrán mañana.

Deber and Haber De

1. Debo estar allí a las seis.
2. Ud. debe limpiar la casa ahora mismo.
3. Ha de desayunar con nosotros.
4. No debes romper las cosas.
5. Habían de ir a la escuela.
6. He de lavar la ropa.
7. Debemos preguntar al portero.
8. Debo escribir con lápiz.

Numbers from 100

ciento cincuenta y seis casas, trescientas setenta y dos caras, quinientas diez máquinas, ochocientas una escuelas, doscientos quince lápices, cuatrocientos veintidós árboles, seiscientos treinta y nueve perros, setecientos cuarenta equipos, novecientos noventa y un estadios, mil quinientos cincuenta campeones, un millón quinientos mil espectadores, cuatro millones seiscientas cincuenta mil quinientas ochenta personas

el cinco de marzo de mil novecientos sesenta y uno, el cuatro de julio de mil setecientos setenta y seis, el veinticinco de diciembre de mil novecientos ochenta y cinco, el doce de octubre de mil cuatrocientos noventa y dos, el primero de enero de mil novecientos setenta y dos, el doce de febrero de mil ochocientos ochenta y ocho

Definite Article for the Possessive

1. Tenía la cara limpia.
2. Me dolían los pies.
3. Juan se puso la camisa.
4. Se cortó el pelo.
5. Le quité el lápiz.
6. Me dolía la mano.
7. Ella les lavó el pelo.
8. Me quitaron la ropa.
9. Me corté la mano.
10. Te pusiste la ropa.

Lesson 19

Relative Pronouns

1. que	1. la cual	1. la cual	1. El que
2. que	2. del cual	2. el cual	2. Los que
3. quien	3. la cual	3. las cuales	3. Los que
4. quienes	4. la cual	4. los cuales	4. La que (El que)
5. quien	5. la cual		
6. que	6. las cuales		

Subjunctive in Adjective Clauses

1. Buscamos una chica que sea tan bonita como María.
2. Buscamos a la chica que estuvo aquí ayer.
3. Quiero comprar un collar que no sea muy caro.
4. No hay ningunas joyas aquí que sean caras.
5. Quería encontrar un traje que me gustara.
6. Conozco a un señor que habla alemán.
7. ¿Hay alguién que tenga una cuenta corriente?
8. ¿Dónde están los zapatos que yo compré ayer?
9. No hay nadie que pague al contado.

Lesson 20

Subjunctive after Certain Conjunctions

1. Voy a Madrid en cuanto tenga dinero.
2. Estudio antes de dormir.
3. Le di el libro para que lo leyera.
4. Leía el periódico cuando él entró.
5. Vinieron sin que yo se lo dijera.
6. Me quedo aquí a menos que te moleste.
7. Se detuvieron para descansar.
8. Iremos al parque con tal que no llueva.
9. María esperaba hasta que llegaron sus amigos.
10. Juan salió antes de que nosotros entráramos.
11. Llevo mi abrigo en caso de que llueva.
12. Voy luego que me lo digan.

1. Comeré antes de que llegue.
2. Comí antes de que llegara.
3. Comieron en cuanto llegó.
4. Irán con tal que no nieve.

Subjunctive in *If* Clauses

1. Si yo fuera presidente, ayudaría a los extranjeros.
2. Yo le escribiría si tuviera lápiz.
3. Si no está enfermo, irá a la escuela.
4. No habría ido si hubiera sabido eso.

Subjunctive after *Como Si*

1. Le hablaba como si fuera un niño.
2. Hablaban como si le hubieran conocido.
3. Me mira como si yo fuera un caballero.
4. Come como si se muriera de hambre.
5. Salió como si tuviera miedo.

Por *and* Para

1. Caminaron para la plaza.   (Anduvieron para la plaza.)
2. Caminaron por la plaza.   (Anduvieron por la plaza.)
3. La carta fue escrita por un indio.
4. Me dio diez mil pesetas por la tierra.
,5. Estudio para aprender.
6. Fuimos por tren.
7. María estudió por dos horas.
8. Estas sillas son para la clase.
9. La casa es para mi familia.
10. Gracias por todo.

Quisiera *and* Debiera

1. Ud. no debiera leer tanto.
2. Quisiera ver esa película.
3. ¿Quisiera darme su libro?
4. Debiera visitar a sus amigos a menudo.

Translation Exercises from Combined Exercises

These drills are taken from the Combined Exercises section of each lesson, and are identified by the same letter under which they appear in the lesson. In sentences where the **tú** form or the **Ud., Uds.** forms are not specifically called for in the English, the authors have used them arbitrarily.

Lesson 1

Exercise C

1. Buenos días, alumnos. ¿Cómo están ustedes?
2. Estoy en la clase de español hoy.
3. Las mesas están aquí.
4. Estudia todos los días.
5. Hablamos español aquí.
6. Estudia en casa.
7. Preparamos las lecciones.
8. La mesa y la silla están en la casa.
9. Ustedes compran libros en la librería.
10. Usted prepara la lección en casa.
11. Necesito los libros.
12. Están aquí hoy.
13. Estás en la librería y necesitas comprar el libro.
14. Las mesas y las sillas están en la casa.
15. Estudiamos todo el día.
16. ¿Cómo se llama usted?
17. Me llamo . . .
18. En la clase de español, no hablamos bien el español.
19. Los alumnos compran libros en la librería hoy.
20. Los libros, las mesas y las sillas están en la clase de español.

Lesson 2

Exercise E

1. Los hombres entran en el restaurante pequeño.
2. Mi hermano vive en una casa vieja.
3. Necesitamos escribir una carta hoy.
4. Las sillas nuevas están en la tienda.
5. Paco y yo aprendemos a leer.
6. En la librería hay libros interesantes.

7. La señorita hermosa abre una carta.
8. Escriben unas cartas interesantes.
9. ¿Necesitan Uds. unos libros?
10. ¿Por qué preparas la lección de español?
11. Hay tiendas grandes en Nueva York.
12. Un hombre muy viejo vive aquí.
13. La señora come en un restaurante todos los días.
14. Unos alumnos escriben cartas todos los días.
15. Vendes unas plumas muy hermosas.
16. ¿Dónde vive la señora?
17. Leemos y estudiamos en casa.
18. Abrimos la tienda todos los días.
19. Aprendes a leer el español.
20. ¿Por qué vive Ud. aquí?

Lesson 3

Exercise F

1. Recibimos diez cartas todos los días.
2. Somos amigos y estamos en la misma clase.
3. Trabajamos en el mismo restaurante.
4. A veces olvidas abrir la librería.
5. No comprenden la lección.
6. Leemos un libro triste.
7. El examen es de Juan, pero no está aquí.
8. Uds. son alumnos, pero yo soy médico.
9. Mañana estudio en la casa de Juan.
10. Los hombres son viejos, pero no están enfermos.
11. La clase es fácil, pero hay que estudiar.
12. Somos de México, pero estamos contentos aquí.
13. El hermano de María es un médico bueno.
14. Las lecciones son difíciles, pero interesantes.
15. Hay que trabajar para vivir.
16. Estoy cansado hoy, pero trabajo mañana.
17. También compra una mesa y cuatro sillas.
18. Hay siete alumnos en clase y ocho en casa.
19. ¿Dónde están los hermanos de María?

Lesson 4

Exercise E

1. Tenemos carne, sopa y legumbres, pero no hay pan.
2. Corre a la tienda para comprar unas cosas.
3. Vienen ahora mismo, pero ya es tarde.
4. Espera su comida.
5. Se llama Juan, pero no es muy simpático.
6. Su clase es grande, pero sus lecciones son fáciles.
7. Además de sus dos hermanas, tiene siete hermanos.
8. Nuestros padres esperan a la puerta.
9. Voy a escribir una carta mientras hay luz.
10. Venimos a nuestra clase de español todos los días.

Lesson 5

Exercise F

1. Llega a las seis y media para cenar con nosotros.
2. A propósito, ¿a qué hora sale el avión?
3. Nunca pasa sus vacaciones allí.
4. Tienen casi veinticinco cartas.
5. Voy a traer libros o plumas.
6. Vamos a pasar una semana en Toledo y un mes en Madrid.
7. Tenemos que salir ahora porque son las once de la noche y tengo sueño.
8. Traigo un libro sobre México a la clase.
9. En mi casa nunca cenamos hasta muy tarde.
10. El libro cae de la mesa.

Review Lesson 1–5

Exercise F

1. Las mesas y las sillas están en la tienda.
2. Estudian todo el día.
3. ¿Vives aquí?
4. ¿Por qué abres la tienda todos los días?
5. Hoy está cansada pero no está enferma.
6. El padre de Juan es alumno, pero no es muy joven.
7. Ya tiene algo además de pan.
8. Corre a la tienda para comprar algo además de pan.
9. Pasan el día en Madrid.
10. Son casi las siete y cuarto y ya tengo sueño.

Lesson 6

Exercise D

1. Sé que hace frío en Madrid en el invierno.
2. Voy en seguida a mi cuarto al terminar mi trabajo.
3. En el sur siempre hace calor en el verano.
4. En mi país hace mucho viento en la primavera.
5. Las cuatro estaciones del año son: la primavera, el verano, el otoño y el invierno.
6. En los países al sur del ecuador no siempre hace buen tiempo.
7. ¿Qué tiempo hace hoy? Hace mucho sol.
8. Tengo hambre; voy a llamar al camarero. ¿Qué vas a tomar? Carne y legumbres, por favor.
9. No conozco bien a su hermana, pero parece muy simpática.

Lesson 7

Exercise C

1. Siempre lo pierdo.
2. Me quiere.
3. Las pide.
4. El autobús las lleva.
5. Las llevan.
6. Nos buscan.
7. Le creo.

8. Siempre la ponen aquí.
9. Las hacemos.
10. Me olvida.

Exercise E

1. Busco mis libros. No los tengo.
2. Tengo una novia ahora, y la quiero mucho.
3. Necesito legumbres, y siempre las compro en el centro.
4. Vayan Uds. en el autobús. Los lleva al parque.
5. Corra Ud., no camine. Salga de la tienda y no vuelva.
6. No diga nada más. Le creo.

Lesson 8

Exercise D

1. No exagere, Sr. García.
2. Vende el coche, Juan; véndemelo.
3. Pon el libro aquí, María.
4. Sal ahora, Roberto.
5. Ven aquí, María. Sé buena.
6. Haga el trabajo ahora, Sr. Mora; no lo haga mañana.
7. Quiero comprar la silla, Sr. López; véndamela.
8. ¿Cómo estás? ¿Qué hay de nuevo?
9. El viene conmigo. María va contigo.
10. Vive lejos, pero me trae muchos libros.

Lesson 9

Exercise C

1. Me despierto a las ocho, pero no me levanto hasta las nueve.
2. Despiértate ahora.
3. ¿Por qué se sentó allí?
4. Entró en un restaurante y comió mucho.
5. Fueron al campo pero el viaje salió caro.
6. Aquel coche anda bastante bien, pero éste anda mejor.
7. Perdieron la mitad de esa película.
8. ¡Qué estupendo tener su propio coche!
9. Queremos levantarnos temprano para ir al centro.
10. Estudió la lección, pero no la aprendió.

Exercise D

1. Ponlo en la mesa y ven aquí.
2. Dime la verdad.
3. Quiere dármela.
4. Quiere dárselo a ellos.
5. El coche le costó mucho, pero lo compró.
6. Nos lo vendió.
7. Venga Ud. conmigo y le llevo a ver una película (al cine).
8. Los visité el año pasado.
9. No estudie hoy. Puede hacerlo mañana.
10. Al fin me compró un coche.

Lesson 10

Exercise D

1. Vamos a bailar. Bailemos.
2. No salgas de este barrio, Juan.
3. Vamos a levantarnos ahora. Levantémonos ahora.
4. No grites, María.
5. Teresa y María están aquí; ésta es bastante gorda.
6. María y Juan son extranjeros; éste es de México.
7. Quiero ir, pero no quiero que vayan ellos.
8. No nos levantemos temprano mañana.
9. Dame el periódico, Juan; no se lo des a él.
10. Pon la revista aquí, María; no la pongas en la mesa.
11. Siéntate aquí, Roberto; no te sientes allí.
12. Tráigamelo, Sr. Robles; no se lo dé a ellos.
13. Quiero comprar este libro, esa revista y esos periódicos.
14. Quiere que yo viva en este barrio.
15. Nos dicen que estudiemos todos los días.

Dialogue Practice

La Sra. Alvarez aconseja a Margarita que no hable con su padre ahora porque está de mal humor. Pero Margarita no puede esperar; tiene que hablarle ahora. Buscan chicas para cuidar a los niños en un hotel en el Parque Nacional; le encantan los niños, y dan habitación y comida y un pequeño sueldo. Su padre no permite que vaya a un sitio tan lejano. Quiere que esté en Santiago este verano. Margarita y su madre van a esperar hasta mañana para hablarle.

Review Lesson 6–10

Exercise F

1. En el invierno no podemos hacer nada.
2. Varios policías están en la esquina.
3. El parque está lejos, pero el autobús cuesta catorce pesetas.
4. No conozco muy bien Madrid, pero sé que hoy hace frío.
5. El coche anda bien, pero los frenos no funcionan.
6. La ventaja es que puedo dormir en el coche.
7. Haz el trabajo ahora, Juan; no lo hagas mañana.
8. Nos despertamos a las nueve y nos levantamos a las diez.
9. Vamos a levantarnos tarde mañana. (Levantémonos tarde mañana.)
10. Quieren que trabaje en casa.

Lesson 11

Exercise E

1. Quise estudiar, pero no pude.
2. Nací el veintiuno de diciembre, pero mi esposa nació el primero de enero.
3. Insistió en pagar todas sus cuentas los sábados.
4. El martes vino a la casa y nos dijo la verdad.
5. Hace una hora que pienso, y naturalmente todavía no sé la fecha.
6. ¿Cuál es la fecha? Hoy es viernes, nueve de abril.
7. ¿De veras hiciste (preparaste) esa comida? Quise hacerlo, pero no pude.
8. ¿Siempre tienes que ganar? No, no me importa.
9. De repente mi esposa me dijo que no trajo dinero.

10. Condujo rápidamente, pero no pudo ver claramente.
11. Le conocí en el cine.
12. ¿Cuánto tiempo hace que estás aquí? Hace tres días que estoy en la ciudad.

Exercise F

1. Quieren que vaya al cine.
2. Me aconseja que me siente.
3. Quiero que salga.
4. Vamos a salir ahora. (Salgamos ahora.) No, quiero que esperes.
5. Prefiero que Ud. no duerma en la clase.
6. Levántese temprano. Nunca me levanto temprano.
7. Sr. Mora, venga Ud. aquí; no salga.
8. Juanito, ven aquí; no salgas.
9. Démelo a mí. No se lo dé a ella.
10. La pago.

Lesson 12

Exercise B

1. Este libro es mío. ¿Dónde está el suyo?
2. Estos pantalones son suyos. Los míos están en la silla.
3. ¿Dónde están los trajes de baño? El suyo está aquí y el de ella está allí.
4. Me alegro de que se case, pero siento que no se case con Roberto.
5. Es lástima que los niños no puedan nadar en el río.
6. Espero que salga hoy.
7. Espero salir hoy.
8. Temo que hable con mi padre.
9. Temo hablar con mi padre.
10. Me alegro de estar en esta clase.

Exercise E

1. Quiero que esté aquí a las seis.
2. Prefiere que yo le dé el dinero.
3. Insisten en que su hijo sea médico.
4. Aconsejamos que Ud. vaya allí mañana.
5. Pido (ruego) que Ud. sepa bien esta lección.
6. Fuimos allí ayer.
7. Dijo que puso el libro en la mesa.
8. Estuvo aquí dos horas esta mañana, y después tuvo que salir.
9. Trajeron el dinero cuando vinieron.
10. Quise salir pero no pude.
11. Anduvo (caminó) todo el día.
12. Supimos que lo hizo.

Lesson 13

Exercise E

1. No creo que duerma bastante.
2. Se divirtió pero solamente durmió cuatro horas.
3. Se vistieron y fueron al centro.
4. Su hija le preocupaba porque no quiso ir.
5. Cerró la puerta y se durmió.

6. Por supuesto repitió la lección, pero no la aprendieron.
7. Dámelo; no lo dejes allí.
8. Es evidente que Ud. no lo puso allí.
9. Es necesario comer (Hay que comer), pero es lástima que Ud. coma tanto.
10. Se cerró la tienda a las cinco, pero no se cerraron las puertas hasta las cinco y media.

Dialogue Practice

El Sr. Alvarez fue a visitar a su hija que trabajaba en un hotel en el Parque Nacional. Se pagaba bien allí y trabajaba de recepcionista. El Sr. Mendoza dijo que los tiempos cambiaban porque en sus días esto no se permitía. El Sr. Alvarez dijo que tenía confianza en su hija, pero no durmió mucho en el tren.

Lesson 14

Exercise F

1. Llegué a la oficina (al despacho) y empecé a trabajar en seguida.
2. Busqué el café, pero no pude encontrarlo.
3. Creyó al camarero y escogió otro café.
4. Probó el biftec, pero no le gustó.
5. No nos gustó el lugar, y no volvimos.
6. No se sentía bien y quería salir.
7. Hacía cinco años que comían en ese restaurante.
8. Comí allí hace una semana, pero no probé el flan.
9. Después de la comida, todavía les quedaban ciento cincuenta y cinco postres.
10. Escogí sopa primero y después pescado.

Lesson 15

Exercise C

1. Era dudoso que tuviera buenos propósitos.
2. Me alegraba de que hiciera fresco.
3. Fue lástima que salieras temprano.
4. No creía que fuera la mejor manera de aprender una lengua.
5. Es lástima que no contestaran.
6. Es dudoso que comprara el primer coche que vio.
7. Es posible que fuera un estudiante universitario.

Review Lesson 11–15

Exercise F

1. Mi padre no permitió que fuera.
2. Fue lástima que no viniera.
3. Le quedaba una semana, pero le faltaba dinero.
4. Se abrieron las tiendas a las nueve y cuarto en punto.
5. Estas camisas son mías; esas corbatas son suyas.
6. Hacía cincuenta y cinco minutos que escribía.
7. Insistía en conducir.
8. Se casaron el junio pasado.
9. Comíamos cuando entró.
10. Se divirtieron y luego (después) se despidieron.

Lesson 16

Exercise F

1. Había más hombres que mujeres en la cárcel.
2. Este problema es muy aburrido. Lo hago mañana.
3. La ventana fue abierta por mi vecino, pero ahora está cerrada.
4. El ejército se apoderó del gobierno, pero no pueden con esos locos.
5. ¡Qué día! Tenía que comprar siete u ocho cosas y estaba lloviendo a cántaros.
6. Los niños se llamaban Juanito e Isabel.
7. Cuando salí de la clase, dejé mis libros allí.
8. Seguía durmiendo en la sala aunque a su esposa no le gustaba.
9. No dejes de leer ese libro pronto. No deje Ud. de leer ese libro pronto.
10. Trajo su comida a la cárcel, y estaba comiéndola allí.

Lesson 17

Exercise B

1. No nos dijo que el equipaje había llegado.
2. Sabíamos que habían ido a la luna.
3. Dentro de dos años habíamos ganado el campeonato.
4. Mi hermano mayor es mejor jugador que Tomás.
5. Mi hermana menor es la mejor alumna de la clase.
6. Hay más de veinte equipos, pero hay solamente un campeón (. . . no hay más que un campeón).
7. Su equipo jugó mal, pero el suyo jugó peor. Sí, pero el nuestro jugó peor que todos.
8. Es una mujer hermosísima.
9. Es un hombre inteligentísimo.
10. Me dijo que el equipo no tiene más que nueve jugadores (. . . tiene solamente nueve jugadores). El nuestro tiene más de quince.
11. Supieron que habíamos ganado el partido.
12. Es el menos inteligente de la familia.

Lesson 18

Exercise D

1. ¿Qué hora será?
2. Serán las diez, pero no estoy seguro.
3. Limpiaría mi cuarto pero mi tía ya lo ha hecho.
4. En los Estados Unidos cenamos sobre las seis.
5. Alguien le cortó el pelo; sería su abuelo.
6. No se sentía bien porque había gastado tanto dinero.
7. La limpieza es importante; debes lavarte las manos a menudo.
8. He de cenar con María. ¿Dónde vivirá?
9. Hay mil quinientos ochenta y seis alumnos en la escuela, pero trescientos cincuenta y ocho están enfermos hoy.
10. Le quité el lápiz, pero no le gustó.

Dialogue Practice

María, vi un anuncio en el periódico de esta mañana. Los Sres. Alonso buscan una chica (sirvienta), y viven en esta misma calle, de modo que podemos vernos todos los días. Hablarás con los Sres. Alonso mañana, ¿verdad? La cocinera es amiga mía, y le pagan bien. Tendrás que cuidar a los dos niños, Roberto e Isabel, durante la tarde.

Lesson 19

Exercise C

1. ¿Dónde está el coche en que vas?
2. Habrá comprado las joyas.
3. Temo que haya comprado las joyas.
4. Habría comprado el traje.
5. Temía que hubiera comprado el traje.
6. Busca un traje que no cueste mucho.
7. Buscaba un traje que no costara mucho.
8. En esta tienda no hay bolso que quiera comprar.
9. En esa tienda no había bolso que quisiera comprar.
10. La tienda cerca de la cual vive tiene muchas gangas.

Dialogue Practice

Juana, mira esa blusa de nilón que hay en el escaparate, la que está delante del vestido de mangas cortas. Vendrá muy bien con la falda que me regaló mi padre. ¿Cuánto costará? ¿Tendrán otra parecida que sea menos cara? No compremos nada aquí. Un amigo de mi padre, el cual trabaja en una joyería, me dijo que allí tienen unas verdaderas gangas. Vamos allá. Temo que hayamos perdido mucho tiempo aquí.

Lesson 20

Exercise D

1. Nos detuvimos hasta que dejó de llover.
2. ¿Te has fijado en las variaciones en la política de ciertos países?
3. Le molestaba tener que trabajar demasiado.
4. Este país es una maravilla, pero me gustaría visitar otros.
5. Cada país tiene su propio ambiente. Por ejemplo, México es una tierra de muchos mestizos e indios.
6. No es (ninguna) molestia. Además, me encanta ver tantas rubias y morenas.
7. Iré al cine contigo con tal que pagues.
8. Trabajé para él hasta que salió para los Estados Unidos.
9. Hice el trabajo en cuanto me lo pidió.
10. Si hubiera estudiado, habría sabido la lección.

Review Lesson 16–20

Exercise F

1. Paco es más alto que Juan, pero no es el más alto de la familia.
2. Me puse el sombrero y salí, pero dejé mi abrigo.
3. Le dijeron que no habíamos estudiado.
4. He de estar allí a las ocho, pero primero debo limpiar mi cuarto.
5. ¿Quién será esa muchacha? Será María.
6. Había quinientos cincuenta árboles en el parque el primero de junio de mil novecientos treinta y cuatro.
7. A Juan le dolía la cabeza; estaba aburrido.
8. Cuando venga, se lo diré.
9. Esperó hasta que llegaron sus amigos.
10. Dijeron que probarían la sopa.
11. La puerta está abierta; fue abierta por el profesor.
12. Se abren las tiendas a las ocho y se cierran a las cinco y media.

VOCABULARY
Spanish-English

Abbreviations are as follows: (*adj.*) adjective, (*adv.*) adverb, (*art.*) article, (*demon.*) demonstrative, (*f.*) feminine, (*ind.*) indicative, (*inf.*) infinitive, (*m.*) masculine, (*neg.*) negative, (*neut.*) neuter, (*obj.*) object, (*part.*) participle, (*pers.*) person, (*pl.*) plural, (*poss.*) possessive, (*prep.*) preposition, (*pres.*) present, (*pret.*) preterite, (*pron.*) pronoun, (*refl.*) reflexive, (*rel.*) relative, (*sing.*) singular, (*subj.*) subject, (*v.*) verb.

A

a to, at
abierto (*past part.*) open, opened
abrigo overcoat; **abrigo de piel** fur coat
abril April
abrir to open
abuela grandmother
abuelo grandfather
aburrido: estar aburrido to be bored;
  ser aburrido to be boring
acá here
acabar to finish; **acabar de + *inf.*** to have
  just + *inf.*
acera sidewalk
acercarse (a) to draw near (to)
aconsejar to advise
acordarse (ue) (de) to remember
acostarse (ue) to go to bed
actualmente at the present time
acuerdo: ¡De acuerdo! OK! Agreed!
además besides, moreover; **además de**
  in addition to
adiós good-bye
admitir to admit
aeropuerto airport
afortunadamente fortunately
agosto August
agradable pleasant
agua, el (*f.*) water
ahora now; **ahora mismo** right now
alcoba bedroom
alegrarse (de) to be glad
alemán (*noun* and *adj.*) German
Alemania Germany
algo something, somewhat

alguien someone
algún, alguno, -a some, any
allá there
allí there
almacén (*m.*) department store
almorzar (ue) to eat lunch
almuerzo lunch
alojarse to stay (in a hotel)
alto, -a tall
altura height
alumno (*m.*) student; **alumna** (*f.*) student
amable nice
ambiente (*m.*) atmosphere
amigo, -a friend
andar to run (machinery); to walk
ángel (*m.*) angel
año year; **tener diez años** to be ten
  years old; **todos los años** every year;
  ¿Cuántos años tiene Ud? How old are
  you?; **el año pasado** last year
anoche last night
anteayer the day before yesterday
antes before; **antes de + *inf.*** before +
  pres. part.; **antes (de) que** before
anunciar to announce
anuncio advertisement
apellido surname
apoderarse (de) to take over
aprender to learn; **aprender a + *inf.*** to
  learn + *inf.*
aquel (*adj.*) that (over there)
aquí here
árbol (*m.*) tree
arma (*m.*) weapon
arrancar to start (machinery)
arreglar to repair, arrange

arroz (*m.*) rice
arte (*m.*) art
ascensor (*m.*) elevator
así que as soon as
asiento seat
asistir (a) to attend
atrasado backward, late
aunque although
autobús (*m.*) bus
automóvil (*m.*) automobile
avenida avenue
avión (*m.*) airplane
ay: ¡Ay de mí! Oh me!
ayer yesterday
ayudar to help

B

bailar to dance
bajar to go down, lower; **bajar de** to get off, get out of (a vehicle)
bajo, -a short, low
banco bank
baño bath
barrio district, neighborhood
bastante enough, rather, quite
beber to drink
biblioteca library
bien well; **está bien** all right
biftec (*m.*) steak
blusa blouse
boca mouth
boda wedding
bolso purse
bonito, -a pretty
buen, bueno, -a good
buscar to look for

C

caballero gentleman
cabeza head
cada each
caer to fall; **caerse** to fall down
café (*m.*) cafe, coffee
calcetín (*m.*) sock
calefacción (*f.*) heating
caliente hot
calle (*f.*) street
calmarse to calm down
calor (*m.*) heat; **hace calor** it is hot; **tener calor** to be hot
cama bed
camarero waiter
cambiar to change
caminar to walk
camino a on the way to
camisa shirt
campeón (*m.*) champion
campeonato championship
campo countryside
canción (*f.*) song
cansado, -a tired
cantar to sing

cantidad (*f.*) quantity
cara face
cárcel (*f.*) jail
carne (*f.*) meat
caro, -a expensive; **salir caro** to be expensive
carretera highway
carta letter
casa house; **en casa** at home
casarse (con) to get married (to)
casi almost
caso: en caso de que in case that
castillo castle
catolicismo Catholicism
catorce fourteen
cena dinner; **cenar** to have dinner
centro downtown, center
cerca (de) close (to), near (to)
cerrar (ie) to close
cielo sky
cierto, -a certain
cinco five
cincuenta fifty
cine (*m.*) movies
ciudad (*f.*) city
claro, -a clear
clase (*f.*) class, kind
clima (*m.*) climate
cobrar to charge, collect
coche (*m.*) car, automobile
cocina kitchen
cocinera cook
coger to get, grasp, catch
collar (*m.*) necklace
comenzar (ie) to begin; **comenzar a + inf.** to begin to + *inf.*
comer to eat
comida meal, dinner, food
como like, as; **como si** as if; **como de costumbre** as usual
¿cómo? how? what?; **¡cómo no!** of course!
complicado complicated
comprar to buy
comprender to understand
con with
condiciones: en malas condiciones in bad condition
conducir to drive
confianza confidence
conocer to know, be acquainted with
conseguir (i, i) to get, obtain
consumir to consume, use
contar (ue) to count, tell
contento, -a happy
contestar to answer
continuo continual
corbata necktie
correr to run
corresponder to fit, suit, correspond
cortar to cut
corto, -a short

cosa thing
costa coast
costar (ue) to cost; **costarle a uno trabajo** to be a lot of work
costumbre (*f.*) custom
creer to believe
criada maid
cruzar to cross
¿cuál? which, which one?
¿cuándo? when
¡cuánta! what a lot of . . . !
¿cuánto, -a, -os, -as? how much? how many?
cuanto: en cuanto as soon as
cuarenta forty
cuarto room, quarter
cuarto, -a fourth
cuatro four
cuatrocientos four hundred
cubierto table setting; (*past part.*) covered
cubrir to cover
cuenta bill; **cuenta corriente** charge account
cuidado care; **tener cuidado** to be careful
cuidar to care for, tend
cura (*m.*) priest
curso course

CH

charlar to chat, talk
chico, -a (*adj.*) small; (*noun*) boy, girl
chocolate (*m.*) chocolate

D

dar to give; **darse cuenta de** to realize; **dar un paseo** to take a walk
de of, from, about, in (*after superlatives*), than (*before numbers*)
deber ought, should, must
decidir to decide
décimo, -a tenth
decir to say, tell
defecto defect
dejar to leave; **dejar de + *inf.*** to stop; (*neg.*) not to fail
delante (de) in front (of)
delgado, -a thin
demasiado too, too much
dentro (de) within
dependiente, -a clerk
deporte (*m.*) sport
derecha right
derecho, -a straight
desastre (*m.*) disaster
desayunarse to eat breakfast
desayuno breakfast
descansar to rest
desde from, since
desear to desire, want
despacho office
despedirse (i, i) (de) to say good-bye (to)

despertarse (ie) to wake up, awaken
después afterward, later; **después de** after
detenerse to stop
detrás (de) behind
día (*m.*) day; **Buenos días** Good morning; **todos los días** every day; **hoy día** nowadays; **todo el día** all day (long); **al día siguiente** on the following day; **día de fiesta** holiday; **¡Qué día!** What a day!
diciembre December
dicho (*past part.*) said
diez ten
diferente different
difícil difficult
dinero money
Dios God; **¡Dios mío!** Oh my goodness!; **¡Gracias a Dios!** Thank heavens!
dirección (*f.*) address
director (*m.*) director
diversión (*f.*) amusement, entertainment
divertido, -a amusing
divertirse (ie, i) to have a good time
doblar to turn, fold
doce twelve
dólar (*m.*) dollar
doler to hurt
domingo Sunday
don title of respect
¿dónde? where?
dormir (ue) to sleep
dormitorio bedroom
dos two
doscientos two hundred
dudar to doubt
dudoso, -a doubtful
durante during
durar to last

E

ecuador (*m.*) equator
educado, -a educated
ejemplo: por ejemplo for example
ejército army
él he
ella she
emocionado, -a excited; **No te pongas tan emocionado** Don't get so excited
empezar (ie) to begin
empleo job, employment
en in, at, on; **en cuanto** as soon as
encantar to charm, enchant, fascinate
encontrar (ue) to meet, find
enero January
enfermo, -a sick
enorme huge
ensalada salad
enseñar to show, teach
entender (ie) to understand
entonces then

entrar (en) to enter
entre among, between
época epoch, period
equipaje (m.) baggage
equipo team
equivocarse to be wrong
escaparate (m.) display window
escoger to choose
escribir to write
escrito (past part.) written
escuchar to listen (to)
escuela school
ese, esa, esos, esas (adj.) that, those
ése, ésa, ésos, ésas (pron.) that (one),
   those
eso (neut. pron.) that; por eso for that
   reason, therefore; eso es that's right
español (m.) Spanish, Spaniard
espectador (m.) spectator
esperar to wait (for); to hope, expect
esposa wife
esposo husband
esquina corner
estabilidad (f.) stability
estable stable
estación (f.) season (of year); station
estadio stadium
Estados Unidos United States
estar to be
este, esta, estos, estas (adj.) this, these
éste, ésta, éstos, éstas (pron.) this (one),
   these
éste (m.) ésta (f.) the latter
este (m.) east
esto this
estropear to damage, ruin
estudiante (m. and f.) student
estudiar to study
estudio study
estupendo, -a stupendous, wonderful
evidente evident
exagerar to exaggerate
examen (m.) examination
explicación (f.) explanation
extranjero, -a foreign, foreigner, abroad

F

facción (f.) faction
fácil easy
falda skirt
faltar to need, lack
fama fame
familia family
favor: por favor please; haga Ud. el
   favor de . . . please
febrero February
fecha date
feliz happy
feo, -a ugly
fijarse (en) to notice

fin end; al fin finally; por fin finally,
   at last; fin de semana weekend
flan (m.) custard
forastero, -a stranger
formar to form
fortuna fortune
francés French
freno brake
fresco, -a fresh, cool; hace fresco it's
   cool (out)
frío cold; tener frío to be cold; hace frío
   it is cold
frito, -a fried
fruta fruit
fuente (f.) fountain
fuerte strong
fumar to smoke
funcionar to function, work
funcionario functionary, public official
fútbol (m.) soccer

G

ganar to earn, win
ganas desire; tener ganas de + inf. to feel
   like + pres. part.
ganga bargain
gastar to spend
gente (f.) people
geografía geography
gobierno government
gordo, -a fat
gozar (de) to enjoy
gracias thank you
gran, grande large, great
gritar to shout
grupo group
guante (m.) glove
guardia (m.) guard
gustar to be pleasing to
gusto pleasure; Mucho gusto Glad to
   meet you

H

haber (used with past part.) to have
había there was, were
habitación (f.) room
hablar to speak, talk
habrá there will be
habría there would be
hacer to do, make; hacer frío, calor, etc.,
   to be cold, warm, etc.; hacer una
   pregunta to ask a question; hacer un
   viaje to take a trip; hacerse to become;
   hace dos años two years ago, for two
   years
hacia toward
hambre (f.) hunger
hasta until, even; hasta luego so long,
   see you later; hasta mañana until
   tomorrow, see you tomorrow; hasta
   que until; hasta pronto see you soon.

hay there is, there are; **hay que** + *inf.* it is necessary + *inf.*

hecho (*past part.*) done

helado ice cream

hermana sister

hermano brother

hermoso, -a beautiful, handsome

hija daughter

hijo son

historia history

¡Hola! Hello! Hi!

holandés Dutch

hombre (*m.*) man

hora hour; **¿Qué hora es?** What time is it?; **¿A qué hora . . . ?** (At) what time . . . ?

hoy today

hubo there was, were

huésped (*m.*) guest, lodger; **huéspeda** (*f.*) guest, lodger

huevo egg

humor: estar de mal (buen) humor to be in a bad (good) mood

I

idioma (*m.*) language

ido (*past part.*) gone

igual equal

ilusión (*f.*) illusion

imaginarse to imagine

importancia importance

importar to be important, matter

impresionante impressive

incluso including, even

indio Indian

inglés (*m.*) English, Englishman

insistir to insist; **insistir en** + *inf.* to insist upon something

interesante interesting

interesar to interest

interrumpir to interrupt

íntimo, -a intimate

invierno winter

invitar to invite

ir to go; **irse** to go away, go off; **ir a** + *inf.* to be going to; **ir de compras** to go shopping; **¡Qué va!** Nonsense! On the contrary; **vámonos** let's be going; **vamos** let's go

irlandés Irish

izquierda left

J

jefe (*m.*) leader, chief, boss

joven (*adj.*) young; (*noun*) young man or woman; **jóvenes** young men or women, young people

joya jewel

joyería jewelry store

jueves Thursday

jugador (*m.*) player

jugar (**ue**) to play

julio July

junio June

junta legislative council

juventud (*f.*) youth

K

kilómetro kilometer (⅝ mile)

L

lado side; **al lado** (**de**) alongside (of), beside

lago lake

lápiz (*m.*) pencil

lástima shame, pity; **es lástima** it's a shame, pity

lavandera washerwoman

lavar to wash; **lavarse** to wash oneself;

lección (*f.*) lesson

leche (*f.*) milk

lechuga lettuce

leer to read

legumbre (*f.*) vegetable

lejano, -a distant

lejos distant, far away

lengua language

levantarse to get up

libre free

librería bookstore

libro book

limpiar to clean

limpieza cleaning, cleanliness

limpio, -a clean

liquidación (*f.*) sale

lista menu

loco madman; **loco, -a** mad, crazy

locura madness, insanity

luego then; **luego que** as soon as

lugar (*m.*) place

luna moon

lunes Monday

luz (*f.*) light

LL

llamar to call, to knock; **llamarse** to be named, be called; **Me llamo . . .** My name is . . .

llegar to arrive

lleno, -a full

llevar to carry, wear; **llevarse** to take away, carry off

llover (**ue**) to rain; **llover a cántaros** to rain hard (bucketsful)

lluvia rain

M

madre (*f.*) mother

magnífico, -a great, magnificent

mal badly; **hace mal tiempo** the weather is bad

maldito, -a cursed
maleta suitcase
malo, -a bad; ill, sick
mamá mother
mañana tomorrow; ¡Hasta mañana! See you tomorrow!
mandar to order, send
manera way, manner
manga sleeve; mangas cortas short sleeves; mangas largas long sleeves
mano (f.) hand
mantequilla butter
manzana apple; city block
máquina (lavadora) (washing) machine
maravilla marvel
martes Tuesday
marzo March
más more
matrimonio marriage
mayo May
mayor older, oldest
media stocking, hose; half
medicina medicine
médico doctor
mejor better, best
menor younger, youngest
menos less, least; a menos que unless
menudo: a menudo often
mercado market
merendar (ie) to have an afternoon snack, to picnic
mes (m.) month
mesa table
mestizo mestizo, of mixed blood
mi, mis my
miedo fear
mientras (que) while; mientras tanto meanwhile, in the meantime
miércoles Wednesday
mil thousand
millón million
ministerio government department
minuto minute
mío, -a (poss. pron.) mine
mirar to look (at)
mismo, -a same
mitad (f.) half
modelo model, make
modo: de modo que so, so that; de todos modos anyhow, at any rate
molestar to bother
molestia bother
montaña mountain
moreno, -a brunette, dark
morir (ue, u) to die
mostrar (ue) to show
muchacha girl
muchacho boy
mucho, -a much; Mucho gusto Glad to meet you
muchos, -as many

muerto (past part.) dead
mujer (f.) woman
mundial (adj.) world
mundo world
museo museum
muy very

N

nacer to be born
nación (f.) nation
nada nothing
nadar to swim
nadie no one
naturalmente naturally
necesidad (f.) necessity
necesitar to need
negar (ie) to deny, refuse
negocio business
nevar (ie) to snow
nilón (m.) nylon
ninguno, -a not any, none
niña girl
niño boy
noche (f.) night; de noche at night; esta noche tonight; anoche last night; por la noche in the evening; Buenas noches Goodnight
norte (m.) north
nota grade
noticia news
novecientos nine hundred
noveno, -a ninth
noventa ninety
noviembre November
novia (f.) sweetheart; novio (m.) sweetheart
nube (f.) cloud; hay nubes it is cloudy
nuestro, -a, nuestros, -as our
nueve nine
nuevo, -a new; ¿Qué hay de nuevo? What's new?
número number
nunca never

O

o or
ochenta eighty
ocho eight
ochocientos eight hundred
octavo, -a eighth
octubre October
ocupar to occupy
oeste (m.) west
oficina office
ofrecer to offer
oír to hear
¡Ojo! Take care! Watch out!
olvidar to forget
once eleven
organizar to organize
otoño fall, autumn

otro, -a other, another

P

padre (*m.*) father
pagar to pay; **pagar al contado** to pay cash
país (*m.*) country
pan (*m.*) bread
pantalones (*m.*) trousers
papá (*m.*) father
par (*m.*) pair
para to, in order to, for, by (a certain time); **para que** in order that; **¿Para qué?** Why? For what reason?
parecer to seem, appear
parecido, -a similar, alike
pariente (*m.*) relative
parque (*m.*) park
parte (*f.*) part
partido game, match
pasar to pass, spend (time); **¿Qué pasa?** What's happening?
paseo walk, ride
patata potato
pedir (**i, i**) to ask (for), request
película film, moving picture
pelo hair
pensar (**ie**) to think; **pensar +** *inf.* to intend + *inf.*
peor worse, worst
pequeño, -a small
perder (**ie**) to lose, miss; **perder el tiempo** to waste time
periódico newspaper
permiso permission
permitir to permit, allow
pero but
perro dog
pesar to weigh; **a pesar de** in spite of
pescado fish
peseta unit of currency (Spain)
pie (*m.*) foot
piso apartment, floor
plato plate, dish
plaza plaza, central square
pluma pen
poco, -a little (in amount)
poder (**ue**) to be able; **poder con** to be able to deal with, cope with
policía (*m.*) policeman; (*f.*) police
política politics
poner to put, place; **poner la radio** to turn on the radio; **ponerse** to put on (clothes), to become, **ponerse a** to begin to
popularidad (*f.*) popularity
por through, along, by, for, on behalf of, for the sake of, in exchange for; **por eso** for that reason; **por favor** please; **por la mañana (tarde, noche)** in the morning (afternoon, evening); **¿Por**

dónde se va . . . ? How do you get to . . . ?; **por supuesto** of course
porque because
¿por qué? why?
portero doorman
postre (*m.*) dessert
practicar to practice, play
precio price
precioso, -a pretty
preciso necessary
preferir (**ie, i**) to prefer
preguntar to ask
primero, -a first
producido produced
pronto soon
propósito intention; **a propósito** by the way
pueblo small town
puerta door
pues well
puesto job, position; (*past part.*) put
puro pure

Q

que that, who, which, than; **lo que** what
qué: ¿Qué? What? Which? **¿Qué hay de nuevo?** What's new?; **¡Qué va!** Nonsense! On the contrary!
quedar to remain, have left; **quedarle bien** to fit one well; **quedarse** to stay, remain
quejarse (**de**) to complain (about)
querer (**ie**) to wish, want, love
quien who
quince fifteen
quinientos five hundred
quinto, -a fifth
quitar to take away; **quitarse** to take off

R

raro, -a strange
rato while
razón (*f.*) reason; **tener razón** to be right
realidad: en realidad as a matter of fact
recepcionista (*m.* or *f.*) receptionist
recibir to receive
recién recent, recently
recomendar (**ie**) to recommend
recordar (ue) to remember
refresco cold drink, refreshment
regalar to give (as a gift)
regatear to bargain, dicker
regresar to return
repente: de repente suddenly
repetir (**i, i**) to repeat
resolver to solve
responder to respond, answer
restaurante (*m.*) restaurant
revista magazine
rico, -a rich
río river

rogar (ue) to beg
romper to break
ropa clothing, clothes
roto (*past part.*) broken
rubio, -a blond
ruido noise

S

sábado Saturday
saber to know (a fact)
sala living room
salir to leave, go out, come out; **salir caro** to be expensive
saludar to greet
sed (*f.*) thirst; **tener (mucha) sed** to be (very) thirsty
seguida: en seguida immediately
seguir (i, i) to follow, continue
segundo, -a second
seguro, -a sure, certain
seis six
seiscientos six hundred
semana week; **fin de semana** weekend
sentarse (ie) to sit down
sentir (ie, i) to feel sorry, regret; **lo siento (mucho)** I am (very) sorry; **sentirse** to feel
señor mister, man; **señores** gentlemen
señora Mrs., lady, wife; **señoras** ladies
señorita Miss, girl
septiembre September
séptimo, -a seventh
ser to be
serio, -a serious
servir (i, i) to serve; **¿En qué puedo servirle?** What can I do for you? May I help you?
sesenta sixty
setecientos seven hundred
setenta seventy
sexto, -a sixth
si if
siempre always
siesta afternoon nap
siete seven
siguiente following
silla chair
simpático, -a nice
sin without; **sin embargo** nevertheless; **sin que** without; **sin más ni más** without more ado, just like that
sino but, on the contrary
sirvienta maid
sitio place
situado, -a located
sobre on, about, over
sol (*m.*) sun
solo (*adj.*) alone
sólo (*adv.*) only
sombrero hat
sonar (ue) to ring, sound

sopa soup
sóquer (*m.*) soccer
sorprender to surprise
su, sus your
subir to go up
sucio, -a dirty
sueldo salary
sueño sleep, dream; **tener (mucho) sueño** to be (very) sleepy
suéter (*m.*) sweater
suficiente sufficient
sur (*m.*) south
suyo, -a (*poss. pron.*) his, hers, yours, etc.

T

tal such, such a; **tal vez** perhaps; **con tal que** provided that; **¿Qué tal?** How are you? How goes it?
también also
tampoco neither, either
tan so; **tanto, -a** so much, so many; **tanto . . . como** as much (many) . . . as; **No es para tanto** It's not all that important
tardar to delay, be late
tarde (*adv.* or *adj.*) late; (*noun*) afternoon; **de la tarde** in the afternoon (*with hour given*); **por la tarde** in the afternoon (*no hour given*); **Buenas tardes** Good afternoon
teatro theater
teléfono telephone
televisión (*f.*) television
tema (*m.*) theme, topic
temer to be afraid, fear
templo temple
temprano early
tener to have; **tener que** to have to; **tener calor, frío,** etc., to be warm, cold, etc.; **tener confianza en** to have confidence in; **tener miedo de** to be afraid of; **tener prisa** to be in a hurry; **tener sueño** to be sleepy; **tener lugar** to take place
tercero, -a third
terminar to end
tía aunt
tiempo weather, time; **los tiempos pasados** the old days, days gone by
tienda store
tierra land
tío uncle
todavía still, yet
todo, -a all, everything
tomar to have (food or drink), take
tomate (*m.*) tomato
tontería silliness, stupid thing
tortilla omelette (*Spain*), cornmeal pancake (*L. Am.*)
trabajar to work

trabajo work; **costarle a uno trabajo** to be a lot of work
traer to bring
tráfico traffic
traje (*m.*) suit; **traje de baño** bathing suit
tratar (**de**) to try (to)
trece thirteen
tren (*m.*) train
tres three
trescientos three hundred
triste sad
tu, tus your
tuyo, -a (*poss. pron.*) yours

U

último, -a last
un, uno, -a a, an, one
universidad (*f.*) university
universitario, -a (*adj.*) university
usted you; **ustedes** you (*pl.*)

V

vacaciones (*f.*) vacation
vamos let's go; **vámonos** let's be going; **vamos a** + *inf.* let's . . .
variación (*f.*) variation
variedad (*f.*) variety
varios, -as several
vaso glass
¡Vaya! Well! For goodness sake!
vecino, -a (*noun*) neighbor
veinte twenty
vender to sell
venir to come; **venir bien con** to look well with; **venga lo que venga** come what may, no matter what happens
ventaja advantage
ventana window
ver to see
verano summer
verdad (*f.*) truth; **es verdad** it is true; **¿no es verdad?** isn't it (so)?; **de veras** truly, certainly
vestido dress
vestirse (**i, i**) to get dressed
vez time; **otra vez** again; **a veces** at times; **muchas veces** often, many times; **alguna vez** ever; **tal vez** perhaps; **a la vez** at the same time
viajar to travel
viaje (*m.*) trip
vida life
viejo, -a (*adj.*) old; (*noun*) old man, old woman
viento wind
viernes Friday
visitar to visit
visto (*past part.*) seen
vivir to live
volver (**ue**) to return
vuelto (*past. part.*) returned

Y

y and
ya already, now

Z

zapatería shoe store
zapato shoe

VOCABULARY
English-Spanish

A

a, an un, uno, -a
able: to be able poder (ue); **to be able to deal with** poder con
about sobre
abroad extranjero
account: on account of por
acquainted: to be acquainted with conocer
addition: in addition to además de
address dirección (*f.*)
admit (*inf.*) admitir
advantage ventaja
advertisement anuncio
advise (*inf.*) aconsejar
afraid: to be afraid temer, tener miedo de
after después de; **afterwards** después
afternoon tarde (*m.*); **in the afternoon** por la tarde (*no hour given*); de la tarde (*with hour given*); **Good afternoon** Buenas tardes
again otra vez
Agreed! ¡De acuerdo!
airplane avión (*m.*)
airport aeropuerto
alike parecido, -a
all todo, -a; **all right** está bien
allow (*inf.*) permitir
almost casi
alone (*adj.*) solo
along por
alongside of al lado (de)
already ya
also también
although aunque
always siempre
among entre
amusement diversión (*f.*)
amusing divertido, -a
and y
angel ángel (*m.*)

announce (*inf.*) anunciar
another otro, -a
answer (*inf.*) contestar, responder
any algún, alguno, -a; **anyhow** de todos modos; **anyone: She doesn't forget anyone** No olvida a nadie; **anything: I never ask for anything** Nunca pido nada
apartment piso
appear (*inf.*) parecer
apple manzana
approach (*inf.*) acercarse
April abril
army ejército
arrange (*inf.*) arreglar
arrive (*inf.*) llegar
as (like) como; **as if** como si; **as soon as** así que, en cuanto, luego que; **as usual** como de costumbre
ask (*inf.*) preguntar; **to ask for** pedir (i, i); **to ask a question** hacer una pregunta
at en (*a place*), a (*time*)
atmosphere ambiente (*m.*)
attend (*inf.*) asistir (a), presenciar
August agosto
aunt tía
automobile coche (*m.*)
autumn otoño
avenue avenida
awaken (*inf.*) despertarse (ie)

B

backward atrasado, -a
bad malo, -a; **badly** mal; **the weather is bad** hace mal tiempo
baggage equipaje (*m.*)
bank banco
bargain ganga; (*inf.*) regatear
bath baño
bathing suit traje de baño
be (*inf.*) ser, estar
beautiful bonito, -a

because porque
become (*inf.*) ponerse
bed cama
bedroom dormitorio, alcoba
before antes; **before + pres. part.** antes
  de + *inf.*; **before** (*before a clause*) antes
  (de) que
beg (*inf.*) rogar (ue)
begin (*inf.*) comenzar (ie), empezar (ie);
  at the beginning al principio; **to**
  begin to comenzar a + *inf.*, ponerse a
  + *inf.*
behalf: on behalf of por
behind detrás de
believe (*inf.*) creer
beside al lado (de)
besides además de
best el (la) mejor
better mejor
between entre
big grande
bill cuenta
block manzana
blond rubio, -a
blouse blusa
book libro
bookstore librería
bored: to be bored estar aburrido, -a
boring: to be boring ser aburrido, -a
born: to be born nacer
boss jefe (*m.*)
bother molestia; (*inf.*) molestar
boy niño, chico, muchacho
brake freno
bread pan (*m.*)
break (*inf.*) romper
breakfast desayuno; **to eat breakfast**
  desayunarse
bring (*inf.*) traer
broken (*past part.*) roto
brother hermano
brunette moreno, -a
bus autobús (*m.*)
business negocio
but pero, sino
butter mantequilla
buy (*inf.*) comprar
by para; (*by a certain time*) por

C

call (*inf.*) llamar; **to be called** llamarse
calm down (*inf.*) calmarse
can (*v.*) poder (ue)
car coche (*m.*), automóvil (*m.*)
care for (*inf.*) cuidar
carry (*inf.*) llevar; **to carry off** llevarse
case caso; **in case that** en caso de que
catch (*inf.*) coger
center centro
certain cierto, -a, seguro, -a; **certainly**
  de veras

chair silla
champion campeón (*m.*); **championship**
  campeonato
change (*inf.*) cambiar
charge (*inf.*) cobrar; **charge account**
  cuenta corriente
charm (*inf.*) encantar
chat (*inf.*) charlar
chicken pollo
chief jefe (*m.*)
chocolate chocolate (*m.*)
choose (*inf.*) escoger
city ciudad (*f.*)
class clase (*f.*)
clean limpio, -a; **to clean** limpiar;
  cleaning, cleanliness limpieza
clear claro, -a
clerk dependiente, -a
climate clima (*n.*)
close (*inf.*) cerrar (ie); **close (to)** cerca (de)
clothes, clothing ropa
cloud nube (*f.*); **it is cloudy** hay nubes
coffee café (*m.*)
cold frío, -a; **to be cold** tener frío; **it is**
  (very) cold hace (mucho) frío
collect (*inf.*) cobrar
come (*inf.*) venir; **to come out** salir;
  come what may venga lo que venga
complain (*inf.*) quejarse (de)
complicated complicado, -a
condition: in bad condition en malas
  condiciones
confidence confianza; **to have confidence**
  in tener confianza en
consume (*inf.*) consumir
continue (*inf.*) seguir (i, i)
contrary: on the contrary ¡Qué va!
cook cocinera
cool fresco, -a; **it's cool out** hace fresco
cope: to cope with poder con
corner esquina
cornmeal pancake tortilla (*L. Am.*)
correspond (*inf.*) corresponder
cost (*inf.*) costar (ue)
count (*inf.*) contar (ue)
country país (*m.*); **countryside** campo
course curso; **of course** por supuesto
cousin primo, -a
cover (*inf.*) cubrir
covered (*past part.*) cubierto
cross (*inf.*) cruzar
cursed maldito, -a
custard flan (*m.*)
custom costumbre (*f.*)
cut (*inf.*) cortar

D

damage (*inf.*) estropear
dance (*inf.*) bailar; (*m.*) baile
dark moreno, -a
date fecha

daughter hija
day día (*m.*); **every day** todos los días;
  all day todo el día; **the old days, days**
  gone by los tiempos pasados; **day**
  before yesterday anteayer
dead (*past part.*) muerto
December diciembre (*m.*)
decide (*inf.*) decidir
defect defecto
delay (*inf.*) tardar
deny (*inf.*) negar (ie)
department store almacén (*m.*)
desire (*inf.*) desear
dessert postre (*m.*)
dicker (*inf.*) regatear
die (*inf.*) morirse (ue, u)
different diferente
difficult difícil
dinner cena, comida; **to have dinner**
  cenar
director director (*m.*)
dirty sucio, -a
disaster desastre (*m.*)
dish plato
display window escaparate (*m.*)
distant lejano, -a; (*adv.*) lejos
district barrio
do (*inf.*) hacer
doctor médico, doctor (*m.*)
dog perro
dollar dólar (*m.*)
done (*past part.*) hecho
door puerta; **doorman** portero
doubt dudar
doubtful dudoso, -a
downtown centro
dream sueño
dress vestido; **to get dressed** vestirse
  (i, i)
drink (*inf.*) beber; **cold drink** refresco
drive (*inf.*) conducir
during durante

E

each cada
early temprano
earn (*inf.*) ganar
east este (*m.*)
easy fácil
eat (*inf.*) comer ; **to eat lunch** almorzar
  (ue)
educated educado, -a
egg huevo
eight ocho
eighth octavo, -a
eighty ochenta
either tampoco, o
elevator ascensor (*m.*)
eleven once
else: **Don't say anything else** No diga
  nada más

employment empleo
enchant (*inf.*) encantar
end (*inf.*) terminar
English, Englishman inglés (*m.*)
enjoy (*inf.*) gozar (de)
enter (*inf.*) entrar (en)
entertainment diversión (*f.*)
epoch época
equal igual
equator ecuador (*m.*)
even hasta, incluso
evening: **in the evening** por la noche
ever alguna vez
every cada; **every day** todos los días;
  everything todo
evident evidente
exaggerate (*inf.*) exagerar
examination examen (*m.*)
exchange: **in exchange for** por
excited: **Don't get so excited** No te
  pongas tan emocionado, -a
expect (*inf.*) esperar
expensive caro, -a; **to be expensive** salir
  caro, -a

F

face cara
fail : **not to fail** no dejar de
fall otoño; **to fall** caer; **to fall down**
  caerse
family familia
far (away) lejos
fascinate (*inf.*) encantar
fat gordo, -a
father padre (*m.*), papá (*m.*)
fear miedo; **to fear** temer
February febrero
feel (*inf.*) sentirse (ie, i); **to feel like**
  tener ganas (de)
fifteen quince
fifth quinto, -a
fifty cincuenta
film película
finally al fin, por fin
find (*inf.*) encontrar (ue)
finish (*inf.*) terminar, acabar
first primer, primero, -a; **at first** al
  principio
fish pescado
five cinco
floor piso
fold (*inf.*) doblar
follow (*inf.*) seguir (i, i); **following**
  siguiente
food comida
foot pie (*m.*)
for para, por; **for example** por ejemplo
foreign extranjero, -a; **foreigner**
  extranjero
forget (*inf.*) olvidar
form (*inf.*) formar

fortunately afortunadamente
fortune fortuna
forty cuarenta
fountain fuente (*f.*)
four cuatro
fourteen catorce
fourth cuarto, -a
free libre
fresh fresco, -a
Friday viernes (*m.*)
fried frito, -a
friend amigo, -a
from de, desde
in front (of) delante (de)
fruit fruta
full lleno, -a
function (*inf.*) funcionar

G

game partido
gentleman caballero
geography geografía
German alemán
Germany Alemania
get (*inf.*) conseguir (i, i), coger; **to get up**
  levantarse; **to get married** casarse (con);
  to get off, get out of (a vehicle)
  bajarse (de)
girl señorita, muchacha, chica, niña
girlfriend novia
give (*inf.*) dar, regalar (*as a gift*)
glad: to be glad alegrarse (de); **Glad
  to meet you** Mucho gusto
glass vaso
glove guante (*m.*)
go (*inf.*) ir; **to go away, go off** irse; **to
  go down** bajar; **to be going to** ir a +
  inf.; **to go out** salir; **to go to bed**
  acostarse (ue); **let's go** vamos; **let's
  be going** vámonos; **let's . . .** vamos a
  + *inf.*; **to go shopping** ir de compras;
  to go up, get on subir
God Dios (*m.*)
gone (*past part.*) ido
good buen, bueno, -a; **Good morning**
  Buenos días; **Good afternoon** Buenas
  tardes; **Good night** Buenas noches;
  good-bye adiós; **to have a good
  time** divertirse (ie, i); **to say
  good-bye (to)** despedirse de (i, i);
  Oh my goodness! ¡Dios mío!; **For
  goodness sake!** ¡Vaya!
government gobierno
grade nota
grandfather abuelo
grandmother abuela
grasp (*inf.*) coger
great gran, grande, magnífico, -a
greet (*inf.*) saludar
guard guardia (*m.*)
guest huésped (*m.*), huéspeda (*f.*)

H

hair pelo
half mitad (*f.*), medio, -a
hand mano (*f.*)
handsome hermoso, -a
happening : What's happening? ¿Qué
  para?
happy feliz, contento, -a; **to be happy**
  alegrarse (de)
haste prisa
hat sombrero
have (*inf.*) tener; **to have to** tener que
  + *inf.*; **to have just** + *past part.* acabar
  de + *inf.*; **What are you going to have
  (food or drink)?** ¿Qué va a tomar?;
  to have left quedar; **to have** + *past
  part.* haber
he él
head cabeza
hear (*inf.*) oír
heat calor (*m.*); **It is hot** Hace calor
heating calefacción (*f.*)
height altura
Hello Hola
help (*inf.*) ayudar; **May I help you?**
  ¿En qué puedo servirle?
her su, sus
here aquí
hers suyo, -a
highway carretera
him le (*dir.* and *indir. object*), él (*after
  prep.*)
his su, sus; (*poss. pron.*) suyo, -a
history historia
home: at home en casa
hope (*inf.*) esperar
hose media(s)
hot (*adj.*) caliente; **It is hot** Hace calor
hour hora
house casa
how? ¿cómo?; **How do you get to . . .?**
  ¿Por dónde se va a . . .?; **how much?**
  ¿cuánto (-a, -os, -as)?; **how many?**
  ¿cuánto (-a, -os, -as)? **How are you?**
  How goes it? ¿Qué tal?
humor: to be in a bad (good) humor
  estar de mal (buen) humor
hundred cien; **two hundred** doscientos,
  -as; **three hundred** trescientos, -as;
  four hundred cuatrocientos, -as;
  five hundred quinientos, -as; **six
  hundred** seiscientos, -as; **seven
  hundred** setecientos, -as; **eight
  hundred** ochocientos, -as; **nine
  hundred** novecientos, -as
hunger hambre (*f.*)
hungry: I'm hungry tengo hambre
hurry: to be in a hurry tener prisa
hurt (*inf.*) doler (ue)
husband esposo

I

I yo
ice cream helado
if si
ill enfermo, -a, malo, -a
illusion ilusión
imagine (*inf.*) imaginarse
immediately en seguida
importance importancia; **to be important** importar; **It's not all that important** No es para tanto
in en, de **(after superlatives); in order that** para que; **in case that** en caso de que; **in spite of** a pesar de
including incluso
Indian indio
insanity locura
insist insistir en; **to insist upon something** insistir en + *inf.*
intention propósito
interest (*inf.*) interesar
interesting interesante
interrupt (*inf.*) interrumpir
intimate íntimo
invite (*inf.*) invitar
it lo, la (*dir. obj.*), él, ella, ello (*after prep.*)

J

jail cárcel (*f.*)
January enero
jewel joya
jewelry store joyería
job puesto, empleo
July julio
June junio
just: just like that sin más ni más; **to have just** + *past part.* acabar de + *inf.*

K

kilometer kilómetro
kind clase (*f.*)
kitchen cocina
knock (*inf.*) llamar
know (*inf.*) saber (*a fact, how to*), conocer (*a person, place, etc.*)

L

lack (*inf.*) faltar
lady señora, mujer (*f.*), señorita; **ladies** señoras
lake lago
land tierra
language idioma (*m.*), lengua
large gran, grande
last (*inf.*) durar; **at last** al fin, por fin; (*adj.*) último
late tarde; **to be late** tardar; **later,** después; **see you later** hasta luego
latter: the latter éste, ésta, éstos, éstas

leader jefe (*m.*)
learn (*inf.*) aprender; **to learn** + *inf.* aprender a + *inf.*
leave (*inf.*) salir (de), dejar
left izquierda; **to have left** quedar
legislative: legislative council junta
less, least menos
lesson lección (*f.*)
let's vamos a + *inf.*
letter carta
lettuce lechuga
library biblioteca
life vida
light luz (*f.*)
like (*prep.*) como; **to like** gustar
listen: to listen (to) escuchar
little pequeño, -a (*size*), poco (*amount*); **a little** un poco
live (*inf.*) vivir
living room sala
located situado, -a
lodger huésped (*m.*), huéspeda (*f.*)
look: to look (at) mirar; **to look (for)** buscar; **to look well with** venir bien con
lose (*inf.*) perder (ie)
lot: a lot mucho; **what a lot of** cuánto
love (*inf.*) querer, amar
low bajo, -a; **lower, go down** (*inf.*) bajar
lunch alumerzo

M

madman loco
madness locura
magazine revista
magnificent magnífico, -a
maid criada, sirvienta
make modelo; **to make** hacer
man hombre (*m.*)
manner manera
many muchos, -as; **so many** tanto, -a, -os, -as; **as many . . . as** tanto, -a, os, -as . . . como
March marzo
market mercado
marriage matrimonio; **to get married (to)** casarse (con)
marvel maravilla
match partido
matter (*inf.*) importar; **as a matter of fact** en realidad; **no matter what happens** venga lo que venga
May mayo
me me (*dir. and indir.*), mi (*after prep.*)
meal comida
meantime: in the meantime mientras tanto
meat carne (*f.*)
medicine medicina

meet (*inf.*) encontrar (ue); conocer (*pret.*); **Glad to meet you** Mucho gusto
menu lista
mestizo (*of mixed blood*) mestizo
milk leche (*f.*)
million millón (*m.*)
mine mío, -a
minute minuto
miss (*inf.*) perder (ie); **Miss** señorita
mister señor (*m.*); señores (*pl.*)
model modelo
Monday lunes (*m.*)
money dinero
month mes (*m.*)
moon luna
more más; **moreover** además
morning mañana; **Good morning** Buenos días; **in the morning** por la mañana
mother madre (*f.*), mamá
mountain montaña
mouth boca
movie cine (*m.*), película (*film*)
Mrs. señora
much mucho, -a; **too much** demasiado; **so much** tanto, -a; **as much . . . as** tanto, -a . . . como
must deber
my mi, mis

N

name nombre (*m.*); **What is your name?** ¿Cómo se llama Ud.?; **My name is . . .** Me llamo . . .; **to be named** llamarse
nap (*afternoon*) siesta
nation nación (*f.*)
naturally naturalmente
near (to) cerca (de); **to draw near (to)** acercarse (a)
necessary necesario, -a, preciso, -a; **it is necessary** hay que + *inf.*
necklace collar (*m.*)
necktie corbata
need (*inf.*) necesitar, faltar
neighbor vecino, -a
neighborhood barrio
neither tampoco
never nunca
nevertheless sin embargo
new nuevo, -a; **What's new?** ¿Qué hay de nuevo?
news noticia(s)
New York Nueva York
nice simpático, -a, amable
night noche (*f.*); **last night** anoche; **at night** de noche; **tonight** esta noche; **in the evening** por la noche
nine nueve
ninety noventa
ninth noveno, -a
noise ruido
none ninguno, -a

Nonsense! ¡Qué va!
no one nadie
north norte (*m.*)
nothing nada
notice (*inf.*) fijarse (en)
November noviembre (*m.*)
now ahora, ya; **right now** ahora mismo
nowadays hoy día
number número
nylon nilón (*m.*)

O

obtain (*inf.*) conseguir (i, i)
occasion vez (*f.*)
occupy (*inf.*) ocupar
October octubre (*m.*)
of de
offer (*inf.*) ofrecer
office oficina, despacho
often muchas veces, a menudo
Oh me! ¡Ay de mí!
O.K. (Agreed) De acuerdo
old viejo, -a; **How old are you?** ¿Cuántos años tiene Ud.?; **to be—years old** tener —años; **older** mayor; **oldest** el (la) mayor
omelette tortilla (*Spain*)
on en, sobre; **on the way to** camino a; **on the following day** al día siguiente
one uno, un, una
only (*adv.*) sólo
open (*inf.*) abrir
opened (*past part.*) abierto
or o
order (*inf.*) mandar; **in order to** para; **in order that** para que
organize (*inf.*) organizar
other otro, -a
ought (*inf.*) deber
our, ours nuestro, -a
over sobre
overcoat abrigo
own propio, -a

P

pair par (*m.*)
parents padres (*m.*)
park parque (*m.*)
part parte (*f.*)
pass (*inf.*) pasar
pay (*inf.*) pagar; **to pay cash** pagar al contado
pen pluma
pencil lápiz (*m.*)
people gente (*f.*)
perhaps tal vez
period época
permit (*inf.*) permitir
picnic (*inf.*) merendar (ie)
picture película (**moving picture**)
pity lástima; **It's a pity** Es (una) lástima

place lugar (*m.*), sitio; **to place** poner
plate plato
play (*inf.*) jugar (ue), practicar
player jugador (*m.*)
plaza plaza
pleasant agradable
please por favor, haga Ud. el favor de . . .
pleasing: to be pleasing to gustar
pleasure gusto
police policía; **policeman** policía (*m.*)
politics política
popularity popularidad (*f.*)
position puesto
potato patata
practice (*inf.*) practicar
prefer (*inf.*) preferir (ie, i)
preparation preparación (*f.*)
prepare (*inf.*) preparar
present (*inf.*) presentar; **at the present time** actualmente
president presidente (*m.*)
pretty bonito, -a, precioso, -a
price precio
priest cura (*m.*)
problem problema (*m.*)
prove (*inf.*) probar (ue)
provided: provided that con tal que
purse bolso
put (*inf.*) poner; **to put on** ponerse; (*past part.*) puesto

Q

quantity cantidad (*f.*)
quarter cuarto
quite bastante

R

rain lluvia; **to rain** llover (ue); **to rain hard (bucketsful)** llover a cántaros
rate: at any rate de todos modos
rather bastante
read (*inf.*) leer
realize (*inf.*) darse cuenta de
reason razón (*f.*); **for that reason** por eso; **For what reason?** ¿Para qué?
receive (*inf.*) recibir
recent (recently) recién
receptionist recepcionista (*m.* and *f.*)
recommend (*inf.*) recomendar (ie)
refreshment refresco
refuse (*inf.*) negar (ie)
relative pariente (m.)
remain (*inf.*) quedar, quedarse
remember (*inf.*) recordar (ue), acordarse (ue) (de)
repair (*inf.*) arreglar
repeat (*inf.*) repetir (i, i)
respond (*inf.*) responder
rest (*inf.*) descansar

restaurant restaurante (*m.*)
return (*inf.*) volver (ue), regresar
returned (*past part.*) vuelto
rice arroz (*m.*)
rich rico, -a
ride paseo
right derecha; **to be right** tener razón
ring sonar (ue)
river río
room cuarto, habitación (*f.*)
ruin (*inf.*) estropear
run (*inf.*) correr; **(machinery)** andar

S

sad triste
said (*past part.*) dicho
sake: for the sake of por
salad ensalada
salary sueldo
sale liquidación (*f.*)
same mismo, -a
Saturday sábado
say (*inf.*) decir; **to say good-bye (to)** despedirse (i, i) (de)
school escuela
season estación (*f.*)
seat asiento
second segundo, -a
see (*inf.*) ver, presenciar; **see you later** hasta luego; **see you tomorrow** hasta mañana; **see you soon** hasta pronto
seem (*inf.*) parecer
seen (*past part.*) visto
sell (*inf.*) vender
September septiembre (*m.*)
serious serio, -a
seven siete
seventh séptimo, -a
seventy setenta
several varios, -as
shame lástima; **It's a shame** Es (una) lástima
she ella
shirt camisa
shoe zapato
shoe store zapatería
short bajo, -a, corto, -a
should deber
shout (*inf.*) gritar
show enseñar, mostrar (ue)
sick enfermo, -a, malo, -a
side lado; **alongside of, beside** al lado (de)
sidewalk acera
silliness tontería
similar parecido, -a
since desde
sing cantar
sister hermana

sit (down) sentarse (ie)
six seis
sixth sexto, -a
sixty sesenta
skirt falda
sky cielo
sleep (inf.) dormir (ue, u); to go to sleep
dormirse; to be very sleepy tener
mucho sueño; (noun) sueño
sleeves: short sleeves mangas cortas;
long sleeves mangas largas
small pequeño, -a, chico, -a
smoke (inf.) fumar
snack: to have an afternoon snack
merendar (ie)
snow (inf.) nevar (ie); snow nieve (f.)
so de modo que, tan; so that para que,
de modo que; so much tanto
soccer fútbol (m.), sóquer (m.)
sock calcetín (m.)
some unos, -as, algún, alguno, -a, -os,
-as; someone alguien; something algo;
somewhat algo
son hijo
song canción (f.)
soon pronto; as soon as en cuanto
sorry: to feel sorry (regret) sentir
(ie, i); I am (very) sorry Lo siento
(mucho)
sound (inf.) sonar (ue)
soup sopa
south sur (m.)
Spanish (adj.) español, -a; (noun)
español (m.)
speak (inf.) hablar
spectator espectador (m.)
spend (inf.) gastar (money); pasar
(time)
sport deporte (m.)
spring primavera
stability estabilidad (f.)
stadium estadio
start (inf.) arrancar (machinery)
stay (inf.) quedarse; to stay in a hotel
alojarse
steak biftec (m.)
still todavía
stocking media
stop (inf.) dejar de + inf., detenerse
store tienda
straight derecho
strange raro, -a
stranger forastero, -a
street calle (f.)
strong fuerte
student alumno, -a, estudiante (m. and
f.)
study (inf.) estudiar; (noun) estudio
stupendous estupendo, -a
stupid: stupid thing tontería

such (a) tal
suddenly de repente
sufficient suficiente
suit traje (m.); bathing suit traje de
baño; to suit corresponder
suitcase maleta
summer verano
sun sol (m.); It is (very) sunny Hace
(mucho) sol, Hay (mucho) sol
Sunday domingo
sure seguro, -a
surely ¡cómo no!
surname apellido
surprise (inf.) sorprender
sweater suéter (m.)
sweetheart novio, -a
swim (inf.) nadar

T

table mesa; table setting cubierto
take (inf.) tomar, llevar; to take a walk
dar un paseo; to take a trip hacer un
viaje; to take away quitar, llevarse; to
take off quitarse; to take over
apoderarse; Take care! ¡Ojo!; to take
place tener lugar
talk (inf.) charlar, hablar
tall alto, -a
taste (inf.) probar (ue)
teach (inf.) enseñar
team equipo
telephone teléfono
television televisión (f.)
tell (inf.) decir, contar (ue)
ten diez
tend (inf.) cuidar
tenth décimo, -a
test examen (m.)
than (before numbers) de, que
thank: Thank you Gracias Thank
heavens! ¡Gracias a Dios!
that (over there) aquel, aquella, ese, esa
(adj.); ése, ésa, aquél, aquélla (pron.);
eso (neut. pron.); those esos, -as (adj.);
ésos, -as (pron.); for that reason por
eso; that's right eso es; that que
the el, la, los, las
their su, sus
theirs suyo, -a
them los, las (dir. obj.); les (indir. obj.);
ellos, -as (after prep.)
theme tema (m.)
then entonces, luego
there allí, allá; there is, are hay; there
was, were había, hubo; there will be
habrá; there would be habría
therefore por eso
these estos, -as (adj.); éstos, -as (pron.)
they ellos, -as

thin delgado, -a
thing cosa
think (*inf.*) pensar (ie)
third tercero, -a
thirst sed (*f.*); **to be (very) thirsty**
  tener (mucha) sed
thirteen trece
thirty treinta
this este, -a, esto (*neut. pron.*); **this
  (one)** éste, -a
those esos, -as, aquellos, -as (*adj.*); ésos,
  -as, aquéllos, -as (*demon. pron.*)
thousand mil
three tres
through por
Thursday jueves (*m.*)
tie corbata
time hora, tiempo, vez; **What time is it?**
  ¿Qué hora es?; **At what time . . .?**
  ¿A qué hora . . .?; **at times** a veces;
  often, many times muchas veces; **at
  the same time** a la vez
tired cansado, -a
to a, para
today hoy
tomato tomate (*m.*)
tomorrow mañana; **see you tomorrow**
  hasta mañana
topic tema (*m.*)
toward hacia
town (small) pueblo
traffic tráfico
train tren (*m.*)
travel (*inf.*) viajar
tree árbol (*m.*)
trip viaje (*m.*); **to take a trip** hacer
  un viaje
trousers pantalones (*m.*)
true: it is true es verdad; **isn't it (so)
  (true)?** ¿no es verdad?
truly de veras
truth verdad (*f.*)
try (*inf.*) probar (ue); **to try (to)** tratar
  (de); **to try on** probarse (ue)
Tuesday martes (*m.*)
turn (*inf.*) doblar; **to turn on (the radio)**
  poner (la radio)
twelve doce
twenty veinte
two dos

U

ugly feo, -a
uncle tío
understand (*inf.*) comprender,
  entender (ie)
United States Estados Unidos
university universidad, universitario, -a
  (*adj.*)
unless a menos que

until hasta, hasta que
up: to go up subir
us nos (*dir.* and *indir. obj.*); nosotros
  (after *prep.*)
use (*inf.*) consumir

V

vacation vacaciones (*f.*)
variation variación (*f.*)
variety variedad (*f.*)
vegetable legumbre (*f.*)
very muy
visit (*inf.*) visitar

W

wait (for) (*inf.*) esperar
waiter camarero
wake (up) (*inf.*) despertarse (ie)
walk paseo; **to walk** caminar, andar
want (*inf.*) querer (ie), desear
warm: It is (very) warm (*weather*)
  Hace (mucho) calor; **to be (very)
  warm** (*a person*) tener (mucho) calor
wash (*inf.*) lavar; **to wash oneself**
  lavarse
washerwoman lavandera
washing machine máquina lavadora
waste: to waste time perder el tiempo
Watch out! ¡Ojo!
water el agua (*f.*)
way manera; **by the way** a próposito; **on
  the way to** camino a
we nosotros, -as
wear (*inf.*) llevar
weather tiempo; **What's the weather
  today?** ¿Qué tiempo hace hoy?; **The
  weather is bad** hace mal tiempo
wedding boda
Wednesday miércoles (*m.*)
week semana; **weekend** fin de semana
well bien, pues; **Well!** ¡Vaya!
west oeste (*m.*)
what ¿qué?; **for what reason?** ¿Para
  qué?; **What a day!** ¡Qué día!; **What can
  I do for you?** ¿En qué puedo servirle?;
  What a lot of . . . ! ¡Cuánto, -a . . . !;
  what (*rel. pron.*) lo que
when cuando, ¿cuándo?
where donde, ¿dónde?
which que, ¿qué?, ¿cuál?
while (*adv.*) mientras, rato
who que, quien; ¿quién?
why ¿por qué?, ¿para qué?
wife esposa, señora
win (*inf.*) ganar
wind viento; **It is (very) windy** Hace
  (mucho) viento
window ventana
winter invierno
wish (*inf.*) querer (ie)

with con
within dentro (de)
without sin, sin que; **without more ado**
  sin más ni más
woe: Woe is me! ¡Ay de mí!
woman mujer (*f.*)
wonderful estupendo, -a
work trabajo; **to work** trabajar, funcionar;
  to be a lot of work costarle a uno trabajo
world mundo, mundial (*adj.*)
worry (*inf.*) preocupar, preocuparse; **to**
  worry (about) preocuparse (de)
worse peor
worst peor
write (*inf.*) escribir
written (*past part.*) escrito
wrong: to be wrong equivocarse

Y

year año; **last year** el año pasado; **two**
  years ago hace dos años
yesterday ayer
yet todavía
you usted (Ud.), ustedes (Uds.) (*subject*
  and after prep.); le, la, los, las (*dir. obj.*);
  le, les (*indir. obj.*); tú (*subj.*), te (*dir.*
  and indir. obj.); ti (*after prep.*)
young joven; **young man or woman**
  joven (*m. or f.*); **young men or**
  women, young people jóvenes;
  younger menor; **youngest** el, (la) menor
your su, sus, tu, tus
yours suyo, -a, tuyo, -a
youth juventud (*f.*)

INDEX